CRITICAL INSIGHTS

The Great Gatsby

CRITICAL
INSIGHTS

The Great Gatsby

by F. Scott Fitzgerald

Editor
Morris Dickstein
Graduate Center of the City University of New York

Salem Press
Pasadena, California   Hackensack, New Jersey

Cover photo: Hulton Archive/Getty Images

Published by Salem Press

© 2010 by EBSCO Publishing
Editor's text © 2010 by Morris Dickstein
"The *Paris Review* Perspective" © 2010 by Jascha Hoffman for *The Paris Review*

∞ The paper used in these volumes conforms to the American National Standard for Permanence of Paper for Printed Library Materials, Z39.48-1992 (R1997).

Library of Congress Cataloging-in-Publication Data
The great Gatsby, by F. Scott Fitzgerald / editor, Morris Dickstein.
    p. cm. — (Critical insights)
    Includes bibliographical references and index.
    ISBN 978-1-58765-608-8 (alk. paper)
    1. Fitzgerald, F. Scott (Francis Scott), 1896-1940. Great Gatsby. I. Dickstein, Morris.
    PS3511.I9G845 2009
    813'.52—dc22

                                                                    2009026346

Second Printing

Contents_____

The Book and Author_____

Critical Contexts_____

Critical Overviews_____

Critical Readings_____

Resources

About This Volume

Morris Dickstein

Trafficking in mystery and obscurity as part of its subject, oblique in its narrative technique, often lyrical in its style, *The Great Gatsby* is one of a small group of inexhaustible American novels that seem perpetually open to fresh interpretation. This volume brings together a host of approaches that critics have taken without unduly intersecting or stepping on each others' toes. It begins with a fresh contemporary take by Jascha Hoffman, then reaches back to provide a number of contexts for understanding this much-analyzed novel. Jennifer Banach Palladino explores the mixture of social, historical, and autobiographical details that point to its background in the 1920s, the aftermath of World War I: a new mobility, galloping technology, ostentatious wealth, a leisure class on a binge, and more relaxed moral standards. Amy Green focuses on the reception of the book, which was welcomed by Gertrude Stein, Ernest Hemingway, and T. S. Eliot but encountered mixed reviews from critics who found the novel slight, its characters unlikeable, their relationships decadent and offensive.

It was only in the Fitzgerald revival after 1945 that the book achieved its classic status. Dan McCall, Neil Heims, and Charles Lewis offer comparative literary contexts, with McCall emphasizing the influence of Keats on the novel, Heims comparing it with one of Henry James's few popular successes, the brisk novella *Daisy Miller*, and Lewis bringing in a contemporary work, Nella Larsen's Harlem Renaissance novel *Passing*. McCall shows how the dreamy excess of Keats's "Eve of St. Agnes" surfaces in something as mundane as Gatsby's collection of shirts but also in his lush romantic fantasies about Daisy. Gatsby, he says, aspires not to money but to "wealth chastened by a notion of romance, possibilities of great life beyond the rim of the actual." But McCall also notes how, in Keats as in Fitzgerald, dreams fade into disappointment and disillusionment. Heims sees a link between James and Fitzgerald in the two Daisys but also in the way both stories are told from the viewpoint of a partly detached, half-judgmental narrator. But in the end he shows that the true parallel is between Daisy Miller and Gatsby himself, "two emblems of innocence and brashness," both peculiarly American, both troublesome figures to the more conventional people around them, and both finally doomed, in part because they do not fit in. Lewis, in treating Gatsby as a character trying to "pass," draws unusual attention to the role of race in the novel, explicit in Tom Buchanan's white supremacist racial views but also, obliquely, in Gatsby's position as a scorned intruder, self-invented, a "Mr. Nobody from Nowhere," as Tom calls him. He sees racism as the book's often unspoken subtext.

Ambitious critical overviews by longtime Fitzgerald scholars include Robert and Helen H. Roulston's study of the novel as a culmination of the author's early development, Kenneth Eble's close examination of Fitzgerald's careful revisions, which improved the novel even when it was already in proof, and Ruth Prigozy's comprehensive introduction to a 1998 edition. Eble's study illuminates the author's creative process and shows how Fitzgerald adds details that "give Gatsby substance without destroying his necessary insubstantiality." In other words, "Gatsby is revised, not so much into a real person as into a mythical one; what he *is* is not allowed to distract the reader from what he stands for," just as Daisy, too, "moves away from actuality into an idea existing in Gatsby's mind." The Roulstons show how the novel is grounded in Fitzgerald's commercial magazine fiction yet moves beyond it, into a region of ambiguity highlighted by Nick Carraway's role as narrator; by certain paradoxical features of Fitzgerald's prose, such as his fondness for oxymorons ("ferocious delicacy," "meretricious beauty"); and by the balance between vernacular and literary language. Such ambivalence, rooted in Keats's half-ironic conception of romance and in the literary influence of an even more ironic writer, the Victorian novelist Thackeray, is best expressed in Nick. He "both is and is not a spokesman for his creator. He does and does not resemble Fitzgerald himself. The events do and do not support Nick's conclusions." Prigozy approaches the novel both historically and formally. She highlights the changes in American society from the Civil War through the 1920s, including the new wealth, the influx of immigrants, the Wilsonian rhetoric of idealism that turned hollow after the war, and the postwar economic boom, including the powerful impetus to crime offered by Prohibition. But she also stresses the novel's structural originality, with its story filtered through the prism of the narrator and marked by mysteries, fragments, and omissions that contribute to its meaning. Through Nick's quest, she says, "the novel becomes a search for moral order."

Prigozy's observations about Fitzgerald's narrative method are taken up in greater detail in critical readings by Matthew J. Bolton and Dan Coleman. Where the Roulstons call attention to Fitzgerald's oxymorons, Coleman shows the effect of Fitzgerald's "extended metaphors," which "threaten at times to take over the novel's reality altogether." These include the so-called Valley of Ashes, the forlorn dump where important action unfolds, and the ghostly eyes of T. J. Eckleburg as they brood over a fantastic, almost animated landscape. For Coleman the novel's technique, along with Fitzgerald's own outlook, oscillates between "the concrete realism of Myrtle's story and the indefinite fantasy of Gatsby's." Both characters wish to escape their origins, and both die trying, but Myrtle lacks Gatsby's "theatrical ability to make something spectacular of himself and his world." Nick, on the other hand, provides balance and distance by serving as the detached observer of this spectacle. Bolton complements this narrative analysis by analyzing not only the elliptical character of Fitzgerald's tale but its actual reliance on ellipses as punctuation, representing the story's crucial gaps, fissures, and silences, its layered, collage-like method. To Bolton this deliberate vagueness points to what is ineffable in Gatsby's vision. This is epitomized by an incommunicable phrase that Nick tries to recall—"an elusive rhythm, a fragment of lost words"—that he almost remembers but which will remain "uncommunicable forever." Barbara Will's deconstructionist reading takes this even further. Bringing in the work of Jacques Derrida and Julia Kristeva, she sees Gatsby not simply as elusive but as an "absence" in the novel, a "vanishing" figure whose "indeterminacy" points to what cannot be represented. Yet like Lewis she also recasts him as the racial Other, though Fitzgerald himself emphasizes class rather than race and mercilessly mocks Tom Buchanan's racist paranoia.

More specific critical studies in this volume include Lawrence J. Dessner's investigation of the neglected role of photography in the novel, which he relates to Gatsby's desire to freeze time and rerun the past; Daniel J. Schneider's close examination of Fitzgerald's symbolic use of color-motifs, an attention to internal correspondences that typifies a New Critical approach to Fitzgerald's carefully structured novel; and Leland S. Person's sympathetic defense of Daisy Buchanan, a character treated harshly by many critics. They have seen her not simply as a confused and shallow young woman, a product of her time and class, but as amoral, vulgar, and inhuman, a "monster of bitchery." Person portrays her instead as the victim of Gatsby's idealization, which she partly calls up and somehow meets halfway, though it ultimately obliterates her. Person's essay is yet another attempt to see the world of *The Great Gatsby* not strictly through the narrator's judgmental eyes.

THE BOOK
AND
AUTHOR

On *The Great Gatsby*

Morris Dickstein

The Great Gatsby was an unlikely book to become one of the handful of enduring American classics, a book to be read and reread, extravagantly loved and universally taught. Scarcely longer than a novella, it made no great impact when it first appeared in 1925. Its reviews and sales were disappointing compared to the enthusiastic reception accorded to Fitzgerald's apprentice novels, *This Side of Paradise* (1920) and *The Beautiful and Damned* (1922), which made him famous. Along with his articles, interviews, short fiction, and widely reported public antics, those books had turned Fitzgerald and his young wife into icons of the younger generation—rebellious, fun-loving, insouciant, and iconoclastic. It would be twenty years before *The Great Gatsby*, with its tragic and elegiac cast, would come to be seen as the representative book of that raucous decade.

Born in 1896, Fitzgerald was still in his twenties when *Gatsby* came out, but his career, along with his marriage to the former Zelda Sayre, was soon to enter a steep decline, and the mixed, largely critical reviews of the novel suggested that his stock was already falling. Eventually Zelda would be hospitalized after a serious breakdown and Fitzgerald would tumble into alcoholism and Hollywood screenwriting, still believing that the meticulous craft he put into *Gatsby* would one day be recognized. In the mid-1930s, after the relative failure of his next novel, *Tender Is the Night* (1934), he hit bottom and described his crack-up in a series of confessional articles for *Esquire*. He died of a heart attack in Hollywood in 1940. It was only after his college friend, the critic Edmund Wilson, edited his unfinished novel *The Last Tycoon* in 1941 and a collection of his articles in 1945 that his reputation rebounded. Along with Hemingway and Faulkner he became the writer's writer for the post-1945 generation, revered and widely imitated. *The Great Gatsby* was canonized not simply as a document of the Jazz Age but as a key to the American psyche and the national experience.

The Great Gatsby is a deceptively simple work with a plot so flimsy—and told so offhandedly—that the particulars stuck with me only after three or four readings. One of the main attributes of fiction, and one of its glories, is what Henry James called "solidity of specification," the wealth of concrete detail that we recognize as a lived world, even in a fantastic or surreal setting. Both the premise and style of *The Great Gatsby* work against such circumstantial realism. First, we are asked to believe that a young man, newly rich, would buy a Long Island estate just to be across the bay from an old girlfriend, whom he loved five years earlier, who jilted him and married someone else. Instead of moving on he has nurtured the flame, as if committed to "the following of a grail" (155). He gives fabulous parties hoping that she will show up, and when they do meet he expects her to leave her husband and child and run off with him, after telling her husband that she never loved him. This is followed by complications and coincidences that strain credibility, culminating in her rejection and his murder. It would be hard for any writer to make this story believable.

Fortunately, such a summary has little to do with what really takes place in *The Great Gatsby*, for its story trickles out in bits and pieces and its style, fresh and full of surprises, is as sinuous and unpredictable as the narrative. Relying on suggestive language rather than realistic detail, the novel achieves resonance as myth and metaphor rather than as a densely populated fictional world. Gatsby's background remains vague and his feeling for Daisy Buchanan is shrouded in a haze of idealization more typical of romantic poetry than of modern fiction. Of Daisy we learn, for example: "The exhilarating ripple of her voice was a wild tonic in the rain" (92). Gatsby's pursuit of his "grail" tells us we are at least as much in the realm of quest romance as in the contemporary world. When he falls in love, his world goes through a metamorphosis as remarkable for its lyrical prose as for its transcendental leap:

> Out of the corner of his eye Gatsby saw the blocks of the sidewalks really formed a ladder and mounted to a secret place above the trees—he could

climb to it, if he climbed alone, and once there he could suck on the pap of life, gulp down the incomparable milk of wonder.

His heart beat faster and faster as Daisy's white face came up to his own. He knew that when he kissed this girl, and forever wed his unutterable visions to her perishable breath, his mind would never romp again like the mind of God. So he waited, listening for a moment longer to the tuning-fork that had been struck upon a star. Then he kissed her. At his lips' touch she blossomed for him like a flower, and the incarnation was complete. (118)

No other modern novelist could have sounded such a note, though romance writers would grasp at tawdry versions of it. The language is evocative and poetic rather than descriptive; the final image comes directly from the poetry and letters of Keats, Fitzgerald's favorite writer. It is meant to describe Gatsby's own sense of his dreamy aspirations, if not exactly in his own words. The narrator, Nick Carraway, who represents the dry-eyed, skeptical side of Fitzgerald's temperament, characterizes it as "appalling sentimentality." Yet Gatsby's "unutterable visions" strike a chord in him; they remind him of something ineffable, "an elusive rhythm, a fragment of lost words, that I had heard somewhere a long time ago." Like Daisy's love for Gatsby, locked deep in the past, the words cannot be recaptured, and Nick finds that "what I had almost remembered was incommunicable forever" (118).

Fitzgerald's effort to communicate the incommunicable is balanced by his irony and satire. *The Great Gatsby* is at once a social novel that evokes a specific time and place and a poetic novel about a young man's dreams. Fitzgerald's language rises at times to an astonishing eloquence, especially in the near-perfect codas to each chapter and, famously, in the novel as a whole, but it can also be dry and sardonic, as in the wry accounts of Gatsby's parties, of numerous minor characters (such as Gatsby's gangster friend, Wolfsheim), and at times of Gatsby himself. The novel pulls together many strands of twenties culture, from organized crime and illegal booze to Wall Street wealth, young migrants from the Midwest, and the frivolous young flappers of the party scene. But the story, and sometimes the very syntax, also points to the vague and the ecstatic—to intimations, however transient, of another order of being, "a secret place above the trees" where Gatsby feels he could "suck on the pap of life, gulp down the incomparable milk of wonder." Like the Romantic poets, Gatsby yearns for a fullness of being, an emotional transcendence, that is at once uplifting and impossible to sustain, intoxicating but finally disillusioning. This paradox is central to poems like Keats's "Ode to a Nightingale" and Wordsworth's Immortality Ode but hardly material for most novelists, whose stock in trade is the mundane, the ordinary. This is the heightened language of desire, the milk of inspiration, that reaches for the infinite only to founder in frustration. But once the object takes on flesh and blood, once it is incarnated in another person's "perishable breath," it becomes bounded, vulnerable. Gatsby's failure is built into his huge but absurd ambition. This grail can be sought and sighted but never carried home.

Gatsby's origins are shadowy. His background and real identity are not to be revealed till late in the novel. We never learn much about how he made his money, though we can see that it was connected to bootlegging, crime, and Prohibition. By telling the story through the eyes of Nick Carraway and telling it in flashbacks, with gaps and omissions, Fitzgerald keeps Gatsby at a distance, preserving his mystery but also allowing us to make judgments of his dreams and follies, as Nick does. To Tom Buchanan, Daisy's husband, a realist in the worst sense, a man without imagination, Gatsby is no more than a "common swindler," a contemptible competitor simply to be eliminated. But Nick, for whom Gatsby at first represents "everything for which I have an affected scorn" (8), comes to admire not only his self-made identity but his foolish, futile visions of grandeur and romance. "They're a rotten crowd," he tells him. "You're worth the whole damn bunch put together" (160). He grows disenchanted with the scene and leaves New York to return to the Midwest, but he becomes Gatsby's Ishmael, the survivor who will tell his story. While others could sense Gatsby's "corruption," only Nick also grasps his "incorruptible dream" (160).

The book could easily have been called *The Education of Nick Carraway.*

Gatsby is an amorphous figure, more an idea than an actual person, because he aspires to something indefinable, "the incomparable milk of wonder." We first meet him through wild rumors about who he is and where he comes from—the gossip of the spongers and freeloaders who crash his parties. As a self-made man he keeps his biography vague, mixing truth, half-truth, and pulpy legend, like that later piece of self-invention, the young Bob Dylan. He doesn't actually appear until a quarter of the way into the novel, and Nick first greets his tales with "incredulous laughter," though some of the most far-fetched turn out to be true. Tom Buchanan, born to wealth and entitlement, sees through him right away as "Mr. Nobody from Nowhere," engaging in "a presumptuous little flirtation" (136, 138). Gatsby himself had told Nick all those stories because "I didn't want you to think I was just some nobody" (73). The real history of his transformation from James Gatz to Jay Gatsby, from poor boy to lavish party giver, and from penniless soldier to Daisy's lover, comes out by fits and starts, almost in reverse chronological order. Writing in 1924, Nick moves from the summer of 1922, when most of the action takes place, back to 1917, when Gatsby and Daisy fell in love, then to Gatsby's youthful dreams and adventures, to his childhood, and finally, in a daring reach into history, back to the Dutch sailors to imagine their sense of wonder at the new world. In place of the inquest late in the novel, which turns into a tissue of lies, Nick's inquest into Gatsby's life resembles an archaeological dig in which we reach the earliest layers last, or a mystery novel that haltingly yields up its secrets. "So we beat on," the novel concludes, "boats against the current, borne back ceaselessly into the past" (188).

The Great Gatsby is often linked to the American Dream, going back to Benjamin Franklin and Horatio Alger, but that usually stands for material success, not emotional expansion. Gatsby acquires wealth not for its own sake but to fulfill his exalted notion of life's possibilities. As a young man "his heart was in a constant, turbulent riot" (105).

He leaves college after two weeks because of its "ferocious indifference to the drums of his destiny, to destiny itself" (106). His ambition and desire take shape in Daisy, and he makes love to her "because he had no real right to touch her hand." He can offer her no security, for he has "no comfortable family standing behind him," as Tom does. In the Army his social status, or lack of it, is obscured, but "at any moment the invisible cloak of his uniform might slip from his shoulders" (155). The purpose of Gatsby's money, five years later, is to enable him to run that reel backwards, to freeze time and undo the past. But the past resists being rewritten, just as the social hierarchy resists the admission of nobodies. Gatsby offers Daisy "romantic possibilities totally absent from her world" (116), but her own limitations and his exalted demands make failure inevitable.

Standing between Gatsby and happiness is the hard reality of social class in the figure of Tom Buchanan, the former college athlete whose "thick body" is "capable of enormous leverage — a cruel body" (122, 13). His "wholesome bulkiness" (157) once appealed to Daisy; now he seems merely "hulking" (18). Like his mistress, Myrtle Wilson, who teems with frustrated vitality and dies a gruesome death, Tom is as solid and physical as Gatsby and Daisy are gossamer and nebulous. But unlike Myrtle, who thinks Tom will leave his wife and marry her—which links her with Gatsby—Tom has no truck with romantic illusions. Since Gatsby comes from nowhere, he could hardly be a serious rival. At seventeen Gatsby had made himself up: he "sprang from his Platonic conception of himself" (105). Daisy floats through the lives of both men, linked to Tom by bonds of money and class but also to Gatsby by the hopes he has projected on her, colossal illusions to which she could never measure up.

Fitzgerald knits the novel together with such linkages and parallels between the characters. Nick is Daisy's cousin but, increasingly, Gatsby's friend. He went to college with Tom, whose values he quietly despises. He is seeing Jordan Baker, who is a minor echo of her friend Daisy. Tom and Wilson, Myrtle's husband, make "a parallel discovery," (130) within an hour of each other, that there is someone else in their wives' lives. Myrtle and Daisy love the same man but in different ways. By accident or design, Tom provokes Wilson into killing his rival, just as Daisy, driving Gatsby's car, accidentally kills hers. Such correspondences make an intricate mesh of a seemingly haphazard tale. So do many echoing words (such as "careless" and "wonder"), plot devices (such as auto accidents), and symbols (such as the valley of ashes, which evokes T. S. Eliot's *The Waste Land*; the green light sighted by Gatsby on the Buchanans' dock; and the blind but brooding eyes of T. J. Eckleburg, like those of a god who long departed). These leitmotifs structure the novel more tellingly than its action or plot.

The Great Gatsby is more than a triumph of craft; it is a searching foray into the myths and realities of American culture. In Fitzgerald's breathtaking conclusion, the young Gatsby's "milk of wonder," then the "wonder when he first picked out the green light on Daisy's dock," lead us finally to the earliest layer of the novel, the Dutch sailor before the "fresh, green breast of the new world," coming "face to face for the last time in history with something commensurate to his capacity for wonder" (187–88). Gatsby is at once a glorious dreamer, the inheritor of Emersonian notions of self-invention, and a man whose fabricated identity "had broken up like glass against Tom's hard malice" (154)—done in by the resistance of society, the inexorable shifts of time and history, and the iron limits of the real. Gatsby's naive and gigantic demands upon the world give him a claim to greatness, but he is also a kind of frontier showman, an illusionist, the Great Gatsby, who stages his own life. But the crowds at his parties don't show up for his funeral, Daisy abandons him and stays loyal to her class, and Nick, alone among his supposed friends, remains faithful to him and weaves the web of his astonishing story.

Work Cited

Fitzgerald, F. Scott. 1950. *The Great Gatsby*. Harmondsworth, England: Penguin.

Biography of F. Scott Fitzgerald_____
Michael Adams

Early Life

Francis Scott Key Fitzgerald was born September 24, 1896, in St. Paul, Minnesota. His father, Edward Fitzgerald, was a furniture manufacturer, and his mother, Mollie McQuillan Fitzgerald, the daughter of a wealthy St. Paul businessman. After Edward Fitzgerald's business failed in 1898, he became a wholesale grocery salesman for Procter & Gamble in Buffalo, New York. Edward was transferred to Syracuse, New York, in 1901 (when Scott's sister Annabel was born) and back to Buffalo in 1903 before losing his job in 1908. The family then returned to St. Paul to live off the money Mollie had inherited from her father.

Edward Fitzgerald, who had cowritten a novel when he was young, read from the works of Lord George Gordon Byron and Edgar Allan Poe to his son and praised the boy's attempts at writing, but he hoped that Scott would become an army officer. Mollie did not encourage his literary interests and wanted him to be a successful businessman like her father, to make up for Edward's failure and to live up to the illustrious ancestors on his father's side of the family, a long line of wealthy Maryland landowners, politicians, and lawyers (Francis Scott Key was a distant relative).

Because Scott's family believed that he needed discipline, he was sent in 1911 to the Newman School, a Catholic preparatory school in Hackensack, New Jersey. At Newman, Fitzgerald met Father Sigourney Fay, a wealthy intellectual who introduced him to Henry Adams and other well-known literary figures. Fay became the boy's surrogate father and is the model for Monsignor Darcy in *This Side of Paradise* (1920).

In 1913, Fitzgerald enrolled at Princeton University. He dreamed of becoming a college football star but did not make the team. He had worked on school publications throughout high school and began writing for the *Princeton Tiger*, the college humor magazine. He also wrote the books and lyrics for musical productions of the prestigious Triangle Club, and through such literary endeavors he made friends with fellow students Edmund Wilson, who became one of America's most important critics, and John Peale Bishop, later a successful poet. Fitzgerald and Wilson wrote *The Evil Eye* for the Triangle Club in 1915. After a publicity photograph, for that production, of Fitzgerald dressed as a girl ran in *The New York Times*, he received an offer to become a female impersonator in vaudeville.

Earlier that year, Fitzgerald had met sixteen-year-old Ginevra King of Lake Forest, Illinois, at a party in St. Paul. For him, she was the embodiment of the perfect woman: beautiful, rich, socially prominent, and sought after. Ginevra, the model for many of the young women in Fitzgerald's short stories, rejected him eventually because he was not wealthy.

That disappointment was not Fitzgerald's only one in 1915. He was elected secretary of the Triangle Club, meaning that he would be its president during his senior year, but bad grades made him ineligible for campus offices. Fitzgerald had neglected his studies almost from his arrival at Princeton. At the end of the fall semester, poor grades and illness forced him to drop out of school.

Fitzgerald returned to Princeton in the fall of 1916 to repeat his junior year, and he continued to write stories for the campus literary magazine. He never graduated, however, since the United States entered World War I, and he joined the army as a second lieutenant in October 1917. On weekends, he began writing "The Romantic Egoists," an early version of *This Side of Paradise*. In June 1918, he was sent to Camp Sheridan, near Montgomery, Alabama. At a country club dance that July, Fitzgerald met eighteen-year-old Zelda Sayre, and they fell in love two months later. Zelda came from a prominent Montgomery family, her father being a justice of the Alabama Supreme Court. Zelda, considered the most popular girl in Montgomery, was attracted to Fitzgerald because they wanted the same things: success, fame, and glamour.

The war ended just as Fitzgerald was to go overseas. He was disappointed because he wanted to test himself in battle and because he saw the war as a romantic adventure. Yet more disappointments were the rejection of his novel by Charles Scribner's Sons and the disapproval of Zelda's parents, who believed that Scott was not stable enough to take proper care of their high-strung daughter. Nevertheless, Zelda agreed to marry him if he went to New York—where she desperately wanted to live—and became a success.

Fitzgerald began working for the Barron Collier advertising agency in February 1919, writing advertisements which appeared in trolley cars. That spring, he sold his first short story, "Babes in the Woods," to *The Smart Set*, the sophisticated magazine edited by H. L. Mencken and George Jean Nathan. Zelda, however, was too impatient for his success and broke off their engagement that June.

Life's Work

Fitzgerald quit his job in July 1919, and returned to St. Paul to live with his parents while revising his novel. Maxwell Perkins, the legendary Scribner's editor, accepted *This Side of Paradise* that September, despite objections to what his very conservative employer considered a frivolous novel. Perkins, whose suggestions helped Fitzgerald improve the book, said he would resign if Scribner's did not publish it.

Shortly after the novel was accepted, Fitzgerald became a client of agent Harold Ober and began publishing stories in the *Saturday Evening Post*, at that time the highest-paying magazine in the field. Unfortunately, he also began a lifelong pattern of drinking and wild spending. He and Zelda seemed made for each other because of their youth, beauty, ambition, and excesses. They were married April 3, 1920, a few days after *This Side of Paradise* was published.

Scribner's published three thousand copies of Fitzgerald's autobiographical novel about a college student's coming of age, and the book was sold out in three days. By the end of 1921, it had gone through twelve printings of 49,075 copies, a huge success for a serious first novel. *This Side of Paradise*, considered the first realistic American college novel, was read as a handbook for collegiate conduct. By presenting the new American girl in rebellion against her mother's values, the novel also created the prototype of the flapper. Novelist John O'Hara later claimed that a half million Americans between the ages of fifteen and thirty fell in love with the book.

The Fitzgeralds quickly became major celebrities in New York because of Scott's success and the young couple's good looks and flamboyant personalities. (Unfortunately, few photographs capture the charismatic good looks of Zelda, with her wavy hair, almond-shaped eyes, and oval face, and blond, blue-eyed, stocky Scott, whose impact is widely attested in contemporary accounts.) Zelda went from the center of attention she had been in Montgomery to the wife of a famous novelist, and she resented the change. She remained jealous of her husband's artistic success and attempted, in the course of their marriage, to become a ballerina, a painter, and a novelist. *Save Me the Waltz* (1932), her highly autobiographical novel, was written to compete with Scott's *Tender Is the Night* (1934). This sense of competition increased Zelda's drinking and contributed to her mental problems. The birth of their only child, Frances Scott (Scottie) Fitzgerald, in 1921 did little to slow down the Fitzgeralds.

The couple had to lead extravagant lives to live up to their press clippings, and Fitzgerald's work suffered for it. He borrowed from his publisher and agent and wrote short stories to finance the writing of his novels. (Of Fitzgerald's 178 stories, 146 published during his lifetime, about two-thirds are of inferior quality, written primarily to pay bills.) Whenever he got ahead, he spent himself into debt again.

Fitzgerald's early success was followed by two failures. *The Beautiful and Damned* (1922), while actually selling more copies than *This Side of Paradise* because of Fitzgerald's reputation, was not as well received by the critics as his first novel. This examination of how greed corrupts a marriage is Fitzgerald's bleakest, most cynical, least effective novel. Because he had long loved the theater, Fitzgerald wanted to be as good a playwright as he was a novelist. *The Vegetable* (1923), a political satire, opened in Atlantic City, New Jersey, in November 1923, and closed quickly, leaving Fitzgerald's aspirations as a dramatist unfulfilled.

In 1924, the Fitzgeralds made their second trip to Europe; Zelda had an affair with a French aviator on the Riviera and attempted suicide, events that her husband used in *Tender Is the Night*. In Paris, Scott was introduced to Gertrude Stein and other prominent American expatriates. He met the then-unknown Ernest Hemingway and recruited him for Scribner's. Their friendship was a close but rocky one, for both writers were temperamental and suspicious of each other.

Fitzgerald's masterpiece, *The Great Gatsby* (1925), is one of the most widely read serious American novels, but this poetic look at love, wealth, innocence, illusions, corruption, and the American Dream was, ironically, a failure when it first appeared, selling half as many copies as either of Fitzgerald's previous novels. He blamed this failure on the lack of the strong women characters necessary to please the predominantly female reading public. The genius of this almost perfect novel, however, was recognized by many serious readers, including T. S. Eliot, who wrote Fitzgerald that "it seems to me to be the first step that American fiction has taken since Henry James."

Almost a decade would pass before Fitzgerald's next novel appeared. He spent that time writing stories, twice attempting unsuccessfully to become a Hollywood screenwriter, moving back and forth between the United States and Europe, seeing Zelda's mental instability and his own drinking increase. Zelda entered psychiatric clinics in France and Switzerland in 1930 and was in and out of institutions for the remainder of her life.

Fitzgerald's account of the disintegration of fragile Americans living on the French Riviera in *Tender Is the Night* is autobiographical, as is most of his fiction. The novel is considered a masterpiece but was yet another failure in 1934; both readers and critics were puzzled by the flashback structure. Fitzgerald hoped that the novel would be republished with the events rearranged into chronological order, and such an edition finally appeared posthumously, in 1951, but most critics regard it as inferior to the original version.

In the mid-1930s, Fitzgerald reached his nadir. Between 1935 and 1937, he wrote nine stories that no one would publish, and he constantly begged Harold Ober for money. His drinking became so bad that he finally had to be hospitalized. Hemingway offered to have his friend killed so that Zelda and Scottie would receive insurance money.

Fitzgerald's fortunes began improving in the month of July 1937, when Metro-Goldwyn-Mayer hired him as a screenwriter at a salary of one thousand dollars a week, allowing him to pay off many of his debts. That same month, he met gossip columnist Sheilah Graham, and they fell in love. Fitzgerald spent his spare time educating the young Englishwoman while she tried to save him from himself, sticking by him even when he resumed drinking and mistreated her.

Fitzgerald took his film work seriously and even entertained hopes of becoming a director, but the assembly line system of creating scripts at that time was unsuitable for someone of his talent and fragile ego. He received screen credit for only one script, *Three Comrades* (1938), an adaptation of an Erich Maria Remarque novel, but even then the finished product differed greatly from what Fitzgerald had conceived. He protested to producer Joseph L. Mankiewicz, "Oh, Joe, can't producers ever be wrong? I'm a good writer—honest. I thought you were going to play fair." He was sent to Dartmouth College with young writer Budd Schulberg in February 1939, to research a film about the school's winter carnival, only to spend the entire trip drunk, and he was fired.

By October 1939, Fitzgerald had decided to ignore his personal, financial, and professional problems as much as possible and began writing *The Last Tycoon* (1941), the story of an idealist film producer—based on himself and Irving Thalberg, the late head of Metro-Goldwyn-Mayer—who falls in love with a young woman much like

Sheilah Graham. The novel was about half finished when Fitzgerald died of a heart attack at Graham's apartment on December 21, 1940.

Edmund Wilson assembled the unfinished novel and Fitzgerald's outline for the remainder of the book for publication in 1941. Fitzgerald's other posthumous book is *The Crack-Up* (1945), also edited by Wilson, a collection of autobiographical essays about his problems which first appeared in *Esquire* in the 1930s. Zelda Fitzgerald died in a fire at a sanatorium in Asheville, North Carolina, on March 10, 1948, and was buried beside her husband in Rockville, Maryland.

From *Dictionary of World Biography: The 20th Century* (Pasadena, CA: Salem Press, 1999): 1161-1165. Copyright © 1999 by Salem Press, Inc.

Bibliography

Berman, Ronald. *Fitzgerald, Hemingway, and the Twenties*. Tuscaloosa: University of Alabama Press, 2001. An explication of the cultural context of the era and how the works of these two American writers are imbued with the attitudes and icons of their day.

_____. *The Great Gatsby and Fitzgerald's World of Ideas*. Tuscaloosa: University of Alabama Press, 1997. Explores Fitzgerald's political and social views of his era and how he incorporated them into his seminal novel.

Bloom, Harold, ed. *F. Scott Fitzgerald: The Great Gatsby*. New Haven, Conn.: Chelsea House, 1986. A short but important collection of critical essays. This book provides an introductory overview of Fitzgerald scholarship (five pages), as well as readings from a variety of perspectives on Fitzgerald's fiction.

Bruccoli, Matthew J. *Some Sort of Epic Grandeur*. New York: Harcourt Brace Jovanovich, 1981. In this outstanding biography, a major Fitzgerald scholar argues that Fitzgerald's divided spirit, not his lifestyle, distracted him from writing. Bruccoli believes that Fitzgerald both loved and hated the privileged class that was the subject of his fiction.

Conroy, Frank. "Great Scott." *Gentlemen's Quarterly* 66 (December, 1996): 240-245. A reconsideration of Fitzgerald on the centenary of his birth, Conroy argues that one of Fitzgerald's great strengths as a writer was his ability to make the metaphysical beauty of his female characters believable.

Eble, Kenneth. *F. Scott Fitzgerald*. Rev. ed. Boston: Twayne, 1977. A clearly written critical biography, this book traces Fitzgerald's development from youth through a "Final Assessment," which surveys scholarship on Fitzgerald's texts.

Gale, Robert L. *An F. Scott Fitzgerald Encyclopedia*. Westport, Conn.: Greenwood

Press, 1998. Provides everything students should know about Fitzgerald's life and works. Indispensable.

Gross, Dalton, and MaryJean Gross. *Understanding The Great Gatsby: A Student Casebook to Issues, Sources, and Historical Documents.* Westport, Conn.: Greenwood Press, 1998. Part of the *Literature in Context* series. An excellent study guide for students of the novel. Includes bibliographical references and an index.

Hook, Andrew. *F. Scott Fitzgerald: A Literary Life.* New York: St. Martin's, 2002. Part of the *Literary Lives* series. Concise rather than thorough, but with some interesting details.

Jefferson, Margo. "Still Timely, Yet a Writer of His Time." *The New York Times,* December 17, 1996, p. C17. A brief biography of Fitzgerald on the occasion of his centennial year; calls him one of those rare artists with a cultural radar system that is constantly picking up sensations, responses, and fresh thoughts.

Kuehl, John. *F. Scott Fitzgerald: A Study of the Short Fiction.* Boston: Twayne, 1991. Part 1 discusses Fitzgerald's major stories and story collections, part 2 studies his critical opinions, and part 3 includes selections from Fitzgerald critics. Includes chronology and bibliography.

Lee, A. Robert, ed. *Scott Fitzgerald: The Promises of Life.* New York: St. Martin's Press, 1989. An excellent collection of essays by Fitzgerald scholars, this book includes an introduction that surveys scholarship on the texts. Topics addressed include Fitzgerald's treatment of women, his notion of the decline of the West, his "ethics and ethnicity," and his use of "distortions" of the imagination.

Mangum, Bryant. *A Fortune Yet: Money in the Art of F. Scott Fitzgerald's Short Stories.* New York: Garland, 1991. Discusses all of Fitzgerald's stories, both those in collections and those uncollected, focusing on their relationship to his novels and their role as a proving ground for his ideas.

Meyers, Jeffrey. *Scott Fitzgerald: A Biography.* New York: HarperCollins, 1994. In this biography, which uses previously unknown materials about Fitzgerald's life, Meyers discusses how such writers as Edgar Allan Poe, Ernest Hemingway, and Joseph Conrad influenced Fitzgerald's fiction.

Miller, James E., Jr. *F. Scott Fitzgerald: His Art and His Technique.* New York: New York University Press, 1964. An expanded version of *The Fictional Technique of Scott Fitzgerald,* originally published in 1957, this book emphasizes Fitzgerald's technique, focusing on the impact of the "saturation vs. selection" debate between H. G. Wells and Henry James; it also adds critical commentary and interpretations of the later works.

Oxford, Edward. "F. Scott Fitzgerald." *American History* 31 (November/December 1996): 44. A biographical sketch that notes that Fitzgerald was able to convey the energy and image of the 1920s, only to become an ironic witness to the death of that era. Discusses Fitzgerald's life with Zelda and his literary career.

Petry, Alice Hall. *Fitzgerald's Craft of Short Fiction.* Ann Arbor: UMI Research Press, 1989. A study of Fitzgerald's short stories in relationship to his novels, American society, and his personal life. Summarizes and critiques critical reception to his short-story collections and discusses his relationship with his editor Max Perkins; analyzes all the major stories and a number of minor ones.

Tate, Mary Jo. *F. Scott Fitzgerald A to Z: The Essential Reference to His Life and Work*. New York: Facts on File, 1998. A comprehensive study of the man and his oeuvre. Provides bibliographical references and an index.

Taylor, Kendall. *Sometimes Madness Is Wisdom: Zelda and Scott Fitzgerald, A Marriage*. New York: Ballantine, 2001. An examination of one of literature's most famous couples and their symbiotic marriage.

the PARIS
REVIEW

The *Paris Review* Perspective

Jascha Hoffman for *The Paris Review*

The Great Gatsby has an almost sacred status among modern American novels, but it wasn't always that way. When it was first published in 1925, F. Scott Fitzgerald's short novel—the tale of a summer of love and intrigue among the upper classes of Long Island—did not sell well. Some contemporary critics thought its plot shallow and its characters, like the nasty Tom Buchanan and his reckless wife Daisy, noxious and thinly drawn. "The story becomes rather a bitter dose before one has finished with it," Edmund Wilson wrote to Fitzgerald just after the book was published. "Not that I don't admire Gatsby or see the point of the whole thing, but you will admit that it keeps us inside the hyena cage." He had a point: only Nick Carraway, the ambivalent Yale graduate who narrates Gatsby's rise and fall, and whose retreat to the Midwest at the novel's end is tinged with regret, survives the summer with some dignity.

After long struggles with alcoholism and screenwriting, and having never seen much profit from *The Great Gatsby*, Fitzgerald died of a heart attack in 1940. His death, however, accomplished something Fitzgerald could not do in life: it sold copies of the book. More than a dozen new versions of *The Great Gatsby* were published in the following decade, including an armed services edition distributed to tens of thousands of soldiers coming home from the Second World War. By the late 1950s the critics were catching up, and the book soon became a staple of the high-school English curriculum. And so Fitzgerald seems to have lived up to at least two of the three standards of literary reception he laid out after the success of his first novel, *This Side of Para-*

dise: "An author ought to write for the youth of his own generation, the critics of the next, and the schoolmasters of ever afterward."

What about the novel has attracted readers from so many generations? A conventional reading takes it as a cautionary tale: James Gatz, an ambitious bootlegger from a poor Midwestern background, tries to lure back a lost lover by throwing lavish parties with his new money under the name Jay Gatsby, but he pays for this charade with his life. His spectacular failure serves as a warning against a narrow interpretation of the American dream, one that sees salvation as something that flows from the bank. Others, however, have found something admirable in Gatsby's striving. One high-school student recently told *The New York Times* that reading the book had only strengthened her resolve to get into Harvard. Likewise, in his recent book *The Runner*, journalist David Samuels presents a surprisingly charitable portrait of a modern-day Gatsby: a bicycle thief who conned his way into Princeton and charmed the student body until he was unmasked and kicked out, only to surface ten years later doing the same thing in Colorado.

But class-climbing audacity is only part of the appeal of *Gatsby*. It is also a story of violent love, in which a long-burning crush pulls a man deep into a risky game he cannot sustain. Blinded by love, Gatsby convinces himself that he has the ability not only to master his future but also to effectively bring back a moment from the past. Although Tom Buchanan's rage leads him to break a woman's nose, it is Gatsby's cold passion that proves even more dangerous. In one of his more fevered passages, Fitzgerald describes Gatsby's desire for Daisy as an urge to climb to the stars to "suck on the pap of life, gulp down the incomparable milk of wonder." If this phrase sounds less like love than the satisfaction of some bestial craving—maybe it is.

That gauzy phrase—"the incomparable milk of wonder"—points to perhaps the greatest strength of the novel: the dizzying range of diction Fitzgerald has snuck into his sentences. Much of the novel's momentum comes from its disorienting alternation of high and low registers, from Jazz Age slang to free flights of poetry. When Nick first learns that Gatsby's great show of wealth is meant only to lure Daisy back to him, he expresses his surprise by saying, "He came alive to me, delivered suddenly from the womb of his purposeless splendor." The words are too big for the job, but the effect is nonetheless grand. A few lines later, when Nick learns that Gatsby wants him to play host to his reunion with Daisy, his response is more casual but no less chilling: "The modesty of the demand shook me."

And it is true, as Alfred Kazin once observed, that Gatsby doesn't want all that much from life. He doesn't want to change the world. He only wants to buy back a moment he imagined he had shared with Daisy. The tragedy is that this one thing is not for sale. It is Gatsby's refusal to accept this fact, and the way he ultimately has to pay for this refusal with his life, that makes him both stupid and brave—almost a martyr, one could say, for the particularly American idea that money can buy love, and that love will stop time.

Works Cited

Bloom, Harold, ed. 1999. *Bloom's ReViews: F. Scott Fitzgerald's "The Great Gatsby."* New York: Chelsea House.

Fitzgerald, F. Scott. 1926. *The Great Gatsby*. New York: Penguin.

_____. 1989. *The Short Stories of F. Scott Fitzgerald: A New Collection*, edited by Matthew Bruccoli. New York: Scribner.

"Francis Scott Key Fitzgerald." 2001-2007. *The Columbia Encyclopedia*, 6th ed.

Rimer, Sara. 2008. "Gatsby's Green Light Beckons a New Set of Strivers." *The New York Times* (February 17).

Samuels, David. 2008. *The Runner: A True Account of the Amazing Lies and Fantastical Adventures of the Ivy League Impostor James Hogue*. New York: New Press.

CRITICAL
CONTEXTS

Gatsby in Context

Jennifer Banach Palladino

In the Preface to the 1992 Macmillan printing of *The Great Gatsby*, prominent F. Scott Fitzgerald scholar Matthew J. Bruccoli aptly notes that *"The Great Gatsby* does not proclaim the nobility of the human spirit; it is not politically correct; it does not reveal how to solve the problems of life; it delivers no fashionable or comforting messages. It is just a masterpiece" (Fitzgerald, viii). In light of the observations which precede this last laudatory affirmation, one must ask what it is that has made the novel such a tremendous success. The work, considered a commercial failure during the author's own lifetime, was listed second among The Modern Library's list of the top 100 novels of all time and has become a standard component of high school, college, and university curricula. It has inspired film renditions, operatic adaptations, and theatrical versions and has influenced the work of countless authors and artists. Most notably, it has stood the test of time, weathering the fickle fluctuations of literary criticism and popular taste. Bruccoli follows up his initial remarks with the observation that "the best reason to read literature is for pleasure" (vii) and correctly asserts that "many admiring readers are unaware of the complexity of *The Great Gatsby* because the novel is a pleasure to read" (vii). In fact, it is this combination of pleasurable readability and intense complexity which has equipped the novel with its staying-power. *The Great Gatsby* is at once autobiographical, fantastical, and historical. Although concerns were initially expressed about its brief length, which failed to match standard word-counts of novels of the time, Fitzgerald may have gotten the last laugh. For, above all else, *The Great Gatsby* is thorough. While the novel fully captures the essence of the Roaring Twenties, it also speaks more generally of human nature. For these reasons it remains supremely relatable to readers of all backgrounds. This is due in large part to Fitzgerald's choice of themes—the pursuit of love, the pursuit of wealth and success, and more generally, the pursuit of a dream—embodied in memorable characters such as Jay Gatsby. Put another way, after all these years, readers enjoy reading about Gatsby's pursuit because they understand it—it is, after all, a mirror of our own pursuits. Preeminent literary critic Harold Bloom explains:

> It is reasonable to assert that Jay Gatsby is *the* major literary character of the United States in the twentieth century. No single figure created by Faulkner or Hemingway, or by our principal dramatists, is as central a presence in our national mythology as Gatsby. There are few living Americans, of whatever gender, race, ethnic origin, or social class, who do not have at least a little touch of Gatsby in them. Whatever the American Dream has become, its truest contemporary representative remains Jay Gatsby. . . . (1)

Like all great fiction the novel has its roots in more tangible material than the stuff simply of the imagination of its author. Fitzgerald's *The Great Gatsby* is the epitome of the writer's motto "Write what you know." One does not have to look far to see that the story was inspired by elements of Fitzgerald's own life and surroundings. After the birth of their child, the author and his wife Zelda moved to a section of Long Island called Great Neck where they were exposed to the workings of the upper class and experienced firsthand the division between old and new money. Those people who had acquired newfound wealth were Fitzgerald's neighbors in Great Neck, while Manhasset Neck across the bay was home to those who came from old money. These polarized sites became the setting for the novel, albeit with the fictional names of West Egg and East Egg. In addition to the setting, Fitzgerald's life was echoed in each of the characters of *The Great Gatsby* as well as in the plot. Daisy Buchanan is said to have been modeled after the author's first love, Ginevra King, although many critics and scholars also find traces of his wife Zelda in her character. More specifically, the unrequited romance between Daisy and Gatsby is reminiscent of the author's own relationship with both Ginevra and Zelda, women who were concerned with wealth and status, which a young Fitzgerald had not yet attained at the time of either courtship. Certainly then, Fitzgerald's choice to describe Gatsby's misfortune in being unable to marry Daisy due to his dismal financial status stemmed from his own misfortunes, as the young Fitzgerald was dismissed by Zelda until his career had taken off and their secure future was assured. Meanwhile Nick Carraway, the narrator, and Jay Gatsby exhibit countless obvious traces of Fitzgerald's own personality and background. Like Fitzgerald, these characters were born in the Midwest. All traveled to take advantage of business opportunities on the East Coast. All enlisted in the army. And Nick and Fitzgerald share a penchant for story-telling, while Gatsby seems content to act as a character pursuing his own storybook ending. Of course, that ending never comes to fruition for Gatsby, and it is difficult not to think of the author himself, who died believing that he was a failure, as someone who missed out on his own storybook ending.

It is in Fitzgerald's intimate recollection of the people and events from his own life and the subsequent translation of this information into fiction that something greater takes place. Fitzgerald's willingness toward candid observation, combined with his careful craftsmanship and eye for detail, transformed *The Great Gatsby* into a document of social history—quite specifically, American social history. Like many great authors—Dickens and Joyce in particular come to mind—Fitzgerald has imbued his story with a distinct sense of time and place. Particularly, Fitzgerald is able to capture the essence of Long Island and New York in 1922. The setting lends credence to the sincerity of what we are reading. It is a setting with which Fitzgerald was familiar as it was the setting for the author's own life, but it is convincing not simply for this reason. The setting adds to the book's plausibility mainly because every last detail of the book has been carefully crafted within this setting so that nothing disrupts the world Fitzgerald has created or tips us off that we are, in fact, reading fiction. The author, notorious for his extreme and ongoing process of revision, took particular pains with this novel to get it right, working even after the galleys were produced to come closer to matching his internal vision. The novel is, therefore, ultimately a successful chemistry of personal history—semi-autobiographical experiences veiled in fiction (although what elements were consciously inserted and what found its way subconsciously remains a matter of debate)—and social history laid bare for all to see. It is this underlying cultural and historical context of the work which functions as the story's skeleton, giving the novel structure and allowing readers a strong foothold. Literary critic Malcolm Cowley recognized that "Fitzgerald never lost a quality that very few writers are able to acquire: a sense of living in history. Manners and morals were changing all through his life and he set himself to the task of recording the changes" (57). Because of Fitzgerald's commitment to chronicling life during this period, *The Great Gatsby* is now regularly consulted as historical documentation of 1920s American society, and Fitzgerald's tendencies toward intimate revelation and his ability to see the world with a critical eye have produced a work with themes which have successfully transcended the time period in which they were written, remaining relevant to modern readers whose experiences are very different. But perhaps most astonishingly, in *The Great Gatsby* Fitzgerald is able to work some magic. The author does much more than report on his own era as a sort of biographer or reporter. Rather, he does so with the eye of an anthropologist and the foresight of a clairvoyant. Fitzgerald, a participant in the era, produced a work which a historian might have produced if asked to characterize the decade years later.

A major factor in the accomplishment of this task lies in Fitzgerald's utilization of the narrator, Nick Carraway. Many critics and scholars have envisioned Nick as the thinly veiled voice of Fitzgerald himself. However, Nick is a character who is more than an autobiographical footnote. As a transplant from the Midwest who has not yet attained wealth and status, and as a second cousin of Daisy Buchanan and a resident of West Egg, he is both insider and outsider, and thus, his employment as narrator and the specific details of his background are supremely functional. He can infiltrate the scenes Fitzgerald wishes to describe and provide objective observations in the guise of recollections of days gone by. Nick begins by speaking in the first person, recounting the happenings of the summer of 1922, but the narrative voice shifts throughout the story into the third person as Nick becomes invested in the events—entering into a relationship with Jordan Baker, becoming friends with Gatsby—now thoroughly entangled in what is taking place. This oscillation between first- and third-person narration provides the reader with a wider lens and an all-encompassing view not typically available in novels. Readers have the benefit of an insider's knowledge of what is taking place, combined with the objectivity and truth that can only come from an observer who remains just removed from the action. This is particularly significant because Nick's observations are perhaps the only truths one may find throughout the novel. They, therefore, orient us and provide perspective. If we are skeptical, as we often should be of narrators, we have Nick's assurances of his total willingness to be honest. We receive this assurance via his reflections on his father's advice: "Whenever you feel like criticizing anyone . . . just remember that all the people in this world haven't had the advantages that you've had" (5). Nick recognizes that the advice is not only a suggestion to refrain from criticizing others, it is also a reminder that "a sense of the fundamental decencies is parceled out unequally at birth" (6). Nick indicates that he has previously been generally successful at heeding this advice in his tolerance of the faults of others, but, he confesses, "after boasting this way of my tolerance, I come to the admission that it has a limit" (6). At this point, Nick is ready to tell it like it is. Meanwhile, all of the other characters remain ensnared in their own lies, deceit, and hypocrisy throughout the course of the story. Tom Buchanan has an affair with Myrtle Wilson but becomes furious when he realizes Daisy's affair with Gatsby. Jordan Baker lies about leaving the top of a car down in the rain and also cheats to win a golf tournament. Even the great Gatsby cannot be trusted, creating elaborate fictionalized accounts of his youth comparable to the outlandish stories created about him by complete strangers. The fact that all of the other characters are incapable of honesty lends credibility to Nick's observations, and thereby readers are made to pay closer attention to what he has to say. Literary scholar David Stouck recognizes that "While Nick's focus is on Gatsby, we must remember that ours can only be on Nick; the latter's perception not only determines the novel's shape, but actually provides its content" (65). But what is the content and why are we drawn in?

Nick captures our attention with what seems to be simply the tragic story of the failure of a rekindled romance between a man and a woman. Even this might be reason enough for us to listen to what he has to say. However, the novel is much more than the story of one couple's failure. Through Nick's tale and the revelation of the unrequited love between Gatsby and Daisy readers come face to face with the dynamic portrait of an entire era, unfailing because of its immense and convincing detail and its unabashed honesty. Each character, each symbol, and each carefully worded description lends itself to this greater vision. As literary critic R. W. Stallman put it: "Now the truth is that Gatsby exists in relation to everything in the novel . . . and nothing is in the novel that does not exist in relation to everything else" (55). The view that Fitzgerald presents is remarkably thorough, inclusive of the era's grandeur, its excess, the sense of opportunity and possibility, and ultimately, its overwhelming failures. It is this last subject which is the most significant, for it is at the very core of the novel. Scholar Marius Bewley states that "The theme of Gatsby is the withering of the American dream" (37), but if our words are chosen as carefully as Fitzgerald's are, one would have to revise this statement to say that a major theme of *The Great Gatsby* is the *corruption* of the American dream, "corruption" being more accurate than "withering," which connotes a natural process free and clear of accountability. As readers, we are acquainted with another failed romance—that between the dreamer and the dream, in this case, the American Dream. As it happens, the corruption of the American dream that Fitzgerald observes is entangled in a specific period in history, namely the 1920s—the time that falls between World War I and the Great Depression. And so, quite ambitiously, it is this that Fitzgerald reveals.

* * *

The Great Gatsby is set in 1922 in the midst of the Jazz Age, a prosperous but complex time following America's emergence from World War I. As the country transitioned from wartime to peacetime, the economy boomed. Mass production took off with major advancements in transportation and communication, and consumerism increased as these new technologies became accessible. One of the primary industries to rise out of this period of burgeoning industrialism was the automobile industry. Cars, which had previously only been available to the rich, were now becoming accessible to a greater population, and people looking to capitalize on this new industry opened gas stations and other related businesses, although not often with success. As a result of the economic upswing, there was a sense of opportunity and a new emphasis on individualism as citizens sought to realize the American dream of finding success and happiness as self-made men and women. The idea was that anyone could become a millionaire regardless of one's background. The actual attainability of this dream gave birth to a class of nouveaux riches, who were generally looked down upon by those who came from old money. In many cases the nouveaux riches were considered unnecessarily flamboyant and without style or good taste.

Regardless of one's social position, the decade was a time of immense social change. Following the horrors of the war, the old traditions and societal rules and regulations no longer seemed applicable. The rise of psychology and the writings of Freud influenced behavior, drawing attention to the acceptability of sexual awareness. Many people began experimenting with hedonism, allowing themselves to put more focus on individual satisfaction and less focus on any moral or societal responsibility. This included women. With the ratification of the Nineteenth Amendment women gained the right to vote, and with it, the belief that they were moving closer to attaining social equality. Women were freer and were able to express their sense of individuality. They no longer had to choose between family life and a career or personal fulfillment. Many women cut their hair short and wore it in a bob, and shortened their dresses, gaining notoriety as flappers. Despite advancements in the cause for women, however, the greater Civil Rights Movement still had many obstacles. Racism was rampant, and groups like the Ku Klux Klan were at their peak with millions of members. Additionally, prohibition, the outlawing of alcohol under the Eighteenth Amendment and the Volstead Act in 1919, led to an increase in illegal activities and crime as bootleggers and mob-run speakeasies became more prominent.

In less than two hundred pages, Fitzgerald was able to capture the essence of the era in its entirety, including its glory, its flaws, and its contradictions. Each social class found representation in *The Great Gatsby* via the setting and the characters. The fictional West Egg of Long Island, where Tom and Daisy Buchanan live, is the fashionable part of the area and where the old money resides. The fictional East Egg, home to Nick Carraway and Jay Gatsby, is the less-desirable area and home to new millionaires eager to flaunt their wealth. Fitzgerald makes the divide between these classes strongly felt by depicting residents of East Egg as flamboyant and over-the-top. Gatsby himself appears in a pink suit and his mansion is covered in so many lights that it resembles a circus or carnival, suggesting that Gatsby is a kind of oddity, his life a veritable sideshow. The residents of West Egg appear to be more refined (visually speaking), but they are also depicted as being more emotionally removed. George and Myrtle Wilson, who hail from the unfortunate valley of ashes, function as representatives of the lower class—those who had not found their way out of poverty, still pining after that which they believed the rich possess.

Nick and Gatsby serve as representatives of the Lost Generation. Both are soldiers who have emerged from the war hungry for success, although somewhat cynical. While Nick represents the recognition that innocence cannot be regained, Gatsby represents the unrelenting human desire to regain what has been lost by revisiting, and even repeating, the past. "'Can't repeat the past?' he cried, incredulously. 'Why of course you can!'" (116). It is more than Gatsby's personal opinion; it is a commentary on the nature of history itself (which, by the end of the story, readers may recognize as a warning).

Despite the fictionalized accounts of Long Island, Fitzgerald uses New York City as an undisguised symbol of the swiftly changing American landscape, while his home, the Midwest, remains a symbol of the pure, untainted American landscape of the past. The changes to American society were more visible in the East, especially in developing urban centers. Fitzgerald sensed the significance of this shift from rural to urban living, as well as the impact of the increased industrialism, and recognized this in his novel. Myrtle Wilson's husband, George, runs a failing auto repair shop and gas station, and the climactic scene of the novel, of course, includes cars, which Fitzgerald cleverly uses as a metaphor for the moral status of the characters. As is the case with much of the dialogue in the novel, Nick's dialogue with Jordan about her driving skills has a second meaning when considered more carefully:

"You're a rotten driver," I protested. "Either you ought to be more careful or you oughtn't to drive at all."

"I am careful."

"No, you're not."

"Well, other people are," she said lightly.

"What's that got to do with it?"

"They'll keep out of my way," she insisted. "It takes two to make an accident."

"Suppose you met somebody just as careless as yourself."

"I hope I never will," she answered. "I hate careless people. That's why I like you." (63)

The dialogue does more than hint at the characters' disregard for others, their selfishness, and their air of apathy when it comes to moral responsibility, and it is important to remember that this exhibition of moral vacancy was more than a trait assigned to this particular character. It was, for Fitzgerald during the 1920s, representative of the great flaw of an entire era, an entire nation. In the novel those who are reckless drivers are morally reckless, with little concern for anyone beyond themselves. Fitzgerald makes this point felt by repeating the bad driver motif through the story. The freeloading Owl Eyes gets into an accident following one of Gatsby's parties. Daisy kills Myrtle with her bad driving. It even appears less literally in Nick's description of Tom and Daisy: "They were careless people . . . they smashed up things and creatures and then retreated back into their money or their vast carelessness, or whatever it was that kept them together, and let other people clean up the mess they made" (187–188). This is not the only example of Fitzgerald using characters as metaphors. The women of the novel—Daisy, Jordan, and even Myrtle—are clichés of the new 1920s woman. They are primarily concerned with their own needs and desires, abandoning traditional maternal roles. Daisy, mother of young Pammy Buchanan, treats her daughter at worst like an afterthought and at best like a doll. We only meet the child once and it is only in an effort at displaying her for Gatsby.

"The Bles-sed pre-cious! Did mother get powder on your yellowy hair? Stand up now and say how-de-do . . ."
"I got dressed before luncheon," said the child, turning eagerly to Daisy.
"That's because your mother wanted to show you off." (123)

The male characters of the novel have an equally significant role. Major social problems are embodied in the hulking Tom Buchanan. His repeated references to works such as Goddard's "The Rise of the Coloured Empire" and his dissertations on the significance of not allowing other races to surpass the so-called Nordic race draw attention to the prevalent racism of the day. Fitzgerald makes Tom's ignorance impossible to ignore. Even his wife Daisy rolls her eyes and winks at her husband's remarks. But Tom is also the character chosen to make the announcement that Fitzgerald ultimately wishes to make. "'Civilization's going to pieces,' broke out Tom violently" (17). Minor characters such as Meyer Wolfsheim, a double for the nonfictional Arnold Rothstein who was accused of fixing the 1919 World Series, allowed Fitzgerald to address other issues such as the corruption of the American pastime and the dangers of bootlegging. While we view the characters drinking throughout the novel, there is a good degree of hypocrisy involved as they also outwardly disdain bootlegging.

While Fitzgerald has employed the characters as metaphors, it is equally important to recognize that he has chosen to make all of the main characters transplants. They are loosely characterized as being from the American West. They have attained wealth, however, the American dream for them has remained an illusion. Despite their wealth, none of the characters are happy in their current circumstances. Tom Buchanan, a former college athlete, begins an affair with Myrtle Wilson. Daisy is restless and dealing with the knowledge of this affair. Even Nick, who has moved east with the intention of learning the bond business, retreats disillusioned to his home at the end of the summer. Of course the most prominent example of this is Jay Gatsby, formerly James Gatz from North Dakota. Much time is spent on revealing this character and it is difficult to discern. The American dream, which used to be about attaining security for one's self and one's family and happiness, has been corrupted by people who want money for money's sake, for status, and for other shallow and selfish reasons. Gatsby, who was successful in attaining a fortune, has to resort to illegal activities to create this persona and still, in the end, does not win what he truly desires—namely, the love of Daisy. Myrtle, who comes from the valley of ashes, is also tied up in the dream of riches. When Nick visits the apartment where she meets with Tom, she changes into a chiffon dress. Nick notes that "with the influence of the dress her personality had also undergone a change" (35). Later in the scene she reflects on her husband, saying, "I thought he knew something about breeding but he wasn't fit to lick my shoe" (39). The novel has been labeled the Great American Novel, quintessentially American because it is about money. Although money infiltrates much of the story and much of the story revolves around social class, the story is about more. It is about greed, the insatiability of human nature, and the failed pursuit of a dream.

If the accomplishments of Fitzgerald that we have already discussed were not yet enough, the book also made literary headway, opening the door for new methods and a more relatable form of modern American literature. The particular style of the book evidenced Fitzgerald's desire for something new. The book, considered by many to be the first successful work of modern American literature, evidenced the tensions between modernist principles and the more traditional elements of Victorian literature. In *The Great Gatsby*, Fitzgerald used complex timelines, rejected any sense of Victorian optimism, and set his sights on a new romanticism with greater focus on realism, which included emphasis on issues of social concern without sacrificing the personal, intimate nature of the story. As culture changed, so too did literature, art, and music. Fitzgerald's new style reflected these changes as well, showing cinematic tendencies, text in the form of collage, and the rhythm inherent in jazz. A careful reader will note that music can be found throughout the novel, whether it comes from an orchestra at Gatsby's party, a song about "in-between time" being played on the piano, or in the sound of Daisy's voice. Even in the rhythm of the sentences and the exchange of language between the characters is the complex music of the era. Literary critic Lionel Trilling recognized this, maintaining that "Gatsby . . . comes inevitably to stand for America itself" (215). The novel encapsulated the cultural conflict of the time and has come to stand for America itself, for the human spirit itself, in both content and style.

Yet, it is important to recognize that *The Great Gatsby* has survived the ebb and flow of changing literary criticism not simply because it is a tremendous portrait of the 1920s in America, but because its themes, which address a larger human spirit and human morality, transcend any specific and final classification, speaking within a broader cultural context. Literary critic Harold Bloom correctly asserts, "Perhaps Gatsby does not suffer, being so lost in his dream. We suffer for Gatsby, as Carraway does, but what mitigates that suffering is the extent to which we too, as Americans, are lost in the same dream of love and wealth" (4). However, while this is true, it is not where the conversation should end. The late professor Kenneth E. Eble gets it right when he explains:

> What I am suggesting here is that if there is such a thing as the great American novel, it will not be because of the American-ness of what it is about . . . Fitzgerald's novel is animated by and makes its impact through a writer's intensely devoted attempt to understand a portion of human experience, the personal dimensions of that experience that reach into the hearts of human beings and the contexts that always complicate and alter such personal responses. From one perspective, these contexts are indubitably American, as much so as they seem to convey the pulse beat of the urban American 1920s. But from another, they are no more American than Ithaca is Greek or Bleak House British. What is kept before the reader . . . are the longings for love, wealth, power, status, for dreaming and realizing dreams and facing the realities of which dreams are compounded and by which they are compromised. (85)

Certainly one does not need to be American to understand the pursuit of a dream, the failures brought about by maligned or misguided intentions.

Works Cited

Bewley, Marius. 1968. "Scott Fitzgerald's Criticism of America." In *Twentieth Century Interpretations of The Great Gatsby*, edited by Ernest H. Lockridge. New Jersey: Prentice-Hall.

Bloom, Harold, ed. 1991. *Gatsby*. New York: Chelsea House.

Bruccoli, Matthew J. 1992. Preface to *The Great Gatsby*, by F. Scott Fitzgerald. New York: Macmillan Publishing Company.

Cowley, Malcolm. 1985. "The Romance of Money." In *F. Scott Fitzgerald*, edited by Harold Bloom. New York: Chelsea House.

Eble, Kenneth E. 1985. "*The Great Gatsby* and the Great American Novel." In *New Essays on Fitzgerald's The Great Gatsby*, edited by Matthew J. Bruccoli. Cambridge: Cambridge University Press.

Stallman, R. W. 1991. "Gatsby and the Hole in Time." In *Gatsby*, edited by Harold Bloom. New York: Chelsea House.

Stouck, David. 1991. "*The Great Gatsby* as Pastoral." In *Gatsby*, edited by Harold Bloom. New York: Chelsea House.

Trilling, Lionel. 1950. *The Liberal Imagination: Essays on Literature and Society*. New York: Viking.

The Critical Reception of *The Great Gatsby*_____

Amy M. Green

The Great Gatsby now holds an undeniable place among the master-pieces of twentieth-century American literature. The green light at the end of Daisy's dock and the spell it casts over Gatsby as he tries to force the world into his version of the American Dream endures as an iconic symbol of both optimism and failure. Despite the critical acco-lades now showered upon *The Great Gatsby*, the novel followed a path to success marked along the way by stinging criticism and lackluster sales at the time of its publication. Fitzgerald understood that his new novel would prove problematical for publishers, as "his story con-tained material that put it well outside the moral boundaries" (Hook, 63) of the commercial literary magazines of his day. Given Fitzgerald's often perilous financial situation, concerns about the marketability of the novel held potentially grave consequences for the author. Indeed, several literary magazines would not serialize *The Great Gatsby* due to concerns about moral issues raised by the story, including adultery and overt sexuality. The novel finally did find a home and was published by Charles Scribner's Sons on April 10, 1925. On the craft of writing, Fitzgerald commented, "An author ought to write for the youth of his own generation, the critics of the next, and the school masters of ever afterward" (Scribner, 22). These words proved prophetic as they relate to evolving critical and popular opinion of *The Great Gatsby*.

Literary luminaries within Fitzgerald's immediate circle, including Gertrude Stein, Ernest Hemingway, and T. S. Eliot, immediately show-ered his new novel with praise. Given that these authors emerged as the vanguard of the modernist movement in literature, their praise bol-stered Fitzgerald's sense of having accomplished something truly liter-ary. Unfortunately, the high esteem in which fellow authors held *The Great Gatsby* did not transfer to the reading public at large or the novel's profitability as "sales remained deeply disappointing," despite the often enthusiastic responses from friends and fellow writers (Hook,

71). Overall, however, the critical response to *Gatsby* immediately following its publication proved less than resounding endorsements for the novel. Influential critic H. L. Mencken reviewed the novel shortly after its publication and commented that the story was "no more than a glorified anecdote" (Mizener 1963, 2), finding the overall plot arc lacking in depth. However, Mencken did not believe that the novel was wholly without merit. He believed that it marked the evolution of Fitzgerald as an author and craftsman, writing that "the story, for all its basic triviality, has a fine texture, a careful and brilliant finish" (Mencken, 157). Furthermore, Mencken praised Fitzgerald's depiction of the decadence of the rich, including their ennui, their questionable morals, and their ever-changing habits—portraits he found accurate. Critic Laurence Stallings, who like Mencken reviewed *The Great Gatsby* in 1925, concurred with the prevalent critical view that the novel showcased Fitzgerald's ability to improve upon his previous novels and short stories. Stallings's overall praise of the novel proves conditional at best. He asserted that "the earlier Fitzgerald was barbarous; those who followed him have aped his barbarity" (Stallings, 155). Yet despite the improvements Stallings found in *The Great Gatsby*, he concluded that the novel did not rise to the level of masterpiece. He wrote, "I do not think for one moment in reading this book that 'here is a great novel' or even, that 'here is a fine book'" (154) and believed that the novel felt unfinished, much like a plan without fineness of execution, a view mirrored by Mencken.

Fitzgerald's acknowledgment of the novel's problematic issues of morality and sexuality contributed to *The Great Gatsby*'s lackluster reception by critics. One anonymous reviewer, writing in 1926, focused on his or her utter contempt for the characters in the novel, finding them unlikeable. The reviewer contended that the novel needed "perhaps an excess of intensity to buoy up the really very unpleasant characters of this story" (New Novels, 176). Modern critics would likely view such criticism as backhanded praise, given that Fitzgerald's story hinges upon the decadence and corruption of nearly every character the reader meets. It will also be the modern critic who recognizes Fitzgerald's realization in *Gatsby* of a theme he visited in earlier works, that of the decline of the wealthy, lazy, and ignorant brought to life by defining "convincingly the reasons for their defeat" (Mizener 1972, 61). However, at the time of its publication, the reading public seemed genuinely taken aback by Fitzgerald's frank depiction of moral decay. Other reviewers proved even less kind in their assessment, evidenced by the headline of a New York newspaper in 1925 which stated simply, "F. Scott Fitzgerald's Latest a Dud" (Hook, 70).

The Great Gatsby remained in critical and literary purgatory until the 1940s, when interest in the novel began to pick up in earnest, a trend which continued into the 1950s (Mizener 1963, 2–3). Critics G. Thomas Tanselle and Jackson R. Bryer see the year 1945 as pivotal to *Gatsby* scholarship and that a "revival" in the novel may have been ushered in by the publication of a scholarly essay praising heretofore neglected merits of the novel. Specifically, interest centered on "Fitzgerald's preoccupation with failure" and the difficulties of living in an industrialized "modern" world (Tanselle and Bryer, 182, 190). In *Gatsby*, Fitzgerald masterfully realizes both of these themes in the crafting of his titular character and indeed, critics took notice of Gatsby himself as a source for close examination. Where previous critics faulted the novel for its perceived lack of scope, the literary scholars of the 1940s recognized the complexity of Gatsby, "for Gatsby, divided between power and dream, comes inevitably to stand for America itself" (Trilling, 17). Whatever the plot may lack in terms of a far-reaching arc across time or exotic locales it makes up for in abundance with its "intellectual intensity" (17). Shortly thereafter in 1948, critic George Garrett recalls attending a class at Princeton in which Fitzgerald's works, including *Gatsby*, were taught for the first time (Garrett, 29), marking the start of *Gatsby* making headway into the classrooms of academia.

Interest in the novel continued into the 1950s. During this decade, scholarly commentary on *Gatsby* began to focus on the irony inherent in the character of Gatsby—a romantic man surrounded by, and even participating in, corruptive acts. The American Dream, once revered as an attainable, an almost holy icon of American culture, now found itself subject to scrutiny. Gatsby exemplifies the man who obtains, at least for awhile, the outward trappings of financial wealth only to see the empire he envisions for himself ultimately fail to materialize. Leslie Fiedler, writing in 1951, posited that *Gatsby* needed time in order to "catch on" with the reading public and critics alike in large part due to "Fitzgerald's refusal to swap his own lived sentimentalities for the mass sentimentalities of social protest that swamp the later Hemingway" (Fiedler, 75). Fiedler's insight into Fitzgerald prefigures by a scant few years the emergence of feminism as a counter to the idealized image of woman as happiest in the role of housewife, a hallmark of the American Dream of her decade. Additionally, critics of this era started to view *Gatsby* through a wider lens, where previous studies looked only at issues of biography or Fitzgerald's place as an author in the Jazz Age (Perosa, 222). Fitzgerald exposes the darkest aspects of human nature in *Gatsby*—from the fragile, ephemeral nature of dreams to the inability of wealth to provide any sort of lasting happiness—and this resonated with critics of the 1950s. The 1960s, a decade of social protest, continued to tear down the myth of the American Dream and the acceptability of the status quo. With some four decades now passed since the initial publication of the novel, critics and readers alike seemed better able to recognize the universality of Gatsby's flaws without fixating on Fitzgerald's depiction of "unreal characters" (Tanselle, 181). Arguably, Fitzgerald never set out with the intention of writing a novel which strictly adhered to the tenets of realism, a discipline steadily giving way to the modernist era by 1925. Yet his contemporaries seemed extraordinarily uncomfortable with the novel, perhaps less out of a dislike for its break with realism and more out of discomfiture at the possibility of the decadent world inhabited by Gatsby, the Buchanans, and Nick Carraway.

Jackson R. Bryer describes the 1970s as an era of "consistent and serious attention" to Fitzgerald's writings (248). Bryer himself is a critical figure in Fitzgerald scholarship, compiling criticism, book reviews, and scholarly pieces. He asserts that *Gatsby* benefits from critical focus much more so than all other Fitzgerald fiction but *Tender Is the Night* (259). The year 1973 emerged as a pivotal one for *Gatsby* studies. Scholar Matthew J. Bruccoli published an edited edition of *Gatsby* which included both rejected passages and emendations made to the text as it moved from manuscript form to publication in 1925. Bruccoli's painstaking work with *Gatsby* led to many interesting points for textual study, including the discovery that Daisy's green dock light was not a part of the novel in its earliest form (Perosa, 233). In addition to the new edition of *Gatsby*, Bruccoli also contributed bibliographies, detailed listings of all of Fitzgerald's works, and editions of the author's letters. These scholarly works greatly facilitated those working in the field of Fitzgerald studies by providing a storehouse of information heretofore uncollected. From the 1970s to the present day, *Gatsby* criticism continues to branch out to include individual character studies, close readings, essays placing the novel in "the context of a wider vision of America and the American Dream" (Bryer, 262), freeing the work from the confines of the Jazz Age alone. By 1980, over fifty books "entirely devoted to Fitzgerald" had been published (247).

Critics continue to turn to *Gatsby* as a source of literary study. The complexity of the story and its biting social commentary lend itself to any number of critical perspectives, from New Historicism, to Feminism, to Queer Theory and beyond. *Gatsby* allows the reader to "clearly discern where we have been and where we have come from" (Garrett, 35) and the continuing healthy sales of the novel attest to its continuing power. Journal articles, books, and edited collections covering the spectrum of topics relating to *Gatsby* continue to emerge and the novel remains a critical component of literary studies, from the high school to collegiate levels. Critic Arthur Mizener, writing in the late 1990s, commented about the accessibility of *Gatsby*, since Fitzgerald so masterfully "makes the fate of his chosen people an image of the fate of Western society" (Mizener 1999, 93).

Gatsby eventually becomes the book "that would acquire classic status, and had written off those critics who had regarded [Fitzgerald] as too immature and unintellectual ever to produce a major literary work" (Hook, 79). Yet Fitzgerald did not enjoy such critical accolades during his lifetime, as the tide of opinion toward Gatsby turned only in the years following his death. Although members of the intellectual and literary elite immediately recognized Gatsby as a profound contribution, the public needed time and distance in order to come to the same level of appreciation. Recent decades have seen more copies of Fitzgerald's works, of which Gatsby remains a perennial favorite, sold each year than were sold during the whole of the author's lifetime. Publishing scion Charles Scribner III cautions that critics and readers alike should avoid approaching Fitzgerald's writings with the intention of looking for flaws. Instead, one should celebrate the poetic beauty of his prose, his ability to transform the ordinary and transport the reader (Scribner, 24). Rather than scorning the novel for its perceived lack of realism or complexity, readers and critics alike began from the 1940s onward to understand the profound social commentary embedded within the story of Gatsby's rise and fall. The varied and intensive scholarly study which continues to focus on the novel acts as a testament to the genius of its author.

Works Cited

Bryer, Jackson R. 1980. "Four Decades of Fitzgerald Studies: The Best and the Brightest." *Twentieth Century Literature* 26, no. 2, F. Scott Fitzgerald Issue (Summer): 247–267.

Fiedler, Leslie. 1963. "Some Notes on F. Scott Fitzgerald." In *F. Scott Fitzgerald*, edited by Arthur Mizener. Englewood Cliffs: Prentice-Hall. 70–76.

Garrett, George. 2000. "The Good Ghost of Scott Fitzgerald." In *F. Scott Fitzgerald: New Perspectives*, edited by Jackson R. Bryer et al. Athens: University of Georgia Press. 28–35.

Hook, Andrew. 2002. *F. Scott Fitzgerald: A Literary Life*. New York: Palgrave MacMillan.

Mencken, H. L. 1991. "As H. L.M. Sees It." In *F. Scott Fitzgerald: Critical Assessments*, edited by Henry Claridge. Vol. 2. East Sussex: Helm Information Ltd. 156–159.

Mizener, Arthur. 1963. Introduction to *F. Scott Fitzgerald*. Englewood Cliffs: Prentice-Hall.

_____. 1999. *F. Scott Fitzgerald*. 1972. New York: Thames and Hudson.

_____. "New Novels." 1991. In *F. Scott Fitzgerald: Critical Assessments*, edited by Henry Claridge. Vol. 2. East Sussex: Helm Information Ltd. 176–177.

Perosa, Sergio. 1980. "Fitzgerald Studies in the 1970s." *Twentieth Century Literature* 26, no. 2, F. Scott Fitzgerald Issue (Summer): 222–246.

Scribner, Charles III. 2000. "F. Scott Fitzgerald: A Publisher's Perspective." In *F. Scott Fitzgerald: New Perspectives*, edited by Jackson R. Bryer et al. Athens: University of Georgia Press. 22–27.

Stallings, Laurence. 1991. "The First Reader—Great Scott." In *F. Scott Fitzgerald: Critical Assessments*, edited by Henry Claridge. Vol. 2. East Sussex: Helm Information Ltd. 153–155.

Tanselle, G. Thomas, and Jackson R. Bryer. 1991. "*The Great Gatsby*: A Study in Literary Reputation." In *F. Scott Fitzgerald: Critical Assessments*, edited by Henry Claridge. Vol. 2. East Sussex: Helm Information Ltd. 181–194.

Trilling, Lionel. 1963. "F. Scott Fitzgerald." In *F. Scott Fitzgerald*, edited by Arthur Mizener. Englewood Cliffs: Prentice-Hall. 11–19.

"The Self-Same Song that Found a Path":
Keats and *The Great Gatsby*_____

F. Scott Fitzgerald's favorite author was John Keats. Of the "Ode on a Grecian Urn" Fitzgerald wrote, "I suppose I've read it a hundred times. About the tenth time I began to know what it was about, and caught the chime in it and the exquisite inner mechanics. Likewise with the 'Nightingale' which I can never read without tears in my eyes." And "The Eve of St. Agnes" has "the richest, most sensuous imagery in English, not excepting Shakespeare."[1]

Even without such an explicit statement from Fitzgerald, we might assume Keats meant something like that to him. In *This Side of Paradise* (II, ii), Amory Blaine declaims "the 'Ode to a Nightingale' to the bushes" and then talks about poetry, distinguishing between Keats and himself on what each finds "primarily beautiful." In the opening chapter of *The Great Gatsby* there is a nightingale singing in the Buchanan yard, the "very romantic outdoors." Several scenes in *Gatsby* take place in starlit nights; it is there that we so often see the title figure in his most characteristic pose, and it is the pose of the speaker in the Keats lyric: the man under the wandering stars who wants to comprehend and join his life to a precious being of eternal beauty. Fitzgerald quite consciously draws upon Keats's language; near the end of the fifth chapter, "there was no light save what the gleaming floor bounced in from the hall" is clearly an echo of Keats's phrase in the "Nightingale": "there is no light, / Save what from heaven is with the breezes blown. . . ." And another line from that poem will provide the title for Fitzgerald's most ambitious work, *Tender Is the Night*.

Keats's influence on *The Great Gatsby* should not be understood exclusively in the terms of "literary imitation."[2] The distinguishing and complicated similarity is in a realization of the ambivalence of beauty. Lionel Trilling has suggested in his essay on "The Fate of Pleasure" that Keats is our greatest poet of pleasure, that Keats understood pleasure with a greater intensity than any other figure in our literature.[3] There is a preoccupation in both Keats and Fitzgerald with the saturation of sense in beakers of wine, "the purple-stainéd mouth." Yet the traditional intoxicant to make us forget the world's pain is not heady enough; the effort is to confront a kind of total beauty in an exalted moment, where all the senses are throbbingly alive and "thou art pouring forth thy soul abroad / In such an ecstasy!" Fitzgerald wrote of the happiest moment of his life that he was "riding in a taxi one afternoon between very tall buildings under a mauve and rosy sky; I began to bawl because I had everything I wanted and knew I would never be so happy again."[4] The surrounding force of a real world will not allow the moment to be sustained. The "real" world—real by virtue of its oppressiveness—denies the existence in time of the ecstatic exaltation. When Nick Carraway says you can't repeat the past, Gatsby cries out "incredulously," "Can't repeat the past? Why of course you can!" And he looks "around him wildly, as if the past were lurking here in the shadow of his house, just out of reach of his hand." What he must touch, what all his money is intended to buy back, is the moment of joy on an autumn night five years previously when he had kissed Daisy and "wed his unutterable visions to her perishable breath." Gatsby is trying to escape time and "return to a certain starting place." Keats surrounds his joy of the nightingale's song with the bitter temporal world which renders the dream powerless because "Beauty cannot keep her lustrous eyes." Both Keats and Fitzgerald posit an idea of the beautiful moment, testing it and understanding it against the forces of time.

But there is finally a drastic contradiction in the beautiful moment itself. In the poetry of Keats and in *The Great Gatsby*, the greatest threat of all may come not from the outside, that cold rude world, but from an overabundance of the beautiful. In "Lamia" Keats writes that "Love in a palace is perhaps at last / More grievous torment than a hermit's fast." And in the "Ode on Melancholy,"

Pleasure nigh,
Turning to poison while the bee-mouth sips:
Ay, in the very temple of Delight
Veiled Melancholy has her sovran shrine. . . .

From the impulse to beauty, the visionary figure passes from dream to dream, finds himself "too happy in thine happiness," and becomes "half in love with easeful death." In the work of Keats the love of beauty becomes so intense, wrought to such a pitch, that it becomes almost indistinguishable from pain. Complete fulfillment is death. At the beginning of Fitzgerald's career he wrote that Amory Blaine's romantic commitment to beauty was an "overwhelming desire . . . to sink safely and sensuously out of sight" into "that long chute of indulgence which led, after all, only to the artificial lake of death."[5]

When Nick Carraway recounts the story of Gatsby's kissing Daisy he is "reminded of something—an elusive rhythm, a fragment of lost words, that I heard somewhere a long time ago." Perhaps on the Eve of St. Agnes. Both Keats's poem and Fitzgerald's novel are drenched in a spirit of ancient revelry. Keats's palace is the ancestral home of Gatsby's mansion where "The silver, snarling trumpets 'gan to chide: / The level chambers, ready with their pride . . . glowing to receive a thousand guests. . . ." Keats's hero partakes of the "magical glory" that Gatsby will; on the Eve of St. Agnes young Porphyro stands the way Gatsby later will stand, "with heart on fire . . . beside the portal doors, / Buttressed from moonlight" imploring "all saints to give him sight of" his beloved. Porphyro's fondest wish will become Gatsby's: "that he might gaze and worship all unseen; / Perchance speak, kneel, touch, and kiss. . . ." We get the lush exotic feel of gorgeous gifts from foreign places that the lover brings to his lady. In chapter five of *Gatsby*, after the tea party at Carraway's house in West Egg, the trio of Jay and Daisy and Nick wander over to Gatsby's mansion. In his "own apartment" Gatsby took out a pile of shirts and began throwing them, one by one, before us, shirts of sheer linen and thick silk and fine flannel, which lost their folds as they fell and covered the table in many-colored disarray. While we admired he brought more and the soft rich heap mounted higher—shirts with stripes and scrolls and plaids in coral and apple-green and lavender and faint orange, with monograms of Indian blue. Suddenly, with a strained sound, Daisy bent her head into the shirts and began to cry stormily.

"They're such beautiful shirts," she sobbed, her voice muffled in the thick folds. "It makes me sad because I've never seen such—beautiful shirts before."

In "The Eve of St. Agnes" Madeline dreams in an "azure-lidded sleep, / In blanched linen, smooth and lavendered" when her suitor "from forth the closet brought a heap" of

> Candied apple, quince, and plum, and gourd;
> With jellies soother than the creamy curd,
> And lucent syrops, tinct with cinnamon;
> Manna and dates, in argosy transferred
> From Fez; and spicéd dainties, every one,
> From silken Samarcand to cedared Lebanon.

When all "these delicates he heaped with glowing hand" on bright baskets and golden dishes he plays upon "her hollow lute" and—as Daisy wept into Gatsby's shirts—so, in the Keats poem, "fair Madeline began to weep" at the tune proclaiming "every sweetest vow."

Henry Dan Piper, in *F. Scott Fitzgerald: A Critical Portrait*, has suggested that the Keats stanza is echoed in the third chapter of *Gatsby*, the presentation of the refreshments at Gatsby's first party.[6] It is true that there we can see Fitzgerald consciously imitating the poet's description of sweetmeats; Fitzgerald's adjectives have a richness ("garnished," "glistening," "spiced") that Keats's do ("candied," "lucent," "silken," and, again, "spiced"). But the more resonant echo is perhaps the less consciously imitative one, the scene with the shirts and Daisy. There Fitzgerald is not just drawing up a menu which indicates that he had a copy of his Keats open beside him; he modulates the whole emotional importance of the moment, the meaning of the foreign treasures to the young man and woman, and the intense feeling that the objects stand for an occasion in their minds. The pervasive influence of Keats upon Fitzgerald will not be adequately understood if we confine ourselves to the abundant technical similarities and ironic imitations that Fitzgerald made of any particular Keats passage; these surface similarities are expressions of the fact that Keats's work touched Fitzgerald at the deepest reaches of his ideas and emotions.

The lovers, Porphyro and Gatsby, are both "famished pilgrims" who seek to be "saved by miracle." There is a religious quality to their service: just as Porphyro proclaims "Thou art my heaven, and I thine eremite" so Gatsby seeks through Daisy to go "to a secret place above the trees" and by kissing her "forever wed his unutterable visions to her perishable breath." At the very moment of the kiss she might blossom for him "like a flower and the incarnation" could be "complete." Porphyro and Gatsby come from afar to the inaccessible saintly girl— "high in a white palace the king's daughter, the golden girl"—and seek by strategy, by gifts, and by devotion to take her away forever into a land of sensuous delight and eternal, abiding love.

In the "Ode to a Nightingale" the speaker is alone with his desire, listening to the haunting music of a lovely presence; the devotion to the ideal beauty is so intense that the young man is blinded to the lesser things around him:

> I cannot see what flowers are at my feet,
>   Nor what soft incense hangs upon the boughs,
>   But, in embalmed darkness, guess each sweet. . . .

The same emotion and echoes of that language persist in *Gatsby*. Both Keats and Fitzgerald are able to impart an opulent sensuous surface to their writings, and they are at their very best when the imagery is chiefly visual, though other senses are often called upon to deepen and enrich the appeal. One of Keats's finest technical accomplishments was his rich and subtle presentation of one sensory experience in terms of another: wine tastes of color and sound. Similarly in *The Great Gatsby* Fitzgerald writes of "yellow cocktail music."

Fitzgerald's use of the technique in *The Great Gatsby* reflects a general cultural urge which his visionary bootlegger represents. One of the most difficult things to account for in the novel is the content of Gatsby's vision—to account, that is, for its imaginative power, the sheer thrill of it and the dangerous dark attraction it has for us. We know that the actual mechanics of a moneyed empire did not engage Fitzgerald. Max Perkins was terrifically enthusiastic about the manuscript that Fitzgerald had sent him from St. Raphael in the fall of 1924, but Perkins had some objections, mainly to the figure of Gatsby himself and to the nature of his wealth. Perkins wrote back,

> Now almost all readers numerically are going to be puzzled by his having all this wealth, and are going to feel entitled to an explanation. To give a distinct and definite one would be, of course, utterly absurd. It did occur to me, though, that you might here and there interpolate some phrases, and possibly incidents, little touches of various kinds, that might suggest that he was in some active way mysteriously engaged. . . .

Fitzgerald replied in December, from Italy; he thought he had located the real basis of the objection:

> *I myself didn't know what Gatsby looked like or was engaged in* and you felt it. If I'd known it and kept it from you you'd have been *too impressed with my knowledge to protest.* This is a complicated idea but I'm sure you'll understand.
>
> Anyhow after careful searching of the files (of a man's mind) for the Fuller McGee [*sic*] case . . .[7]

The point is that the actual sources of Gatsby's wealth, and the nature of his manipulations of it, were not an essential part of the vision Fitzgerald had. What did engage him was the presence and elaboration of signs of wealth as a signal of power exercised in the service of beauty. Gatsby's massive heaps of imported shirts are expressions of his devotion to a woman who had money in the sound of her voice. He presents such magnificent piles of luxury—in the sight and touch of his clothes, the joyous rhythms of his parties—to overwhelm her with beauty, an appeal to all her senses. He must get her to forget her husband and child and situation; to do that he must re-create the past by stocking and opening vast closets of sensory pleasure for a fairy princess. The commercial enterprise, in this way, becomes a function of amorous energy and a visible expression of it. The Chivalric Hero does not stand in armor, the Knight who slays the dragon for the love of the lady; he is, instead, a man "in a white flannel suit, silver shirt, and gold-colored tie" (Gatsby's incredible costume for the Carraway tea party) whose very splendor is nothing armed, all his aggression having been spent in the acquiring of "gorgeous rags."

When Fitzgerald would count up the five good things he had done in his revisions he would include "I've accounted for his money." But that accounting comes to us only in hints and nods that Fitzgerald gleaned from the newspaper accounts of Edward M. Fuller. Nick hears Gatsby say into the phone: "Well, he's no use to us if Detroit is his idea of a small town." Gatsby is quite right, the man is of no "use" to him, for Gatsby's perception of the sizes of American things is part of "the colossal vitality of his illusion." His sense of American geography is so vastly inaccurate that he is of the same breed as the unnamed business connection; on the ride in his fabulous open car, Gatsby does place San Francisco in the Middle West.

The essence of Gatsby's vision is willful ignorance, a refusal to recognize the unalterable distances of the world. Keats expresses again and again in the "Ode to a Nightingale" the desire to "Fade far away"; as the contrast between his imagined participation in beauty and his sad circumstance becomes unbearable, he cries out "Away! away! for I will fly to thee. . . ." To be an inhabitant of this world, to see oneself in it, is agony. There are "sleeping dragons all around," and true lovers must fly "o'er the Southern moors" to home. All around Gatsby's pleasure dome there are dragons sleeping in the valley of ashes. "The waste land" is presided over by Dr. T. J. Eckleburg, and "ashes grow like wheat into ridges and hills and grotesque gardens." Gatsby must get away from that corroding presence, refuse to inhabit the mundane world as anything other than "an ecstatic patron of recurrent light."

When Nick tries to find out what the source of Gatsby's money is, his neighbor admits that he was "in the drug business" and he was "in the oil business" and then says, "But I'm not in either one now." Fitzgerald's point is that Gatsby is in the pleasure business itself—his teeth set "at an inconceivable pitch of intensity." Where Gatsby gets all his wealth is where Porphyro in "The Eve of St. Agnes" gets all his treasures, from the immensity of devotion. The lover is true only if he creates "a world complete in itself." Wealth, in *The Great Gatsby*, is not the familiar notion of American money as the expression of a raw and ruddy frontier power; it is wealth chastened by a notion of romance, possibilities of great life beyond the rim of the actual. Wealth is beauty; it has been brought from all over the world, as Keats's treasures were "in argosy transferred from Fez" and "silken Samarcand" and "cedared Lebanon."

There is also the sense in *Gatsby* that to obtain beauty is to lose it. No present pleasure, realized and consummated, can fulfill the yearning for "the orgiastic future." In his autobiographical first novel Fitzgerald wrote of his hero, "it was always the becoming he dreamed of, never the being." And in *Gatsby*, after she cries in his shirts, Gatsby takes Daisy out to survey his grounds; he says, "You always have a green light that burns all night at the end of your dock." And Nick Carraway observes, "Daisy put her arm through his abruptly, but he seemed absorbed in what he had just said. Possibly it has occurred to him that the colossal significance of that light had now vanished forever." At the moment that was supposed to be the greatest triumph, the ecstasy, Gatsby loses sight of the "golden girl." Daisy accessible is not Daisy. At last when they can touch, when she does what he thinks is exactly the distinguished thing that all his effort will finally make her do—"put her arm through his"—Gatsby is lost. His vision had provided "a satisfactory hint of the unreality of reality" and promised him that the solid earth was finally malleable, if only his dream could be sufficiently large and intense. Gatsby knows that he must create a privileged community of abundant wealth; to live in that community is supposed to provide a heightened perception of the world, to extend one's awareness into a realm where the moment of splendor puts the dreamer in touch with the truth of a "Platonic conception." Fitzgerald conceives of truth in this novel much as Keats does in his poem on the Grecian Urn: those semitragic, semihistorical poses of immaculate desire where love is "forever warm and still to be enjoyed."

> Bold Lover, never, never canst thou kiss,
> Though winning near the goal—yet, do not grieve;
> She cannot fade, though thou hast not thy bliss,
> Forever wilt thou love, and she be fair!

Winning too near the goal results in grieving. Daisy can only exist for Gatsby so long as he cannot have her, so long as she is "as close as a star to the moon." And when he finally does have her again, "his count of enchanted objects" must necessarily be "diminished by one."

The ecstasy of longing is thwarted by possession. *The Great Gatsby* properly ends with images of running after, beating backward against the tide, a hopeless commitment of the self to the unobtainable. When Jordan Baker tells Nick that "Gatsby bought that house so that Daisy would be just across the bay" the overt implication is that some evening, sooner or later, she would be able to come over to him, wander into the blue ken of his yard; but the real power of Jordan's line, as the book displays Gatsby to us, lies in the covert meaning that the distance set up is exactly the right one. It is far enough to need the green light shining into the mist, far enough to establish the appropriate distance for the preservation of the dream as dream.

Critics have noted that there is a good deal of death imagery in *The Great Gatsby*. Henry Dan Piper writes that "the entire novel seems to have been conceived by Fitzgerald as the expression of a death wish."[8] In the first chapter, in a passage which Fitzgerald later revised, Nick Carraway said, "I suppose the urge to adventure is one and the same with the obscure craving of our bodies for a certain death." And in another draft of the book when Nick first sees Gatsby's car he is immediately reminded of a hearse.[9] On the ride into New York Gatsby and Nick pass a funeral procession, another of the several symbols in the book which connect the automobile and death.

But we should not understand these images of death merely as the counterpart to a dream of youth. When Nick says he is giving us "a story of the west after all" he is connecting Gatsby with the voyagers to the New World, linking Gatsby's dream to the dream of Columbus. Here the modern explorer sets out to find his New World. But to reach it he must go back, from West to East, just as he must go back in time, attempting to regain his youthful love affair. Spatially and temporally, *The Great Gatsby* is a voyage into the past, and the passion is in the voyage itself. Gatsby is a man of infinite will attempting to free himself of the known world's boundaries; he reaches blindly back to a moment of beauty, attempting to give it permanent status. To overpower the valley of ashes, massive creative devotion must recapture a lost state of amorous beatitude.

Death is at the center of the dream. For Fitzgerald as for Keats "the dreamer venoms all his days." In the "Ode to a Nightingale" the longing at the moment of greatest happiness is not for life:

> Now more than ever seems it rich to die,
> To cease upon the midnight with no pain. . . .

"Rich to die." And the ultimate meaning of the nightingale's song goes back into the world of the dead to become a historical recapitulation of lost dreams. The vision of ecstasy, pitched at death, reaches to "emperor and clown" in "ancient days" and the "self-same song that found a path / Through the sad heart of Ruth, when, sick for home, / She stood in tears amid the alien corn. . . ." Nowhere do we see the influence of Keats on Fitzgerald more strongly than in this notion of the ultimate extension of the yearning for ecstasy as visionary encapsulments of mortality. Keats hears the nightingale's "high requiem" fading away from him into the neighboring countryside. Gatsby on his blue lawn finds his dream "already behind him . . . where the dark fields of the republic rolled on under the night." The nightingale's song and the green light flow into richly storied scenery; for Keats beauty is "buried deep in the next valley glades" and for Gatsby the dream "vanished" into "the old island." The self describes the scene into which the personification of desire recedes, a lyric epiphany of loss. The romantic desire for mystical union with the beautiful drives both Keats and Fitzgerald back into legends of "vast obscurity," visionary dreams and loves surrendered to time.

Notes

1. From a letter to his daughter, August 3, 1940. Included in *The Crack-Up*, ed. Edmund Wilson (New York, 1959), p. 298.

2. See R. L. Schoenwald, "F. Scott Fitzgerald as John Keats," *Boston University Studies in English*, III (Spring, 1957), 12–21, and also John Grube, "*Tender Is the Night*: Keats and Scott Fitzgerald," *Dalhousie Review*, XLIV (1964), 433–441. Schoenwald mentions Keats's influence on *The Great Gatsby* very briefly (pp. 16–17), and Grube not at all.

3. Trilling includes the essay in *Beyond Culture: Essays on Literature and Learning* (New York, 1965), pp. 57–87. He maintains that Keats "may be thought of as the poet who made the boldest affirmation of the principle of pleasure and also as the poet who brought the principle of pleasure into the greatest and *sincerest* doubt" (p. 67).

4. *The Crack-Up*, pp. 28–29. There is a recurring concentration throughout his work on the moment of beauty *as moment*. "After all," he wrote, "any given moment has its value; it can be questioned in the light of after-events, but the moment remains. The young prince in velvet gathered in lovely domesticity around the queen amid the hush of rich draperies may presently grow up to be Pedro the Cruel or Charles the Mad, but the moment of beauty was there." Quoted by Malcolm Cowley in his introduction to *The Stories of F. Scott Fitzgerald* (New York, 1951), p. xiv.

5. *This Side of Paradise* (II, v).

6. New York, 1965, p. 313, n. 16.

7. Piper presents the letters, pp. 112–113.

8. P. 107.

9. See Piper's discussion of the Princeton manuscripts, p. 109.

Paradox, Ambiguity, and the Challenge to Judgment in *The Great Gatsby* and *Daisy Miller*_____

Neil Heims

I

F. Scott Fitzgerald's short novel *The Great Gatsby* (1925) and Henry James's novella *Daisy Miller* (1878) both begin with a narrator offering a series of confidences that seem to demand the reader's indulgence. They both seem to suggest that these revelations will reward the reader with some moral instruction that will benefit his or her ability to judge others, or convince them to refrain from judging others, even when behavior may appear to be or may in fact be different from what usually passes for acceptable.

James begins with a description of the Swiss town of Vevey, set at the end of the nineteenth century, and its many hotels "of every category," sounding almost like a tourist's guidebook. Indeed, *Daisy Miller* turns out to be some kind of guidebook, but one that despairs of offering suitable guidance for evaluation of human character or behavior, except for the postulations that motive is ambiguous, personality difficult to fathom, and perception subjective and not entirely reliable.

Problems of understanding, ambiguity, and perception plague the vacationing Winterbourne, for whom the authorial narrator seems to be a discreet surrogate who presents the story from Winterbourne's point of view. The conflict that the title character, young American Daisy Miller, provokes for Winterbourne's settled value system casts him as the principal character. Daisy remains constant. She does not change, though Winterbourne's understanding of her does. Indeed, he undergoes a potentially transformative experience through their interaction.

The elegant hotel *Trois Couronnes*, "classical" and distinguishable "from many of its upstart neighbors by an air of both luxury and of maturity," offers a normative standard that its guests can be measured by.

June is the time of year when many American tourists descend on Vevey, and the hotel takes on some of their characteristics, notably their uninhibitedness, becoming "an American watering place." However, lacking European cultivation, the visitors fail to display the decorum that the setting demands.

The conflict in *Daisy Miller*, and within Winterbourne himself, is between refinement, restraint, and adherence to social rules (elements of Winterbourne's character) and doing as one pleases, even in defiance of established rules of conduct (characteristic of Daisy Miller). It is not necessarily clear by the end of the tale which attitude is preferred, but Daisy's charming mixture of innocence and determination elicits strong reader sympathy while the proper society ladies who censure her appear snobbish, limited, and unyielding.

II

Paradox, rather than ambiguity, governs the ethical revelations evinced by the denouement of *The Great Gatsby*. Despite Gatsby's underworld past and associations, which narrator Nick Carraway finds contemptible, Gatsby bears a noble sensibility. He defies oppressive society by trying to conform to it. No matter how deeply it may be the result of a need to transform himself from a no-account impoverished youth into a man who can be proud of his accomplishments, Gatsby touches such depth that he sacrifices himself for the woman he loves, Daisy Buchanan. He never reveals that she was driving his car when it struck and killed Myrtle Wilson. Tom and Daisy Buchanan, on the contrary, are part of "a rotten crowd" and seem to be merely creatures of surface, who would sacrifice themselves for no one. Nick regards them as "careless people," who "smashed up things and creatures and then retreated back into their money or their vast carelessness . . . and let other people clean up their mess." Despite his vulgarity and past criminal activities, Gatsby is "worth the whole damn bunch put together." The reader will likely feel something similar about Daisy Miller, who is rejected by society, and in some measure even by Winterbourne, because social arbiters like Mesdames Costello and Walker see as vulgar what others consider youthful spontaneity. Might not the reader sense that it is social condemnation that drives Daisy Miller to the recklessness that society condemns?

The more refined and sophisticated Winterbourne (an American who resided for a considerable period of time in Geneva) is sipping coffee in the garden of the *Trois Couronnes* one evening, when the embodiment of American excess and lack of constraint first appears in the form of an American boy of nine, Randolph Miller, Daisy's brother. He is carrying "a long alpenstock, the sharp point of which he thrust into everything that he approached—the flower-beds, the garden-benches, the trains of old ladies' dresses." He stops in front of Winterbourne and demands a lump of sugar. With permission to take one, Randolph takes three. Winterbourne engages him in conversation, learning much about his family, their itinerary, and their home in Schenectady, until Daisy approaches. Because of this acquaintance with her brother, Winterbourne feels comfortable that he is not violating etiquette by initiating a conversation. She is not only entrancingly beautiful but is as forward in her speech as she is self-contained. He cannot decide whether she is deep or shallow, naïve or reckless. He never takes her seriously. He condescends to her. He sees her as capricious, and decides that she does not really have the sense to govern herself. His aunt's refusal to see her, too, is an insult that he does not entirely repudiate. These elements of disrespect are what Daisy reproaches him for in a "message before her death which [he] did not understand at the time."

III

Like *Daisy Miller*, *The Great Gatsby* begins with movement from self-centered, contextual exposition to introduction of characters and dialogue. Upon first appearance, a sense of mystery surrounds both Daisies. The preceding exposition in *The Great Gatsby* is more conversational and personal than in *Daisy Miller.* James's narrator is authorial, confident, dry, ironic, and untouched by moral ambiguity, delivered with insight into the characters tempered by modest sobriety in the face of human complexity. The focus of *Gatsby* is the life story and sentiments of its narrator. Nick immediately admits to his involvement in the tale and to the powerful effect it has had on his life. Unlike Winterbourne, he is anything but disinterested.

The year is 1922. A Midwesterner, Nick has returned from the First World War and traveled to New York to seek his fortune as a bond trader. He is so emotionally immersed in the "riotous" story he tells—being a principal actor in its events—that after he returns home to write about what has happened, he longs for a world governed by the sort of discipline that puts everyone in uniform and in a stance of continual "moral attention." Unlike Winterbourne, he does not doubt his own values or internal balance; he doubts the world's. Winterbourne, his value system jolted, withdraws, as his refined character would dictate, behind the convention of a detached, third-person narrator, avoiding violent emotion and injecting distance, balance, and ambiguity. He is torn between his appreciation of and desire for Daisy Miller and his respect for what is proper; he remains suspended between attraction and repulsion. Nick is not conflicted by the disturbing allure of a woman. Being married, Daisy Buchanan is unavailable to him in any event, and her friend Jordan Baker provides a surrogate, shallow romance, one of no great consequence to the plot or to his own development, except for the opportunity it affords him to assert his independence from the entire New York milieu, which he is both attracted to and repulsed by.

Nick Carraway's presence as narrator of *Gatsby* does not provide objective distance or worry the reader with the awful consequences of the ambiguity of knowing. It seeks to excite the reader, to draw the reader in, even to persuade the reader to be governed by and acquiesce in Nick's values, judgments, and enthusiasms. It dazzles, disorients, and, finally, disenchants the reader—paralleling the arc of Nick's journey. Unlike Winterbourne, Nick is quick to experience strong sentiments, even revulsion and disappointment, and to make judgments. He is emphatic about the fact that the events of this story have shaken him and changed him, subdued his ardor for experience. Winterbourne was a rather subdued fellow before he met Daisy Miller, which, the tale suggests, is his problem. The encounter seems only to make him more committed to the kind of reserve that Daisy Miller challenges.

The focus of *Gatsby* is not human or moral complexity. The issues are clear and the characters sharply drawn as fleshed-out stereotypes: Tom the scoundrel; Daisy is spoiled and unstable, defeated and ironic; Jordan Baker is proud and dishonest; Myrtle, Tom's mistress, is vulgar, discontented, and grasping; and Gatsby is the sacrificial lamb, consumed by a society trivialized by class distinctions and an egoism that yearns for those distinctions. All of the players in *Gatsby* are in one way or another posing, always striving to maintain an image. The characters in *Daisy Miller* are established in themselves and defined by their class, the embodiment of their roles. Only Daisy can be suspected of taking on a role, playing at her own actual disposition, and defensively flaunting it when challenged and condemned. Nick Carraway tries not to pose. He seeks his identity. His rite of passage involves discerning other people's stances and is completed once he sees through them. His experience fills him with passion while releasing him from passion, leaving him philosophical and exhausted, a man whose only pose is not to pose. He has "seen the skull beneath the skin" and enters the realm of those who have been subdued by experience.

IV

The irony of *The Great Gatsby*, despite its focus on class distinctions, does not result from the clash of the human character, in all its subtle complexity, with a formal and exclusive social order, as in *Daisy Miller*. Fitzgerald's irony stems from the fact that people are often the opposite of what they appear to be and that, in their particular desires, they are often set in conflict with each other. Tom Buchanan, a wealthy, established, conservative ex-football player, is a vulgar and brutal egoist, a hypocrite, an immoral upholder of conventional morality. Despite his social and economic status, Tom is perpetually driven by one motive—to assert his mastery. The upstart mobster Gatsby is an innocent and a gentleman impelled by an ideal, by an apparition of success that he takes for the real thing. To win Daisy Buchanan's love signifies for Gatsby a triumph of the creative power of his imagination. To possess her would indicate a successful transformation from the poor and outcast James Gatz to the wealthy and independent Jay Gatsby.

Nick begins his narration by taking us into his confidence with a sort of confession that quickly turns into a piece of advice. He relates that his father told him, "Whenever you feel like criticizing anyone, just remember that all the people in this world haven't had the advantages that you've had." This reflection is perfectly applicable to *Daisy Miller*, if the word "advantages" is replaced by "breeding," for what she lacks is the breeding required to be admitted to the society of Mesdames Costello or Walker. A want of regard for the rules of the game allows Daisy's behavior to be as free of social constraint as it is and makes it the fulcrum of ambiguity upon which the moral as well as the interpersonal issues of *Daisy Miller* turn. Nick's father's admonition, proffered as a guide to temper criticism of others, applied as mitigation in considering Gatsby, can also encourage condemnation of Tom and Daisy Buchanan.

As the entrance of the Millers into the hotel garden sets in motion Winterbourne's tale, so does Nick's invitation to Tom and Daisy's (his second cousin) mansion for dinner. The *Trois Couronnes* and the Roman drawing room of Mrs. Walker in *Daisy Miller* are essentially symbolic representations of the social norm of their social setting, which in turn provides the point of view from which the events are seen. Likewise, the motive forces in *Gatsby* are the milieu of upscale Long Island and the socioeconomic inequalities of American society.

V

Nick's cottage is set in West Egg, in the midst of fabulous and extravagantly vulgar mansions and imitation European castles, commissioned by the newly rich to broadcast their wealth. Tom and Daisy Buchanan live across the bay in East Egg, which claims equally wealthy, if not wealthier, inhabitants whose tastefulness reflect [sic] the tact of those more secure in their wealth and social position. However, as in Tom, their vulgarity is concealed behind a façade of respectability. Born to money, Tom need not strive and struggle to find identity in a world governed by wealth in the way that Gatsby, born to poverty, does. In fact, where Gatsby desires to enter the rarified realm represented by Daisy, Tom's tastes tend toward the vulgar, as his liaison with Myrtle Wilson attests.

In the same way Randolph prepares Winterbourne and the reader for the first appearance of Daisy Miller by serving as her context, Tom serves as context and prelude to Daisy Buchanan's arrival. While Randolph points to the kind of world Daisy Miller comes *from*, Tom represents the kind of world Daisy Buchanan lives *in*. He is the force of nature that defines her. Unlike Daisy Miller, Daisy Buchanan is not in rebellion against the mores of her society, but acquiesces to them with narcissistic irony. Daisy Miller is neither melancholic, ironic, nor narcissistic. She is simply vivacious in her innocent lack of concern for forces that would stifle her. Moreover, she has a natural grace, expressed in the tasteful way she dresses. Of course, she is hampered by the mores of society, and so is Winterbourne, who betrays her trust, primarily because he has internalized the rules of the game so deeply. And so Daisy is cut off from her social world, and Winterbourne is cut off from the realization of his desire and from the gift of contact with her.

Like Daisy Miller, Daisy Buchanan is hampered by the gender roles assigned by society in a way that Tom and Winterbourne are not. Unlike Daisy Miller, Daisy Buchanan acquiesces to society in the same way she acquiesces to her subordinate status as a woman. By acquiescence, Daisy Buchanan survives and moves from the intriguing interlude with Gatsby to a comfortable domesticity with Tom. Daisy Miller's indiscretion harms no one but herself, while Daisy Buchanan's affair results in Myrtle Wilson's death, something for which Daisy receives no sanction and about which she appears to experience little concern. The night of Myrtle's death, Tom and Daisy are seen sitting together contentedly in their kitchen, enjoying a late supper. Ultimately, she shows no less contempt for her social inferiors than does her husband.

The disproportionate nature of gender privilege is only reinforced by Fitzgerald's inclusion of Myrtle Wilson's infidelity in the plotline. Her rebellion against her husband, garage man George Wilson, is not a sign of her liberation from the constraints of gender; it indicates her submission to Tom's superior sexual potency and class privilege. Tom is thirty, no longer a college football star, but Nick sees in his features signs of hardness, arrogance, superciliousness, dominance, and aggressiveness. From early on Tom regarded himself as part of the master race.

VI

Daisy Miller is a psychological enigma to Winterbourne, to the narrator, and ultimately to the reader. She is caught in a world of conflicting values and perceptions but retains her independence, absorbing and returning the scorn of society. Daisy Buchanan, oppressed and resigned, but nevertheless comfortable, is not perplexing in the least. While Tom too can also be seen as a captive of his circumstances, it is because of those circumstances he is able to thrive, without suffering or needing to reflect. After Myrtle's death, that he "cried like a baby" when he shut down the apartment he had rented for her indicates not his suffering but his self-indulgence. He was weeping for his own lost youth. Nick imagines Tom as always being on the make and seeking, without ever recapturing, "the dramatic turbulence of some irrecoverable football game."

Tom, whose money is his power, is the determining force in his own life. Consequently, he is more like Daisy Miller, as she asserts herself and outrages custom, than Daisy Buchanan is. Tom's gender and class, however, grant him privilege and power that Daisy Miller cannot have: he gets away with his indiscretions. Only Nick realizes the outrage. Daisy Buchanan, too, escapes sanction because of the protection of men: Gatsby and Tom. She cannot assert as Daisy Miller did, "I have never allowed a gentleman to dictate to me, or to interfere with anything I do." Indeed, Nick says of Daisy Buchanan, after Gatsby goes off to war and before Tom arrives, "She wanted her life shaped . . . by some force—of love, of money, of unquestionable practicality. That force took shape . . . with the arrival of Tom Buchanan."

VII

Nick first sees Daisy Buchanan stretched out on an enormous couch alongside Jordan Baker, their skirts billowing in a breeze that wafts through the room, which is blocked when Tom closes some windows. Daisy is a picture of boredom and idleness. Her face gives off a sense of sadness despite the loveliness Nick sees in it. She chatters to Nick, who is thrilled by her voice, with flighty energy, avoiding saying anything meaningful. Similar to Daisy Miller, she is a force that kindles desire in others. Her chatter is mannered and self-conscious, rather than innocently direct and uncannily accurate like Daisy Miller's. Only when Jordan, hearing Nick say he lives in West Egg, asks if he knows a man named Gatsby does Daisy rise from her lassitude and become animated. But a call to dinner prevents Nick from saying anything about his neighbor or learning the cause of her sudden interest. What Nick learns at dinner is that there is strain in the relationship between Tom and Daisy because Tom has a mistress.

Nick Carraway portrays Daisy Buchanan as a figure clouded in mystery, but the mystery that Nick must penetrate about her is not the same as the one Daisy Miller presents to Winterbourne. Unlike Daisy Miller, Daisy Buchanan is no puzzle. Her mystery is not "the mystery of a young girl's sudden familiarities and caprices." It is the mystery of particular past events in her life that are revealed during the course of *The Great Gatsby*. Her circumstances are puzzling at first, as are her remarks, only because narrative information is withheld. Why does she despair at being a woman? Is she teasing Tom when she blames him for hurting her little finger or alluding to his violent side? What is the cause of her lethargy, or her cynicism, or her banter? Unraveling the circumstances that make her what she is comprises a significant amount of the substance of *Gatsby*. But while her circumstances and mysteries are historical, in *Daisy Miller* they are psychological and ethical. In the final accounting, Winterbourne may be just as perplexed about his powers of observation as he is about Daisy Miller. Once all is known, Daisy Buchanan's behavior, her speeches, her attitudes are entirely understandable and explainable. Nothing is hidden from Nick's understanding. Nor does he doubt his judgments. Daisy Buchanan is shallow, transparent, and selfish in a way that Daisy Miller is not.

There is a kind of tragic nobility in Daisy Miller, as there is in Gatsby. They both sacrifice themselves: he to love, she to a will that defies social convention. As *Gatsby* unfolds, the reasons why Daisy Buchanan is flighty, cynical, and unsure are revealed. She was disappointed in a first love and then entered into marriage with Tom, despite reservations, only to find deeper humiliation because of his brutality and jealousy and his contempt for any interest but his own. Nothing, however, is directly revealed about Daisy Miller or the reasons for her behavior. Understanding her must be the fruit of interpretation based on hints, like her final message regarding esteem. We are never told whether she is intensely naïve or astonishingly deep, or whether she is a flirt and a tease or a dangerously ignorant young American girl. We don't know whether she behaves in Rome as she does out of innocence and spite, violating all propriety by going unescorted wherever she pleases with Giovanelli, or if she is acting out of frustration at Winterbourne's coldness and disrespect. Then again, perhaps all these speculations miss the mark and she is simply a young lady inclined to follow her own impulses despite the objections of others. How are we to judge that?

Winterbourne is actually as much an enigma for Daisy Miller as she is for him. He maintains an attitude toward her of an older brother, despite feeling annoyed and jealous about her receptivity to Giovanelli's advances. He maintains a calm exterior despite his fantasy that they will elope when they meet in the hotel lobby before traveling to a castle in Chillon. The reader, though, is fully aware that he is more troubled by the fact that she favors Giovanelli than by her violation of social taboos.

Daisy Miller is accurate in her description of Winterbourne as stiff. His behavior is quite obtuse. In conversation with her at Mrs. Walker's, he reproaches her with the fear that her "habits are those of a flirt." "Of course" they are, she acknowledges, and asks if he has "ever hear[d] of a nice girl that was not," and supposes that "you will tell me that I am not a nice girl." Winterbourne, ever the gentleman and repressed suitor, attests that he thinks she is very nice, but says, "I wish you would flirt with me." Her response is pure flirtation: "You are the last man I should think of flirting with. . . . As I have had the pleasure of informing you, you are too stiff." "You say that too often," Winterbourne answers, quite stiffly, unable to sense she is flirting with him. Daisy chuckles and says, "If I could have the sweet hope of making you angry, I would say it again." Ever blind to her playfulness, Winterbourne responds that being angry would make him stiffer, and once again admonishes her, "if you won't flirt with me [stop flirting with Giovanelli]." Even then Daisy Miller continues to tease him. Is it not because of her affection for him and her frustration at his assumed superiority?

Unlike Daisy Buchanan, Daisy Miller seems not to have a back story. No report of circumstances is offered to account for how she speaks and acts, except that she is American and not European. There is an arch suggestion throughout that Winterbourne has a back story, but it is only hinted at and never limned. Daisy Miller is as much a cultural emblem or allegorical figure as she is a psychologically complex fictional character. She combines the strange American mixture of innocence and brashness or, as Winterbourne notes, confounded by her ease in talking to men, "audacity and puerility."

There is no ambiguity, obscurity, or psychological complexity regarding Daisy Buchanan's feelings about Gatsby. She is torn between two attachments. As she was first presented as a windblown creature, she is carried off by the bigger gust. She does not follow her own preferences but acquiesces to the stronger man. Her rejection of Gatsby for Tom is a statement about each man's power, not about the intensity of her love.

VIII

When Nick returns to West Egg after his first dinner with the Buchanans and lingers in his yard to enjoy the bright summer night, he sees the figure of his neighbor, Gatsby, regarding the starry sky and then the water of the bay that touches the edge of his lawn. A sense that Gatsby wishes to be undisturbed prevents Nick from calling out. Like Daisy Buchanan, Gatsby is a mysterious figure only because there is a yet-untold story behind him. However, it is intertwined with hers and will be revealed during the course of *The Great Gatsby*. He is introduced to the reader as a fragment of a conversation, then appears as a figure seen in the distance surrounded by night, then as a man who recognizes Nick at one of his stupendous parties but whom Nick does not recognize, and always as a conundrum until after his death, when his entire story is unraveled. Like Daisy Miller, Gatsby in death becomes an emblematic figure for some aspect of American life. Just as Tom is the vacuous, self-satisfied, privileged American boy-man, Gatsby is the dissatisfied, disenfranchised American boy-man trying to claw his way to social acceptance and self-regard by gathering wealth and breaking into high society. Both he and Daisy Miller are socially unacceptable, and both have a strong desire to be accepted, but Daisy Miller has no intention of transforming herself. Gatsby, on the other hand, is all about self-transformation, even during childhood, as the resolutions written inside the Hopalong Cassidy book his father later shows Nick indicate. Once known, Gatsby's history dissolves his mystery and simultaneously reveals and debunks the American myth of possibility and upward mobility.

Since Gatsby and Daisy Buchanan have a prior connection, since there is a back story for them, his story will illuminate her obscurity just as hers will give meaning to his. In this way they are like Winterbourne and Daisy Miller: they define and illuminate each other. Whereas Winterbourne and Daisy Miller interact on what can be called a subconscious level—each bringing out the defenses the other relies on in order to maintain composure—Gatsby and Daisy Buchanan have had a relationship, even if secret. They have experienced the piercing excitement of acknowledged desire in each other's presence.

Like Daisy Miller, Gatsby is emblematic of innocence and brashness: reputedly American characteristics. Despite his murky career, he is an innocent, one who does not think to reflect on the ethics and morality of his desires or the actions taken in their pursuit. Gatsby's is a story of class envy, of how James Gatz, a child of squalor, transforms himself into Jay Gatsby, a man of mythic splendor and flamboyance, and how Daisy becomes a symbol of the unattainable he is determined to possess.

Despite the confusion he experiences in his attempt to understand Daisy Miller, Winterbourne retains the reserve, propriety, and emotional neutrality that his acculturation and class have bestowed upon him. Nick Carraway, narrator and participant in the story he tells, experiences its events "within and without, simultaneously enchanted and repelled by the inexhaustible variety of life." For Winterbourne, experience is something that only lightly brushes him as it passes by, leaving his buried self untouched. Nick's experience touches him, seduces him, and then bowls him over. With an analytic eye, James penetrates the environment he composes and shows it to be constricting and claustrophobic, notwithstanding its opulence. The settings, gardens, parks, drawing rooms, and carriages in the Pincio are backdrops where characters meet and converse and enact the psychodrama of the human encounter. Crossing beyond the boundaries of that environment, as Daisy does, can be most dangerous, even deadly. It is not wealth but behavior that matters in this world, and her behavior diminishes her personal value. The setting of *The Great Gatsby* is magnetic, seductive in its opulence, compelling even when lurid, unstable, and fraught with violence. Only wealth matters. Daisy Buchanan, after all, whose voice even sounds like money, is a highly desirable commodity. Indeed, her market value soars as a result of the competition for her between Gatsby and Tom. The events of the tale ultimately lead Nick to resign himself to the fraudulence of wealth and opulence as ideals, to discover their emptiness, their cruelty, their disregard for human lives.

Works Cited

Fitzgerald, F. Scott. 1992. *The Great Gatsby*. New York: Macmillan.
James, Henry. 1878. *Daisy Miller: A Study in Two Parts*. New York: Harper & Brothers.

Babbled Slander Where the Paler Shades Dwell:
Reading Race in *The Great Gatsby* and *Passing*_____
Charles Lewis

[Passing is] such a frightfully easy thing to do. If one's the type, all that's needed is a little nerve. (Nella Larsen, *Passing* 25)

He hurried the phrase . . . or swallowed it, or choked on it, as though it had bothered him before. And with this doubt, his whole statement fell to pieces, and I wondered if there wasn't something a little sinister about him, after all. (F. Scott Fitzgerald, *The Great Gatsby* 43)

The resemblances between F. Scott Fitzgerald's *The Great Gatsby* (1925) and Nella Larsen's *Passing* (1929) are remarkably extensive and largely unrecognized.[1] These two short novels offer surprisingly similar portraits of an America whose bright notes of progress and prosperity were dampened by widespread racism and nativism, so it is no coincidence that novels about racial passing, such as Larsen's, proliferated in the 1920s, nor is it altogether an anomaly when we encounter (in Fitzgerald's story of a different sort of passer) Tom Buchanan's lightly veiled reference to Lothrop Stoddard, arguably the most widely known race theorist in America at the time.[2] Yet critics generally have not linked what is now one of America's more widely studied novels about racial passing with our most familiar canonical emblem of American self-invention and social mobility, despite their historical proximity, thematic overlap, and formal similarity.

In each novel, the main character is a passer closely observed by another admiring but ambivalent character whose relationship with the passer is fraught with tension and ambiguity, whose own position in society similarly entails an element of passing, and whose perspective infuses the narrative with a highly charged mix of desire and dread. The plots of these novels feature the protagonists' attempts to return to an earlier state of affairs that is itself folded into the narrative structure, and their problems are prominently rendered in terms of marriages to similarly racist husbands. The presence of race in each novel is variously literal and figurative, a distinction that is itself both underscored and undermined by the position and practice of the passer. In each novel, then, the fictional rendering of passing is not only a dramatization of the social complexities of racial identity but also a trope for reading, whereby racial figuration links race to reading (as Ellison might have put it) on a broader frequency. Passing is, in this sense, not so much just *what* we read as it is a trope for *how* to read, for although race operates in these novels as what Henry Louis Gates has described as "the ultimate trope of difference" ("Writing 'Race'" 5), passing invites us to read race as something more like a final twist: a trope for the difference that is figuration itself. In this sense, the passer conducts us through a racialized territory marked with key questions about literary form, operation, meaning, and value. The passer, at least in literary fiction, is more than a person in society, serving as a textual trope for the "double-consciousness" of race whose "two-ness" of figurative play is conjoined not only in our segregated readings of this fiction, but also in the critical passage between—and beyond—them. Indeed, the ties forged here between these two novels are themselves bound in a kind of critical pass that invokes literal and figurative charges of plagiarism intended to prefigure the passer's own figurative play and interrogation of our reading practices. A character like Clare Kendry, who literally passes racially, therefore suggests important (and potentially disturbing) connections to one like Jay Gatsby, whose passing is figuratively rendered in terms of racial blackness.

While Clare's story in *Passing* is a literal (or more conventional) instance of racial passing, her identity is nevertheless problematic; her father is white, she is raised by white relatives, and her appearance is taken for white, so the claim that she is black poses familiar questions about not only the legal definition and social construction of race but also its literary representation and figurative signification in fiction. Indeed, Clare's passing anticipates the critical reception of Larsen's novel, which has been described as a narrative that is itself passing as a fiction of racial passing—and whose true identity can be interpreted more accurately in terms of modernist psychology, homosexual desire, or class conflict.[3] In this sense, passing is a figurative trope by which readers have read beyond (or through) the literal depiction of race in order to take critical possession of *Passing*. Similarly, Fitzgerald's many references in *The Great Gatsby* to race and breeding generally, as well as his figurative and dramatic depiction of blacks in particular, frame Tom Buchanan's more pointed accusations about Gatsby in such a way as to blur the distinction between the literal presence and figurative representation of race. When Tom Buchanan insists that letting "Mr. Nobody from Nowhere" make love to his wife is the first step to "intermarriage between black and white," we cannot really know whether he has just proposed that Gatsby represents a literal position on a gradated scale of racial Others (i.e., blacks, Jews, Slavs, Italians, and Irish as non-white), that race is here a metaphor for something else (e.g., class or region), or some uncertain combination of both.

Werner Sollors has addressed how, although parvenus, arrivistes, and other passers of various sorts have long been a staple of literature, racial passing has a particularly significant and peculiar place in American history and literature. In her introduction to *Passing and the Fictions of Identity*, Elaine K. Ginsberg similarly notes that the "genealogy of the term *passing* . . . associates it with the discourse of racial difference and especially with the assumption of a fraudulent 'white' identity by an individual culturally and legally defined as 'Negro' or black" (2–3). Ginsberg also addresses the more varied configurations and complexities of passing:

> By extension [of its traditional meaning], "passing" has been applied discursively to disguises of other elements of an individual's presumed "natural" or "essential" identity, including class, ethnicity, and sexuality. . . . And although the cultural logic of passing suggests that passing is usually motivated by a desire to shed the identity of an oppressed group to gain access

to social and economic opportunities, the rationale for passing may be more or less complex or ambiguous and motivated by other kinds of perceived rewards. (3)

Accordingly, Pamela Caughie has argued that "passing at once reinforces and disrupts the binary logic of identity that gives rise to the practice to begin with. . . . Thus, while the concept of passing is understood within a binary logic of identity, the practice actually functions in terms of a double logic: it is both the problem and the solution" (21–22). Gayle Wald has therefore suggested that "by approaching these [passing] narratives. . . . we begin to see how they. . . . articulate needs and interests that do not merely respond to or replicate the wishes of the dominant culture" (30). In this sense, we need to grasp how the "binary logic" of race is marked and then remarked by the "double logic" of the passer whose play in the dark and light of literal and figurative identities and relations can even implicate the needs and interests of the literary reader more generally. We can begin to explore these claims by examining more closely the racialized aspects of *The Great Gatsby*.

II

Fitzgerald's novel is profoundly and variously concerned with race and ethnicity, social identity, and the possibilities of passing.[4] Tom Buchanan commences the race talk just pages into the novel:

"Civilization's going to pieces," broke out Tom violently. "I've gotten to be a terrible pessimist about things. Have you read 'The Rise of Colored Empires' by this man Goddard?"

"Why, no," I answered, rather surprised by his tone.

"Well, it's a fine book, and everybody ought to read it. The idea is if we don't look out the white race will be—will be utterly submerged. It's all scientific stuff; it's been proved. . . . This fellow has worked out the whole thing. It's up to us, who are the dominant race, to watch out or these other races will have control of things. . . . This idea is that we're Nordics . . . we've produced all the things that go to make civilization." (9)

Later in Chapter 1, Daisy tells Nick that Jordan Baker is "'[from Louisville. Our white girlhood was passed together there. Our beautiful white—'" (13). When Tom interrupts with a question about her talk with Nick minutes before, she says, "'I think we talked about the Nordic race'" (13).[5] The theme of racial purity is developed further in Chapter 2 as Nick and Tom drive through the valley of ashes (landscape in blackface?) to visit Tom's mistress, Myrtle Wilson. They go to New York, where they encounter a "gray old man who bore an absurd resemblance to John D. Rockefeller. In a basket swung from his neck cowered a dozen very recent puppies of an indeterminate breed" (18). Myrtle inquires, "'What kind are they?'" (18), and the man replies, "'All kinds. What kind do you want, lady?'" (18). What then ensues is the first overt instance of passing in the novel, in which the mongrel dog is to pass as the purebred "police dog" Myrtle desires:

> "That's no police dog," said Tom.
> "No, it's not exactly a police dog," said the man with disappointment in his voice. "It's more of an Airedale." (18)

Nick is also doubtful ("undoubtedly there was an Airedale concerned in it somewhere, though its feet were startlingly white" [18]), and the confusion about passing continues with regard to gender:

> "Is that a boy or a girl?" she asked delicately.
> "That dog? That dog's a boy."
> "It's a bitch," said Tom decisively. (18)

The three of them and the dog go on to rendezvous with Myrtle's sister Catherine and Mr. and Mrs. McKee, where the race talk continues.

Mrs. McKee announces to everyone, "'I almost married a little kike who'd been after me for years. I knew he was below me'" (23), whereupon Myrtle explains how she came to marry George: "'I married him because I thought he was a gentleman. . . . I thought he knew something about breeding, but he wasn't fit to lick my shoe'" (23). Later, the Jewish gangster Meyer Wolfsheim makes a similar claim about Gatsby's breeding to Nick: "'I knew I had discovered a man of fine breeding after I talked with him an hour'" (47).

Daisy alone unequivocally possesses the necessary credentials of good breeding and racial whiteness, as is apparent in all the proximate figurations of whiteness associated with her—a dress (5–6), a roadster (49), a string of pearls (50), and a white palace (80). But Gatsby will not be able to pass as Daisy's shade of pale, and Tom challenges him directly in the next scene. But before he does, the narrative offers us a sort of dress-rehearsal of passing in the odd, almost surreal scene in which the characters discuss Biloxi, the mysterious guest at the Buchanans' wedding, for he, too, is a passer whose familial, geographical, and social identity is neither quite believable or [sic] entirely implausible. As Susan Marren puts it, "'Blocks Biloxi' appears . . . apparently out of nowhere, and inserts himself smoothly into the social circle by presenting a narrative of identity. . . . Biloxi's narrative is a suggestive backdrop for what follows it, Gatsby's more radical rewriting of the same social framework" (95–96). For Nick's and Tom's suspicions about Biloxi's claim to have attended Yale are virtually repeated when Tom challenges Gatsby's claim to have gone to Oxford.

Just pages earlier, Nick has dismissed race as a source of meaningful difference between people: "it occurred to me that there was no difference between men, in intelligence or race, so profound as the difference between the sick and well" (82). However, in this next scene, the race discourse explicitly casts Gatsby as a racial Other threatening the purity of the Buchanans' world:

"Self-control!" repeated Tom incredulously. "I suppose the latest thing is to sit back and let Mr. Nobody from Nowhere make love to your wife. . . . Nowadays people begin by sneering at family life and family institutions, and next they'll throw everything overboard and have intermarriage between black and white."

Flushed with his impassioned gibberish, he saw himself standing alone on the last barrier of civilization.

"We're all white here," murmured Jordan. (86)

Yet as Walter Benn Michaels has pointed out, "For Tom, as for Stoddard, Gatsby . . . *isn't quite* white, and Tom's identification of him as *in some sense* black suggests the power of the expanded notion of the alien. Gatsby's love for Daisy seems to Tom the expression of *something like* miscegenation" (25, my emphasis).

Note that Michaels's observation, not altogether unlike Tom's, is neither completely literal nor entirely figurative in nature, for it necessarily hedges on a critical claim in a way that articulates—and in some sense replicates—the ambiguity in the novel. Indeed, one might wonder if Fitzgerald would have had answers to these questions, given his struggles during the revision process to develop and clarify Gatsby's background (in part at the request of his editor, Max Perkins). Although Gatsby's identity as a passer suggests elements of both socio-economic class and a possibility of his Jewish background—Gatz is a version of a Jewish-German name—that echo Fitzgerald's own position as an Irish-American *arriviste* from the Midwest, a reading of race and passing in the novel requires giving closer attention to how they are figuratively linked to the trope of blackness and specifically inflected by Fitzgerald's literal depiction of blacks, although these characters appear only twice in the novel.

The first of two literal encounters with blacks is set up by another figurative one that marks the racial theme. On their way into New York with Gatsby at the wheel, Nick and Gatsby are pulled over by a policeman for speeding. Waving a "white card" before the policemen's eyes,

Gatsby is allowed to pass, as the policeman exclaims, "'Know you next time, Mr. Gatsby. Excuse me!'" (45). They ascend the "great bridge . . . with the city rising up across the river in white heaps and sugar lumps" and are passed by two different but not entirely dissimilar parties. First, Nick recalls how "[a] dead man passed us in a hearse heaped with blooms, followed by. . . carriages for friends . . . [who] looked out at us with the tragic eyes and short upper lips of southeastern Europe, and I was glad that the sight of Gatsby's splendid car was included in their somber holiday" (45). In the nativist 1920s, these mourners might very well be marked as nonwhite, and Nick is happy that Gatsby is able, as it were, to wave his own white card in contrast to the ethnic procession of the dead. This racialized spectacle gives way to another as they cross the suggestively named Blackwell's Island:

> a limousine passed us, driven by a white chauffeur, in which sat three modish negroes, two bucks and a girl. I laughed aloud as the yolks of their eyeballs rolled toward us in haughty rivalry.
>
> "Anything can happen now that we've slid over this bridge," I thought; "anything at all. . . ."
>
> Even Gatsby could happen, without any particular wonder. (45)

This disturbing and complex scene, with its bridges and passes and reversals and mirrors, can be read in terms of Nick's (and Gatsby's) identification with and his insistence on difference from—these black characters. Indeed, it is a depiction of both racist and romantic readiness intricately conjoined around the conflated images of the parvenu and the passer.

The only black person who speaks in *The Great Gatsby* is a witness in the investigation of Myrtle's death when she is struck by Gatsby's car, which is driven by Daisy. If not the sole witness to a crime, he is at least the only one who can speak to the incident that is the catalyst for Gatsby's own death at the hands of Myrtle's husband, who, in turn, has been set on his course by Tom:

"What's the name of this place here?" demanded the officer.

"Hasn't got any name."

A pale, well-dressed negro stepped near.

"It was a yellow car," he said, "big yellow car. New."

"See the accident?" asked the policeman.

"No, but the car passed me down the road, going faster'n forty. Going fifty, sixty." (93–94)

Moments later, Nick says that when Tom explains to Wilson that the yellow car was not his, "Only the negro and I were near enough to hear what he said," again suggesting some important place for the black stranger in this episode. The scene then ends with Tom and Nick driving away, and Tom, sobbing, exclaims, "'The God damned coward!'" (95).

This episode possesses a number of aspects that can be linked to passing. The black man is "pale" and Gatsby's car is itself yellow, two terms often associated with passing. Even the other colloquial usage of "yellow," which is invoked by Tom when he calls Gatsby a coward, might be cast in relation to passing, at least in terms of Tom's various challenges to Gatsby throughout the story. The theme of false or mistaken identity is also tied to Myrtle's death since she runs out in the street believing Gatsby's car is Tom's; moreover, she earlier mistook Jordan for Tom's wife. In spite of this trespass and resulting violence, Gatsby's car passes, and the only one who sees him is a black man. Finally, Daisy is the driver, which gives her a responsibility for the entire episode not unlike the culpability Tom assigns to her for the threat of miscegenation in her affair with Gatsby in the first place.

It is clear that this canonical American novel, with all its attention to racial identity and social position, is indeed more than a portrait of "the pure American self divorced from specific social circumstances" (Baym 71). As Toni Morrison has said of American literature more generally, the novel's achievement is realized in part by "playing in the dark." Critics who address race in *The Great Gatsby* have usefully tended to place it within the historical framework of immigration, ethnic diversity, assimilation, and class mobility in the 1920s, in which blackness signifies broader and more varied constructions of nonwhiteness, as well as other sorts of social identity and difference. As noted earlier, Michaels explores how Tom Buchanan's "expanded notion of the alien" suggests that while he somehow sees Jimmy Gatz as black, such a claim needs to be viewed in the broader context of nativism in the 1920s (25). Beth A. McCoy's and Susan Marie Marren's extensive discussions of race and passing in *The Great Gatsby* follow this pattern, as does Jeffory A. Clymer's argument that "Fitzgerald's text works out before the reader's eyes . . . the inexorable process by which issues of class leach into constructions of race. . . . Tom [Buchanan] can only conceptualize Gatsby's lower-class background and affair with his wife in the terms of miscegenation, a transgression of racial boundaries" (185).

Insofar as these readings explore how the trope of blackness signifies a broader social dynamic, they are consistent with Gates's notion of race as the "ultimate trope of difference." Yet reading blackness as a trump trope for all difference everywhere can turn it into a critical metaphor without brakes that is prefigured by the practice of passing. This point can be developed by way of the resemblances between *The Great Gatsby* and *Passing* and exploring the question of how we might read that relation.

III

The importance of race and passing in *The Great Gatsby* is by no means the only link to Larsen's novel. Their three-part plot structures, for example, both involve a reencounter between key characters that precipitates an attempt to return to an earlier state (of identities and relations), and this desire meets resistance and ends in violent death.[6] The story is conveyed in each case by a way of a participant-observer (Nick and Irene, respectively) whose attention is similarly given over almost completely to the main character's "romantic readiness" (as Nick describes Jay Gatsby) and "having way" (as Irene describes Clare Kendry). In both cases, the bond between characters is very strong, an attraction that can be seen, in turn, as variously reconfigured and re-routed through a series of complicated detours, displacements, and in-versions, whereby their attraction also gives way intermittently to re-pulsion and condemnation. Nick and Irene are obsessed with passing in part because they also are passing in order to enjoy economic and so-cial mobility, albeit in more attenuated configurations since both pos-sess a sense of pedigree that makes them feel superior to the main char-acters. Also, Nick and Irene each contend with a companion—Jordan Baker and Brian Redfield, respectively—who is depicted as somewhat discontented, restless, and distant, which again suggests a kind of pro-jective or mirroring relation between character pairs. Finally, both nar-rators are given to occasional lapses and odd ruptures in coherency that can be linked to altered states, such as alcoholic intoxication, surreal rumination, or neurotic or hysterical distortion.

Other characters and their relations present interesting connections. Perhaps most prominent are Tom Buchanan and John Bellew, both of whom have pronounced racist views, are depicted as variously power-ful and clumsy, and are deceived in a way that exposes them to a kind of racial contamination, insofar as Clare is a black woman passing as white and Gatsby is perceived by Tom as a racial Other. Yet another parallel involving these men is their offspring; in each instance, the children play minor roles, but that marginality prefigures a key place in the stories insofar as they represent a bodily threat to desire and the promise of freedom. When Gatsby meets Daisy and Tom's daughter, he realizes that Daisy's life now presents some complication to his ro-mantic longing and his desire to "repeat the past": "Gatsby . . . kept looking at the child with surprise. I don't think he had ever really be-lieved in its existence before" (77). Daisy also displays regret regard-ing her child; she weeps upon learning her newborn's gender, whose fate it will be to become "'the best thing a girl can be in this world, a beautiful little fool'" (12). Clare's concern, however, is that children present a threat to her desire to pass as white because her "true" identity might emerge by way of darker skin: "'I nearly died of terror the whole nine months before Margery was born for fear that she might be dark. Thank goodness she turned out all right. But I'll never risk it again. Never! The strain is simply too hellish'" (36). This threat of the body is suggested similarly when John Bellew jokingly explains to Irene why he calls Clare "Nig": "'Well, you see, it's like this. When we were first married, she was as white as—well—as white as a lily. But I declare she's gettin' darker and darker. I tell her if she don't look out, she'll wake up one of these days and find she's turned into a nigger'" (39).

Other similarities between the novels are worth inventorying briefly: a movement of characters from the Midwest to the East Coast that suggests a relation between regional and class identity; the depiction of fashionable parties for key thematic and dramatic purposes; the appearance of marginal characters whose darker skin color (Liza, Zulena, and Sadie in *Passing*), class status (the Wilsons, McKees, and Wolfsheim in *The Great Gatsby*), or religious-ethnic status (Claude Jones, the "black Jew" in *Passing*, and Wolfsheim in *The Great Gatsby*) complicate the passing binary (or serve to suppress the complications posed by attenuated passers such as Nick and Irene); key scenes in which women (Irene and Daisy) tear up letters from the main characters (Clare and Gatsby, respectively) into "white pieces" that end up dissolving in water; scenes involving fainting and heat exhaustion; the major characters' deployment of the narrators to pursue a desired social position; the portrayal of highly sexualized women—Clare Kendry and Myrtle Wilson—whose bodies are mortally mutilated under ambiguous circumstances (both involving some configuration of mistaken or false identity in which another woman is most likely responsible for their death); some similarity in corresponding characters' names (Jay Gatsby and Clare Kendry; Tom Buchanan and John Bellew); and finally, of course, the deaths of the two passers—a mortal passing similarly linked to the broader seasonal depiction of summer's brilliance, its oppressiveness, and its expiration.

The resemblances between these novels are extensive enough to warrant a consideration of sources and influences—and what these relations imply. Could Fitzgerald have borrowed from the African-American tradition of the "tragic mulatto" narrative? Has Fitzgerald committed a kind of literary plagiarism by taking possession of the trope of racial passing, or might we describe it instead as something more like a blackface forgery?[7] The charge suggests a sort of textual passing that echoes critical discussions of racial passing that have likened it to the practice of plagiarism.[8] In fact, the figuration of blackness and presence of racial trespass in *The Great Gatsby* has been linked in at least one instance not to black sources but to another white writer, in which the similarity between Daisy in *The Great Gatsby* and Mrs. Forrester in Willa Cather's *The Lost Lady* raised the question of plagiarism. Walter Benn Michaels describes the connection as follows:

> In *The Great Gatsby*, published two years after *A Lost Lady*, Gatsby's relation to Daisy seems, at least to Tom, a kind of miscegenation, a threat to the difference between white men and "niggers." Fitzgerald had read and admired *A Lost Lady* while working on *Gatsby* and subsequently wrote Cather a famous note, apologizing for what he described as an act of "apparent plagiarism," an unintentional similarity between descriptions of Mrs. Forrester and Daisy. . . . [T]he connection—with respect to miscegenation—is real enough. (46)

Any claim about Fitzgerald's literary originality or ownership ostensibly ought not to involve either pulling a figurative punch (did he or didn't he?) or confusing a figurative claim with the distinctly literal proposition that he was in fact influenced by these tropes and traditions. Nevertheless, just as the passer challenges the ontological and epistemological status of racial difference by blurring the distinction between figurative and literal identities and relations, so, too, can the plagiarist lead us to revisit how our figurations of textual originality, authorial ownership, and literary value become tangled and babbled in those "gray areas" where, as Howells once analogously located Chesnutt's fiction, "the paler shades dwell."

Clearly, these issues can be especially vexing when discussing the relationship between the works of black and white writers; this is particularly evident in the question of Larsen's sources and influences, her own profoundly damaging experience with plagiarism, and the larger pattern of reading black literature as an imitation of—or as that which is assigned value in relation to—work by white writers. The story of Larsen's plagiarism is well known. In January 1930, Larsen published a short story in *Forum* entitled "Sanctuary" that was almost immediately thought to be plagiarized—an occurrence that is generally viewed as crucial in her ensuing lifelong silence as a writer. Personal friends, as well as readers and the editors of *Forum*, began to speak out about the similarities between Larsen's story and another by Sheila Kaye-Smith entitled "Mrs. Adis," published in *Century* in 1922. The editors at *Forum* invited Larsen to publish an "Author's Explanation" in the April issue, in which she made two key claims. First, she insisted that she heard the story from a black female patient with whom she worked as a nurse. Second, Larsen claims that the plot, which involves a woman's harboring her own child's killer and her silence with legal authorities in the name of racial solidarity, really belonged to the black community: "'in talking it over with Negroes, I find that the tale is so old and so well known that it is almost folklore. . . . It has many variations. . . . A Negro sociologist tells me that there are literally hundreds of these stories. Anyone could have written it up at any time'" (qtd. in Davis 352). In some sense, it is as if Larsen suggested that Kaye-Smith's story was the act of plagiarism.

Any comprehensive and balanced assessment of influences on Larsen's novel would have to locate *Passing* in relation to a number of sources and traditions: first, Larsen's own life, since miscegenation and passing were so central to her own experience; second, a number of longstanding African-American literary traditions, especially the "tragic mulatta" and passing narratives; and, of course, those aspects of American literary modernism within which *The Great Gatsby* would also have to be placed and over which Fitzgerald obviously possessed no proprietary claim, such as technical experimentation with narrative point of view, a psychoanalytical interest in consciousness and subjective perception, close documentation of the rapid social change experienced by the generation coming of age in the twenties, and a deep sense of restlessness or alienation with contemporary culture.[9]

In her biography on Larsen, Thadious Davis identifies key influences on *Passing* that locate the novel in relation to modernism generally. Citing Larsen's "reading in modern literature" and the broad influence of nonliterary thinkers such as Freud and Einstein, Davis suggests that

> Clare Kendry . . . owes her passive nature in part to Gertrude Stein's Melanctha in *Three Lives*. . . . The treatment of the environment and its impact in shaping the lives of individuals owes much to Theodore Dreiser's *Sister Carrie* and Sinclair Lewis' *Main Street*. . . . Irene's narrated monologues and stream of consciousness reflect Larsen's reading of Joyce's *Ulysses*. . . . Larsen depended . . . on the modernist concept of the unreliable observer as represented by Joseph Conrad in *Heart of Darkness*. (310–311)

In her Introduction to *Passing*, Davis quotes from a letter in which Larsen refers to her "mind, warped . . . by the Europeans and the American moderns" (xxviii), and she also cites Gates's observation about passing as a modernist thematic:

> [Clare's] death by going out an open window is so open to speculation and interpretation that it recalls the modernist implications of passing as a thematic. "The thematic elements of passing—fragmentation, alienation, liminality, self-fashioning—[that] echo the great themes of modernism," as Henry Louis Gates, Jr., has observed, are also central concerns in Larsen's text. (xxx)

Other critics have examined connections between Larsen's fiction and these and other important white American and European influences.[10] One interesting reference to Fitzgerald in relation to the writers of the Harlem Renaissance is supplied in an interview with Dorothy West. Responding to a question about the relative influence of Carl Van Vechten and H. L. Mencken, West states, "I certainly heard Mencken's name tossed about at the time, but he was from a different generation. If we were influenced by anyone, it was F. Scott Fitzgerald" (McDowell, "Conversations" 294).[11]

Neither the textual resemblances nor the circumstantial evidence noted here would lead a reader to accuse Larsen of literally plagiarizing Fitzgerald in the conventional sense, and it is perhaps unwise to place too much emphasis on his influence, even if we were to interpret this relation as an instance of some sort of "writing back" on Larsen's part. However, reading the resemblance in terms of plagiarism (in both directions) underscores how passing functions both as a literal theme in the novels and as a figurative trope for reading them not only independently but also in relation to one another, the implications of which are twofold. First, it reveals that we need to consider in more depth how reading race can tell us something about literary interpretation generally by exposing this slippage between literal and figurative formations in both literary works *and* critical practice. Moreover, this passing aspect of race invites us to examine more fully how the literal historical conventions about and social constructions of racial identity and difference have been and continue to be variously reinforced and undermined by what is arguably a literary question of figuration.

As something more like a coda than a conclusion, another recently rediscovered novel illustrates this point. In 2002, Gates discussed in a number of popular media outlets (e.g., *The New Yorker, National Public Radio*, and *The New York Times*) his acquisition and publication of Hannah Crafts's *The Bondswoman's Narrative*, which Gates believes is the first American novel written (in the 1850s) by a female fugitive slave. Suggesting that Crafts "sought to place her autobiographical novel squarely within the republic of letters" (1), Gates locates the influence of other slave narratives, as well as Gothic and sentimental novels, in a broader practice of slaves literally and figuratively "reading from their masters' libraries" and making use of this reading in their own writing (1). This tradition, in which slaves "read, echo, or borrow from" (1) other writers, provides a framework for Gates's description of Crafts's plagiarism and her master John Hill Wheeler's "stealing a little learning from the slave" (2) by way of his library possession of a wide range of African-American works.

Noting that Crafts "closely revised—and sometimes lifted" (1) passages from Dickens's *Bleak House*, Gates suggests, "Of the black writers published before 1865, none *quoted* more texts in her own work than did Hannah Crafts" (1, my emphasis). Crafts "audaciously . . . quilt[s] together . . . a remarkably impressive range of English and American literature" (1), a surprising "creative plundering" (2) matched reciprocally by the "presence of so many slave narratives in her master's library" (2). Citing a long list of African-American authors in Wheeler's library, Gates proposes, "It was as if he read the works of fugitive slaves to study the mind of the enemy, perhaps better to master and control his slaves, and to prevent them from escaping" (2). He concludes that "Crafts and Wheeler, slave and master, cloistered in the library, searching out each other's secrets, enacted a mirror tableau: The slave woman furtively tracking down the letters of her master, the master surreptitiously decoding the language of the slave" (3).

Similarly, the passing resemblance between Larsen's and Fitzgerald's work underscores how the call of and the response to the passer, by anticipating the critical reader of both figurative tropes and literal truths, suggest how we might continue to navigate by losing our way. To ask how Gatsby was black can tell us much about what passes when we talk about race, just as that race talk is the twist in the turn we call reading.

Notes

1. Two dissertations (Marren and McCoy, both in 1995) explore passing in fiction by black and white writers. Both have separate chapters on *The Great Gatsby* and *Passing*, but neither really develops the links between the two novels. Beth A. McCoy closes her analysis of *The Great Gatsby* with the claim that "[o]ne of the most obvious candidates for . . . new and fruitful yoking [with *The Great Gatsby*] is Larsen's *Passing*." McCoy briefly inventories some links and then suggests that "the similarities are many, provocative, and seemingly, just waiting to be mined" (113). Although McCoy voices the concern that exploring these similarities might resemble earlier accusations of plagiarism, she concludes by calling for more textual analysis (114–117). More recently, in an NCTE collection on teaching American literature in high school and college, Rita Teague and Colleen Claudia O'Brien address the passing connection between these novels and suggest that a comparative approach is valuable in helping students understand race, class, and sexuality in this period.

2. I. A. Newby argues that the years "1900 to 1930 . . . were the years in which anti-Negro thought reached its zenith, the years which produced the greatest proliferation of anti-Negro literature, and the years in which that literature enjoyed its broadest appeal" (xi). See Christian for a discussion of passing literature in this period. Walter Benn Michaels addresses the links between nativism and modernism more broadly, including how the Immigration Acts of 1921 and 1924 reflect the anxiety over racial identity and difference during this period. Michaels also notes that Stoddard's *The Rising Tide of Color Against White World Supremacy* was published in 1920 by Scribner's, Fitzgerald's own publisher (144 n. 12). Stoddard's name actually appears elsewhere in *The Great Gatsby*: when Nick encounters "Owl Eyes" in Gatsby's library, this drunken visitor marvels that the books "'have real pages and everything'" (30) and then rushes to the bookcase and pulls down "Volume One of the 'Stoddard Lectures'" (30). James Ellis, however, claims this is a reference not to Lothrop Stoddard but to John Lawson Stoddard, a travel writer whose romantic depictions of the world would have been perfectly appropriate for Gatsby's library. Other readers have suggested that Buchanan's reference was to Henry H. Goddard, a psychologist and eugenicist.

3. See Brody, Tate, and Wald about other interpretive grounds for reading the novel.

4. See Thompson for an extended analysis of racial figuration in *The Great Gatsby*. Although Thompson addresses many of the elements of the novel I survey here, both his argument (about Gatsby being black) and some of the responses to it reflect the sort of slippage between literal and figurative aspects of race I wish to examine by way of the trope of passing. Also, see Goldsmith for a reading of the racialized configuration of passing in the novel.

5. While Daisy's rather odd reference to the "'white girlhood . . . passed'" (13) with Jordan Baker underscores Daisy's white identity, it arguably complicates Jordan's. Noting the relative critical inattention to Jordan, McCoy cites those passages in which Nick observes Jordan's skin, which he repeatedly describes as both "dark" and "wan." McCoy argues that the significance of Nick's reference to "Jordan's fingers, powdered white over their tan" (76) can only be grasped by locating in a "larger system

of racialized signifiers" (100). McCoy even speculates on the possibility that Jordan Baker might have been modeled in part on Josephine Baker (110 n. 45). At the very least, given Daisy's reference at the opening of the book as well as Jordan's tense insistence in Chapter 7 that "'We're all white here'" (86), she occupies an interesting place in the racial discourse of the novel.

6. *The Great Gatsby* is organized into nine chapters whereas *Passing* is divided into three parts, each of which contains four brief chapters. While Larsen's tripartite structure is more apparent (the three parts are titled "Encounter," "Reencounter," and "Finale"), Fitzgerald's nine chapters are discernibly organized into three sets of three: Chapters 1–3 introduce us to the key characters and plot lines (Buchanans, Wilsons, and Gatsby); Chapters 4–6 trace the entire arc of the relationship of Gatsby and Daisy, including background exposition of their initial romance, their reencounter at Gatsby's mansion in West Egg, and Gatsby's insistence to Nick that he can indeed repeat the past; finally, in Chapters 7–9 the characters shuttle back and forth between New York and Long Island as things come apart and the bodies start falling. In Larsen's novel, Part 1 begins with Irene Redfield receiving a letter from Clare Kendry, which precipitates the recollection of their encounter two years earlier (which is itself a reencounter after many years since Clare "disappeared" in order to pass as white); Part 2 is an account of their reestablished relationship; and Part 3 follows the chain of events that result in Clare's death.

7. Fitzgerald once drew a cartoon of himself as a minstrel figure among the Ivy Leaguers. The cartoon appeared in a postcard to a cousin (*Correspondences* 13). See McCoy 1.

8. See, for example, McDowell's introduction to *Passing* and Haviland's article on passing and plagiarism.

9. See Davis and Hutchinson for Larsen biographies. See Christian for a helpful overview of the mulatta tradition, especially 35–61. For an analysis of passing as a kind of trope for modernist/postmodernist identity and subjectivity, see Cutter. Henry Louis Gates, Jr.'s theory of intertextual signification in *The Signifying Monkey* addresses the originality of black writers in relation to both black and white writers. For a psychoanalytical analysis of Larsen's plagiarism of a white female writer, see Haviland.

10. See, for example, Fleming and Lay on Larsen's connections to Sinclair Lewis and Henry James, respectively.

11. In a somewhat different triangulation of influence and resemblance, Charles Scruggs argues that both Fitzgerald and Larsen were influenced by Mencken's literary criticism, suggesting that both Jay Gatsby and Clare Kendry are technically rendered as recommended by Mencken in a review of Somerset Maugham's *The Moon and Sixpence* (16).

Works Cited

Baym, Nina. "Melodramas of Beset Manhood: How Theories of American Fiction Exclude Women Authors." *The New Feminist Criticism: Essays on Women, Literature, and Theory.* Ed. Elaine Showalter. New York: Pantheon, 1985. 63–80.

Brody, Jennifer DeVere. "'True' Colors: Race and Class Conflict in Nella Larsen's *Passing.*" *Callaloo* 15 (1992): 1053–65.

Caughie, Pamela L. *Passing and Pedagogy: The Dynamics of Responsibility.* Urbana: U of Illinois P, 1999.

Christian, Barbara. *Black Women Novelists: The Development of a Tradition, 1892–1976.* Westport: Greenwood P, 1980.

Clymer, Jeffory A. "'Mr. Nobody from Nowhere': Rudolph Valentino, Jay Gatsby, and the End of the American Race." *Genre* 29 (1996): 161–92.

Cutter, Martha J. "Sliding Significations: Passing as a Narrative and Textual Strategy in Nella Larsen's Fiction." *Passing and the Fictions of Identity.* Ed. Elaine K. Ginsberg. Durham: Duke UP, 1996. 75–100.

Davis, Thadious M. *Nella Larsen, Novelist of the Harlem Renaissance: A Woman's Life Unveiled.* Baton Rouge: Louisiana State UP, 1994.

Ellis, James. "The 'Stoddard Lectures' in *The Great Gatsby.*" *American Literature: A Journal of Literary History, Criticism, and Bibliography* 44 (1972): 470–71.

Fitzgerald, F. Scott. *The Correspondence of F. Scott Fitzgerald.* Ed. Matthew J. Bruccoli. New York: Random House, 1980.

_____. *The Great Gatsby.* New York: Scribner's, 1953.

Fleming, Robert A. "The Influence of *Main Street* on Nella Larsen's *Quicksand.*" *Modern Fiction Studies* 31 (1985): 547–53.

Gates, Henry Louis, Jr. "Borrowing Privileges." *The New York Times Book Review.* 2 June 2002: (1–3). 30 Dec. 2006. http://query.nytimes.com/gst/fullpage.html?res=9E05E3D81E38F931A35755C0A9649C8B63&n=Top%2fFeatures%2fBooks%2fBook%20Reviews.com.

_____. "Introduction: Writing 'Race' and the Difference It Makes." *"Race," Writing, and Difference.* Ed. Henry Louis Gates. Chicago: U of Chicago P, 1986.

Ginsberg, Elaine K., ed. *Passing and the Fictions of Identity.* Durham: Duke UP, 1996.

Goldsmith, Meredith. "White Skin, White Mask: Passing, Posing, and Performing in *The Great Gatsby.*" *Modern Fiction Studies* 49 (2003): 443–69.

Haviland, Beverly. "Passing from Paranoia to Plagiarism: The Abject Authorship of Nella Larsen." *Modern Fiction Studies* 43 (1997): 295–318.

Howells, William Dean. "Mr. Charles Chesnutt's Stories." *Atlantic Monthly* 85 (May 1900): 701.

Hutchinson, George. *In Search of Nella Larsen: A Biography of the Color Line.* Cambridge, MA: Belknap-Harvard UP, 2006.

Larsen, Nella. *Passing.* New York: Penguin, 1997.

Lay, Mary M. "Parallels: Henry James's *The Portrait of a Lady* and Nella Larsen's *Quicksand.*" *CLA Journal* 20 (1977): 475–86.

Marren, Susan Marie. "Passing for American: Establishing American Identity in the work of James Weldon Johnson, F. Scott Fitzgerald, Nella Larsen, and Gertrude Stein." Diss. U of Michigan, 1995.

McCoy, Beth Ann. "'Do I Look Like This?': Race, Gender, Class, and Sexuality in the Novels of Jessie Fauset, Carl van Vechten, Nella Larsen, and F. Scott Fitzgerald." Diss. U of Delaware, 1995.

McDowell, Deborah E. "Conversations with Dorothy West." *Harlem Renaissance Re-examined*. Ed. Victor A. Kramer and Robert A. Russ. Troy, NY: Whitson, 1997. 285–303.

_____. Introduction. *Quicksand* and *Passing*. New Brunswick, NJ: Rutgers UP, 1986.

Michaels, Walter Benn. *Our America: Nativism, Modernism, and Pluralism*. Durham: Duke UP, 1995.

Morrison, Toni. *Playing in the Dark: Whiteness and the Literary Imagination*. Cambridge: Harvard UP, 1992.

Newby, I. A. *Jim Crow's Defense: Anti-Negro Thought in America, 1900–1930*. Baton Rouge: Louisiana State UP, 1965.

Scruggs, Charles. *The Sage in Harlem: H. L. Mencken and the Black Writers of the 1920s*. Baltimore: Johns Hopkins UP, 1984.

Sollors, Werner. *Neither Black Nor White Yet Both: Thematic Explorations of Interracial Literature*. New York: Oxford UP, 1997.

Stoddard, Lothrop. *The Rising Tide of Color Against White World Supremacy*. New York: Scribner's, 1920.

Tate, Claudia. "Nella Larsen's *Passing*: A Problem of Interpretation." *Black American Literature Forum* 14.4 (1980): 142–46.

Teague, Rita, and Colleen Claudia O'Brien. "Looking for the Other Side: Pairing *The Great Gatsby* and *Passing*." *Making American Literatures in High School and College: Classroom Practices in Teaching English*. Ed. Anne Ruggle Gere and Peter Shaheen. Vol. 31. Urbana, IL: NCTE, 2001. 137–47.

Thompson, Carlyle V. *The Tragic Black Buck: Racial Masquerading in the American Literary Imagination*. New York: Peter Lang, 2004.

Wald, Gayle. *Crossing the Line: Racial Passing in Twentieth-Century U.S. Literature and Culture*. Durham: Duke UP, 2000.

CRITICAL
OVERVIEWS

Introduction to *The Great Gatsby*

Ruth Prigozy

When F. Scott Fitzgerald was writing *The Great Gatsby* in the summer of 1924, he wrote to his editor, Maxwell Perkins, 'I think my novel is about the best American novel ever written.'[1] He knew, as did few of his contemporaries, that this, his third novel, would far transcend in artistry and lasting significance the two earlier works, *This Side of Paradise* (1920) and *The Beautiful and Damned* (1922). Fitzgerald's remark was, of course, part excitement that the novel was meeting his high expectations, part youthful exuberance (he was only 28), and part hope—perhaps the same kind of hope that animates the character whose name he placed on the title-page.[2] One of his last comments on the novel, in a letter to his daughter, suggests that despite neglect by the public and critics, *Gatsby* had never failed him: 'What little I've accomplished has been by the most laborious and uphill work, and I wish now I'd *never* relaxed or looked back—but said at the end of *The Great Gatsby*: I've found my line—from now on this comes first. This is my immediate duty—without this I am nothing.'[3] He knew (and it is some consolation to us that he kept his faith) that *Gatsby* would endure.

Just how enduring the novel has proved is evident simply in its current sales: every year, *Gatsby* sells over three hundred thousand copies, nearly four times as many as all of Fitzgerald's other works combined. The word 'Gatsby' has entered the world's vocabulary: to call someone 'Gatsbyesque' is immediately to define an individual in terms of his capacity for hope, his romantic idealization of experience. Films and television have made the character part of popular culture in America and abroad. *Gatsby* is celebrated as a major influence by other important writers (notably J. D. Salinger). Hundreds of scholarly articles have been written about the novel in the last forty years. And Fitzgerald would particularly enjoy seeing his creation used to advertise clothing and cologne in a medium with which he was certainly familiar—mass magazines, where he published well over one hundred short stories.

When Fitzgerald died, *Gatsby* had not sold out the 23,870 copies that comprised the first two printings in the first year of the novel's publication; the remainder, under 3,000, were in the publisher's warehouse. Yet Fitzgerald, up to the end, urged his editor to encourage a popular edition of the novel, 'to keep *Gatsby* in the public eye—or *is the book unpopular*? Has it *had* its chance? Would a popular reissue in that series with a preface *not by* me but by one of its admirers . . . make it a favourite with class rooms, profs, lovers of English prose—anybody. But to die, so completely and unjustly after having given so much. Even now there is little published in American fiction that doesn't slightly bare my stamp—in a small way I was an original.'[4] When the Modern Library published an edition in 1934, Fitzgerald, keenly aware of the novel's obscurity, wrote an Introduction which was a passionate defence of his work, stressing again the purity of his artistic conscience during the ten months of its composition, of its truth or 'the attempt at honesty of the imagination', of the appropriateness of his material which some critics had labelled immature. 'But, my God!' he wrote, 'it was my material, and it was all I had to deal with.'[5] As if in wonder that the 1934 edition did not sell, he wrote to his wife, again exclaiming, 'but my God I am a forgotten man'.[6] It is clear that for Fitzgerald his future reputation rested with *Gatsby*, for from the beginning of its composition he knew that he was creating a genuinely new novel, a novel of destiny for him as well as for America.

From his correspondence with Maxwell Perkins, we know that Fitzgerald was well into planning the novel in the spring of 1922 (he may have begun to think about Gatsby's parties and the social world of West Egg as early as 1920 when he spent a summer at Westport, Connecticut, where the wealthy and/or celebrated inhabitants bear a strong resemblance to those portrayed in *Gatsby*). He had decided that its locale would be the middle west and New York (one of the major subjects of the novel is the contrast between the East and West), although in its original conception it takes place in 1885 rather than in the 1922 of the finished work. But perhaps most important, the form of the novel had begun to take shape: '[it] will be centered on a smaller period of time'. He indicated that it would have a Catholic element, but that idea receded during the composition.[7] (The short story 'Absolution' (1924), about a young boy and his encounter with a deranged priest in the midwest, was based on an abandoned section of the novel dealing with Gatsby's youth.)

In looking back over Fitzgerald's correspondence during this period, we realize how much of his creative life he poured into this novel and how determined he was that it would be the artistic consummation of his life: 'I want to write something new—something extraordinary and beautiful and simple + intricately patterned.'[8] He put the novel aside briefly in 1923 when his play *The Vegetable* was produced (and failed) and returned to it with even greater determination in the spring of 1924. He told Perkins that he had to rewrite practically half of it that autumn, his concentration riveted on structural problems. Despite the difficulty of composing a novel whose effect depends as much on what is omitted as what appears on the printed page, he never believed that *Gatsby* would prove less than one of the great books of its time. He was convinced above all of its originality: 'It is like nothing I've ever read before'; 'I feel absolutely self-sufficient + I have a perfect hollow craving for loneliness.'[9]

Although he would admit to his admiration for other writers, notably Joseph Conrad, Fitzgerald wanted to be free of them in order to focus on his own ability to create illusion. He wrote to Perkins from Great Neck where he began work on the novel; 'In my new novel, I'm thrown directly on purely creative work—not trashy imaginings. . . . This book will be a consciously artistic achievement & must depend on that as the first books did not.'[10] Fitzgerald had lived in New York City for six months in the early 1920s, and from mid-October 1922 to 24 April 1923 in Great Neck, a community on the north shore of Long Island, some 20 miles from Manhattan. Both places defined the geography and social world of *Gatsby*. He completed the novel on the Riviera in the summer of 1924, but his revisions before publication continued:

responding to Maxwell Perkins's suggestions regarding the clarity of Gatsby as a character and the narrative structure that reveals his biography (Perkins felt that it needed to be broken up), Fitzgerald wrote to his editor that he had fixed those problems in proof.[11] Chapter VI was completely rewritten, Fitzgerald moving Gatsby's biography from Chapters VII and VIII of the unrevised galleys. Gatsby's association with Dan Cody was moved from the galley of Chapter VIII to the opening of Chapter VI, as were Gatsby's remarks to Nick about Daisy following the party. The major change in Chapter VII was the completely rewritten Plaza Hotel scene in order to stress Gatsby's utter defeat by Tom Buchanan.[12]

The Great Gatsby was published on 10 April 1925 and received mixed reviews. The overriding opinion of the reviewers was that Fitzgerald represented the Jazz Age, and that at best, *Gatsby* was a novel of limited scope, with disagreeable or immature characters, and a trivial subject. Many praised his cleverness, and several concluded that it was a more considerable achievement than his earlier novels. A few critics recognized immediately that it was a masterpiece, notably Lillian C. Ford in the Los Angeles *Sunday Times*, who recognized the elusive quality of the novel, the sense of mystery that Fitzgerald was determined to retain: 'The story is powerful as much for what is suggested as for what is told. It leaves the reader in a mood of chastened wonder, in which fact after fact, implication after implication is pondered over, weighed and measured. . . . Mr Fitzgerald has certainly arrived.'[13] A few major critics (William Rose Benet, Herbert S. Gorman, Harry Hansen, and Laurence Stallings) praised the novel, but H. L. Mencken, while admiring the writing, found the novel merely 'a glorified anecdote'.[14] Only Gilbert Seldes, writing in *The Dial* several months after publication, praised it unreservedly: 'Fitzgerald has more than matured; he has mastered his talents and gone soaring in a beautiful flight, leaving behind him everything dubious and tricky in his earlier work, and leaving even farther behind all the men of his own generation and most of his elders.'[15]

Fitzgerald was deeply disappointed in the reviews and in the poor sales. Letters of praise from writers he admired somewhat assuaged the pain of public rejection, and he revelled in the praise of T. S. Eliot: 'It seems to me to be the first step that American fiction has taken since Henry James'; of Gertrude Stein: 'You are creating the contemporary world much as Thackeray did his in *Pendennis* and *Vanity Fair* and this isn't a bad compliment'; and of Edith Wharton: 'Let me say at once how much I like Gatsby, or rather His Book, & how great a leap I think you have taken this time—in advance upon your previous work.' Wharton felt that Fitzgerald should have given more of Gatsby's history from the point where he first goes to Cody's yacht, but she admitted that would be the 'old way'.[16] Wharton's advice suggests how great a departure from the contemporary novel *Gatsby* proved to be. Without using such modernist devices as stream of consciousness that signalled experimentation with form and style, Fitzgerald succeeded in creating a new kind of novel which critics could not easily categorize and hence rejected.

By May 1925, Fitzgerald wryly conceded *Gatsby*'s poor sales performance, remarking to Perkins, 'The jacket was a hit anyhow.'[17] Finally, the sad finale to *Gatsby*'s odyssey came in Great Britain, where, after rejection by Collins it was published by Chatto & Windus in 1926. Although the reviews were generally respectful it did not appeal to the English reading public, as Collins's editors had suspected.

Neither Fitzgerald nor his contemporaries ever forgot *Gatsby*. In 1930, he wrote to Zelda Fitzgerald, 'I forgot how I'd dragged the great Gatsby out of the pit of my stomach in a time of misery,'[18] and writer Marjorie Kinnan Rawlings wrote to him some years later, after having reread the novel, 'The book resolves itself into the strangest feeling of a crystal globe, or one of the immense soap bubbles we achieved as children, if it could hold its shape and colour without breaking—It is so beautiful, it is so clairvoyant, it is so heartbreaking—.'[19]

When Fitzgerald died in 1940, the critics had not changed their view of *Gatsby*. 'It was not a book for the ages, but it caught superbly the spirit of a decade,' said the *New York Times*, an appraisal that sums up the novel's reputation as reflected in the obituaries for the author. *The New Yorker* appreciated it as 'one of the most scrupulously observed and beautifully written of American novels,' and such writers as John Dos Passos, Malcolm Cowley, John Peale Bishop, Glenway Wescott, and John O'Hara defended Fitzgerald as an important American writer, but some time would pass before the public and the scholars and critics would rediscover *The Great Gatsby*.[20]

The Great Gatsby has generally been regarded, along with Hemingway's *The Sun Also Rises* (1926), as a quintessentially post-World War I novel in which the events of the 1920s are perceived as direct outgrowths of changes in the national sensibility following the Armistice in 1918. But with *Gatsby*, it is not quite so simple; as Ronald Berman suggests, '*The Great Gatsby* is a post-war book, but I think most readers have the wrong war in mind.'[21] Fitzgerald himself, Berman demonstrates, saw the change in his generation of Americans as occurring over a twenty-year period, with the war playing a negligible role in that change. For Fitzgerald, literature and the influence of intellectual leaders like H. G. Wells shaped the attitudes of younger Americans.[22] The public philosophy that William James and others like Josiah Royce and John Dewey were discussing concerned the relation of ethics and literature, and tactically, 'resistance to the temptations of a deeply materialistic culture; moral and intellectual improvement; the conversion of natural energies to worthy purposes; and our social duties in America'. Berman concludes that 'Public Philosophy provides part of the background for the debates in Fitzgerald's narrative concerning family and human relations; and for the hopeful concept of individualism.'[23] Certainly, the issues raised in Gatsby and the elusiveness of the narrative despite its particularity of place and time, suggest that to gain a fuller understanding of the novel we must trace its historical background as far back as the post–Civil War years. These are the years invoked by Nick Carraway when he describes his own family's origins; from that longer perspective we may more clearly view the upheavals wrought by another war and the turbulent years that followed.

The changes that took place in America between the Civil War and the end of World War I were swift, sweeping, and, for many citizens, shattering. Seemingly at once, accepted values and meanings were lost; indeed, Henry Adams saw in this period the erosion of institutions and ideals that had existed since the Middle Ages. The great nineteenth-century writers, Mark Twain, Henry James, and William Dean Howells, as well as others in the fields of science, education, and philosophy, recalled a pre-war world which was lost to them, while a new world had not yet made its outlines clear. Everything seemed to be in flux, and although one could point to specific areas of change in social institutions, economic expansion, the workplace, education, scientific discovery, and population growth, the effects of those changes had been the subject of public discussion and often private despair for more than fifty years—years when F. Scott Fitzgerald, born in 1896, entered young manhood. Some of those radical changes included the rise of wealth. From just a few millionaires before the war, the number reached to over 4,000 by the 1890s.[24] An agrarian society was rapidly becoming industrialized as Congress passed laws that allowed for railroad subsidies and new immigration and tariff increases; concurrently the nation experienced an unprecedented growth in cities to which the new wealth gravitated. At the same time, as poorer farmers were pushed off their land by railroad entrepreneurs, speculators, and drought, with the frontier closed during the last quarter of the century, they drifted into these cities where a new class of urban poor was quickly born. The new technologies—mass newspapers, popular mass magazines, and, later, automobiles—were part of the new taste for popular entertainment, and theatrical producers saw limitless opportunities for productions that appealed to all walks of life (think of Maggie's innocent wonder at her visit to the vulgar music hall in Stephen Crane's *Maggie: A Girl of the Streets* [1893], or Theodore Dreiser's Carrie Meeber who, in *Sister Carrie* [1900], succeeds first as a chorus girl and then as a popular actress on Broadway). Entertainment for this new public was a curious blend of sacred and profane. As a British traveller remarked after listening to an informal song recital in a Western hotel parlour:

> no one in the room except myself seemed to find it in the least incongruous or funny that he sandwiched "Nearer, my God, to thee" between "The man who broke the bank at Monte Carlo" and "Her golden hair was hanging down her back," or that he jumped at once from the pathetic solemnity of "I know that my Redeemer liveth" to the jingle of "Little Annie Rooney."[25]

Not the least of the demands of the new wealth was the lavishly decorated mansion capable of housing the priceless art collections imported by America's millionaires. The city, whether in the East or in the Midwest, was a fact of American life, and it fed the imagination of poets, novelists, and artists of the late nineteenth and early twentieth centuries.

No survey of this era of American history can ignore perhaps the most important occurrence: the waves of immigrants who arrived in a land that itself was undergoing enormous changes. The tensions between native-born Americans and the newcomers were not quickly resolved; the immigrants flooded the cities, bringing energy and hope, and gradually revitalizing culture. By 1885, there were almost a thousand foreign-language newspapers in the United States. Rapid change and growth created in many Americans a sense of alienation as the old values died; even personal identity might be lost or found through the eyes of those who perceived even the slightest shift in one's wealth or social status. Henry Adams, in 1918, described his reaction to these changes: 'in 1865 he was living in a twentieth-century world with eighteenth-century assumptions about order and purpose in change'.[26] This image of the individual battered by new technology and forms of popular entertainment, unable to focus on a balancing belief or value from the inherited past, lost amid the rush of new experience, would haunt the writers of the next generation. This image describes too the American who would face the unexpected and absurd horrors of another war, and a decade of peace in name only.

For America, the war that had begun abroad three years earlier, started on 2 April 1917. It ended with the Armistice on 11 November 1918, but in that short period more than 350,000 Americans had died and over four million had been called to serve. Of the more than thirty-four million men who served in the armies of Britain, France, Italy, and Russia, twenty-one million died in the war.[27] The rhetoric that had prepared the nation for full participation turned hollow in the face of the enormous casualties and the recognition that the very premise upon which the war was fought was not the defence of worldwide democracy, but to secure shaky alliances in a European power struggle. Furthermore, Woodrow Wilson, who had been re-elected in 1916 after pledging to keep America out of the war, entered the fray soon after his second inauguration. Another power struggle among the victorious nations was reflected in the Versailles Treaty, to which Wilson, after early misgivings, lent his full support. Failure of Congress to pass the Treaty on the grounds that it might result in another war only encouraged Wilson to take his case directly to the American people by cross-country train on 3 September 1919. Three weeks into the trip he suffered a stroke, and his presidency fell into the management of his wife and some advisors. Wilson's determination and defeat registered in the hearts and minds of Americans: here was failure on a national scale, and the moral of the story was infinitely adaptable to theorists of many persuasions.

We need only look at a handful of novels to understand how deeply the disaster of the war and its aftermath resonated both in America and abroad: Hemingway's *In Our Time* (1925) and *The Sun Also Rises*, e. e. cummings's *The Enormous Room* (1922), and Erich Maria Remarque's *All Quiet on the Western Front* (1928) offer different reflections on both the agony and the absurdity of the whole enterprise. *Gatsby* is Fitzgerald's post-war novel (however much its ideas reflect issues concerning Americans for more than twenty years), much more so than *This Side of Paradise*, which was started when he was in the army (he did not serve overseas) and rewritten immediately after the war's end. Both Jay Gatsby and Nick Carraway have served abroad and their participation in the war forms a bond between them. Throughout the novel the war is a persistent echo, and Fitzgerald's attitude towards it is complex. Despite Nick Carraway's satiric dismissal of the conflict as a 'delayed Teutonic migration' (Ch. I), the author could see its heroic aspects and romanticize war heroes that he remembered from his Great Neck years, Thomas Hitchcock and Charles C. Rumsey.[28] The two major battles in which Gatsby saw action were the Battle of the Marne and the Battle of Argonne, both in 1918. The latter, the harshest and bloodiest of the war, involved more than a million Americans and resulted in enormous American casualties—26,277 dead and 95,786 wounded. Gatsby's participation in that battle makes his heroism unequivocal, as reflected in Nick's respect for his war service (Chs. IV and VIII).

By Fitzgerald's own account the Jazz Age began about the time of the May Day riots in 1919 and 'leaped to a spectacular death in October, 1929'.[29] The riots involved many new immigrants with socialist or anarchist backgrounds who were now employed in substandard conditions with low wages in factories and manufacturing industries. The Bolshevik revolution in Russia, along with American prejudices against these immigrants, created fears that led mobs to break up socialist May Day parades in several cities in 1919. Mitchell Palmer, the United States Attorney General who supported the mobs, would be for ever linked in history with the 'Palmer raids'.

The Eighteenth Amendment to the Constitution, outlawing the sale of alcoholic beverages, was passed on 16 January 1919, and the Volstead Act, which enabled the law to exact penalties for violating the Amendment, was passed in September of that year. Although Wilson vetoed the law, he was overriden by Congress and the Eighteenth Amendment was in force by the beginning of 1920. Along with Prohibition, the New York underworld was given new life, and *The Great Gatsby* would vividly convey the omnipresence of that world in a decade when all the old boundaries that separated the classes were being broken, and a new wave of instant millionaires, like Gatsby himself, or entertainers and their entourages, mingled with the wealthy polo-players who inhabited the stiff enclaves of the established rich on Long Island's gold coast. Meyer Wolfsheim, one of the immigrants, is a disguised Arnold Rothstein, a well-known underworld figure who was peripherally involved with the Black Sox scandal—the plot to fix the baseball World Series of 1919.[30]

During the 1920s, as the stock market reached new highs, and the rich grew richer, there seemed to be no end to the nation's expansion; the gross national product and the population grew by twenty-five per cent, and five per cent of the population controlled one-third of the nation's wealth by the end of the decade. Sales of automobiles, an important part of the new technology, reached more than 120 million by 1929, and the success stories of men like Henry Ford were familiar to schoolchildren. Fitzgerald's emphasis on the automobile suggests how powerfully the new technology was shaping the beliefs, attitudes, and behaviour of the nation. For that technology included mass media— the fictional magazine *Town Tattle* and the real pulp fiction best-seller *Simon Called Peter* both appear in *Gatsby*—and radio, which in 1920 saw its first licensed station in Pittsburgh's KDKA. Popular music through radio and phonographs was available to every family, and the movies attained a level of artistry and mainstream popularity that they had been striving for since Edwin S. Porter's *The Great Train Robbery* had startled nickelodeon audiences back in 1903.[31] The movies of the 1920s worked hand in hand with the new technology, as viewers' tastes for clothes, cars, home decorations and improvements were stimulated by the images on the big screens.

It was also an age of heroism in sports, where baseball was more popular than ever, and Babe Ruth embodied the values that managed to transcend the corrupt machinations of gangsters, greedy ballclubowners, and morally flawed players. And it was an age of corruption in government, symbolized by the Teapot Dome scandal that rocked the Harding administration, when Albert B. Fall, the Secretary of the Interior, was forced to resign in 1924 after leasing public oil reserves to private interests.

It was an era of parties and good times, both for the wealthy like Gatsby and the Buchanans, and for those less affluent who wanted to take part in the fun, like the guests at Myrtle Wilson's apartment, or the thousands who flocked to speakeasies for liquor, jazz, dancing, and a general relaxation of inhibitions. Living in Great Neck, which was a hub for the New York theatrical world, Fitzgerald observed the lavish parties at Herbert Bayard Swope's estate. Swope was director of the New York *World*, and had been peripherally involved in the Herman Rosenthal case; at lunch with Gatsby, Wolfsheim alludes to the murder of Rosenthal, a minor underworld figure who refused to pay extortion money to a New York City police officer, Charles Becker. Swope, then an editor at the *World*, pressured Rosenthal to tell the story to the newspaper, which resulted in his murder (1912).[32] Swope was also a friend of Arnold Rothstein. Fitzgerald's close Great Neck friend, writer Ring Lardner, lived next to the Swope mansion on East Shore Road, and he and Lardner watched as guests arrived and departed from lavish parties that often lasted until sunrise. Fitzgerald described one such party to his cousin: 'They have no mock-modesty + all perform their various stunts upon the faintest request so its like a sustained concert.'[33]

The Jazz Age ended abruptly with the crash of the stock market which had fuelled the energy of the decade. In four days in late October 1929, the market fell $15 million, and on 29 October it collapsed completely. As Fitzgerald said, 'the most expensive orgy in history was over. . . . It was borrowed time anyhow—the whole upper tenth of a nation living with the insouciance of grand dukes and the casualness of chorus girls.'[34]

For his novel, Fitzgerald drew not only on the Public Philosophy with which he had been familiar since his early youth, but also on a few seminal figures in literature and philosophy whom he acknowledged as influences.[35] In 1940 Fitzgerald declared that Oswald Spengler, who achieved worldwide fame with *The Decline of the West* (1918; revised for English translation, 1926–8), had had a powerful effect on him while writing *Gatsby* (articles on Spengler appearing in magazines and journals that Fitzgerald read would have made him quite familiar with the work before its translation into English). Richard Lehan argues persuasively that although we should not overemphasize the connection, strong parallels exist between Spengler's thesis and Fitzgerald's novel—particularly the idea that 'in historical terms, Culture gives way to Civilization; in human terms, Faustian man gives way to Enlightenment man—the priest-king is replaced by the new Caesar, the man of money and power. When this happens, a primitive sense of race is lost, and the decay embodied in the idea of Civilization begins.'[36] In these terms, Gatsby would be the Faustian man, and Tom Buchanan the new Caesar.

T. S. Eliot's poem 'The Waste Land' (1922) influenced to a greater or lesser degree almost every writer of Fitzgerald's era. In the Valley of Ashes passage in *Gatsby*, 'a fantastic farm where ashes grow like wheat into ridges and hills and grotesque gardens; where ashes take the forms of houses and chimneys and rising smoke and, finally, with a transcendent effort, of ash-gray men, who move dimly and already crumbling through the powdery air' (Ch. II); in Daisy's cry, 'What'll we do with ourselves this afternoon? . . . and the day after that, and the next thirty years?' (Ch. VII), which echoes Eliot's 'What shall we do tomorrow? What shall we ever do?' (lines 133–4); and in the contrast between banality and historical significance that recurs throughout the novel (notably in references to *Town Tattle* and Versailles in Chapter II, and in the Guest List in Chapter IV), Eliot's major themes are adumbrated.

Fitzgerald acknowledged his debt to Conrad in the Introduction to the 1934 edition of the novel;[37] certainly in the selection of narrator, echoes of Conrad's Marlow, however faint, may be detected. But the many comic passages in the novel cannot be traced to Conrad, who had no real gift for humour. And Fitzgerald admired the work of Willa Cather, to whom he wrote in 1925 to explain 'an instance of apparent plagiarism' concerning the similarity between a passage in *Gatsby* and her 1923 novel *A Lost Lady*. Near the end of the novel Cather writes: 'Her eyes, when they laughed for a moment into one's own, seemed to promise a wild delight that he has not found in life.' Fitzgerald was concerned that this sentence resembled his passage in Chapter I of *Gatsby*: 'Her face was sad and lovely with bright things in it, bright eyes and a bright passionate mouth, but there was an excitement in her voice that men who had cared for her found difficult to forget: a singing compulsion, a whispered "Listen," a promise that she had done gay, exciting things just a while since and that there were gay, exciting things hovering in the next hour.' Cather told Fitzgerald that she did not detect any plagiarism.[38]

Throughout his life Fitzgerald acknowledged his debt to his favourite poet, John Keats. In a letter to his daughter in 1938, he confessed that he had adapted a phrase from Keats's 'Ode to a Nightingale' to *Gatsby*. The Keats lines, 'But there is no light, / Save what from heaven is with the breezes blown / Through verdurous glooms and winding mossy ways' becomes in *Gatsby*: 'He lit Daisy's cigarette from a trembling match, and sat down with her on a couch far across the room, where there was no light save what the gleaming floor bounced in from the hall.'[39]

But whatever influences we may adduce, *The Great Gatsby* is an original novel that traces through the history of one shadowy man the history, hopes, dreams, and fate of a nation and ultimately leads us to consider a human quest that lies beyond geographical, even earthly boundaries.

Years after *Gatsby* was published, when Fitzgerald was contemplating a new novel, he wrote, 'It would be short like "Gatsby" but the same in that it will have the transcendental approach, an attempt to show a man's life through some passionately regarded segment of it.'[40] Fitzgerald knew from the outset that the structure of *Gatsby* would be unlike anything he or his contemporaries had attempted, and he refused to relinquish his plan to focus on a mood, or 'hauntedness . . . rejecting in advance . . . all of the ordinary material for Long Island, big crooks, adultery theme & always starting from the small focal point that impressed me—my own meeting with Arnold Rothstein for instance'.[41] *The Great Gatsby* is structured as a series of mysteries which suggest other mysteries, ending not with a solution or resolution, but with a passionate moral commentary on what the narrator, Nick Carraway, has made of the events of a summer over a year before his novel begins. We should not forget that Fitzgerald's structure is Nick's structure; we are reminded by the text that Gatsby's story is contained in a book, a 'history' that Nick is writing as part of his own struggle to make sense of the fragments that comprise his experience of that haunted summer. Ronald Berman notes: 'The novel has a surface and uncharted depth. . . . Nick does not fully see or understand what he perceives, and neither do we.'[42] And Richard Lehan suggests, 'like concentric circles . . . key elements begin to expand and aggregate, creating subsidiary themes, which in turn create more subsidiary themes.'[43] In Gatsby, structure is meaning, and the omissions, suggestions, resemblances, innuendoes, lost memories, 'a fragment of lost words' (Ch. VI) define the structure of the novel as much as the arrangement of chapters and sequence of events.

The mysteries begin with the opening passage where Nick Carraway tries to explain himself in relation to the story of Gatsby, but the questions the opening poses will require the reader to pursue the answers to the very end. What are the 'fundamental decencies'? (Ch. I). When he came back East, why did Nick want the world to be 'in uniform and at a sort of moral attention forever'? Who is Gatsby? Why is Nick's language so charged with feeling when he speaks of Gatsby? If Gatsby is the sort of person for whom Nick has 'unaffected scorn', why is he exempt from Nick's disillusionment? What is the 'foul dust' that floated in the wake of Gatsby's dream? The end is given to the reader in the beginning—for Nick, Gatsby 'turned out all right', but the mysteries have begun to accumulate; they are not dispelled by Nick's remark, for the reader now expects that the rest of the novel will supply the answers. One crucial link in the structure, however, has been established at the outset, that between Gatsby and Nick. Nick accepts Gatsby for his 'extraordinary gift for hope, a romantic readiness such as I have never found in any other person and which it is not likely I shall ever find again'. Gatsby's special gift is clearly shared by Nick, and dictates the structure of the novel. We must find out who Gatsby really is, and we must accept, at the end, Nick's retrospection on the meaning of Gatsby and the fate of his extraordinary gift.

Fitzgerald acknowledged structural problems as he was writing the novel, telling Perkins at one point that he didn't know how to get the characters to New York, that the novel had to build to Gatsby's meeting with Daisy which occurs half-way into the nine-chapter novel. Fitzgerald did, as we have noted, revise some chapters so that the emotional centres were placed after the reader acquires some knowledge of Gatsby over the five-year period before their reunion at Nick's, and later, at the Plaza Hotel, where the antagonism between Gatsby and Tom reaches its ugly denouement.

The novel is structured around parties, both large and small, each ending either in violence or in confrontation, each contrasting both in place and participants with the preceding event. Thus, from the strained dinner party at the Buchanans', Fitzgerald moves in Chapter II to the larger party at Myrtle's, which, although more vulgar and violent than the first, is nevertheless filled with the same tension as Nick's initial evening at the Buchanans'. The next party in Chapter III is the archetypal jazz-age extravaganza, where the mystery of the host's past is deepened by the rumours and gossip that invariably accompany the mere mention of his name. It is at this point that Gatsby makes his first appearance in the novel, but his presence does nothing to dispel the aura of mystery that until the end will surround him. And so the novel moves from the guest list of a typical Gatsby party that opens Chapter IV to the small lunch party with Wolfsheim, to another large party, this time with Tom and Daisy as guests, to the débâcle at the Plaza with only five in attendance. The action seems to occur in waves that echo the sense of drift that is so pervasive in the characters and in the world of the novel.[44] Carefully placed flashbacks fill in the vague outlines of Gatsby's past, but the mystery is preserved until the end when we finally learn who Gatsby really is and just how far he had come to find his dream. The novel is constructed on a pattern of repetitions, of actions and verbal patterns, like the parties, the automobile trips, the dances, the discussions of careless driving and of Gatsby's rumoured history.

Despite the mysteries, the novel is filled with specific reflections of its time. Like E. L. Doctorow's more recent novel *Ragtime* (1975), *Gatsby* blends history (the Rosenthal murder, the Black Sox scandal, the war) with fiction, and its pages are filled with the popular culture of the era—theatrical figures like Joe Frisco, Gilda Gray, David Belasco, movies, mass magazines and newspapers, advertisements, and popular songs. But such evocations of the period swirl around the mystery of the man at the centre; paradoxically, the more we know about the world in and around New York City in 1922, the more elusive the meaning of the novel becomes. The reader has to look beneath the surface, for Fitzgerald parcels out information with sly calculation. The relationship between Nick Carraway and Jordan Baker adds another level of mystery: it is presented in fleeting snatches of dialogue—meetings suggested but barely described—yet it serves as an important counterpoint to Gatsby's romance with Daisy. The justly celebrated ending of the novel, Nick's revelation of the meaning of the summer's events, not only concludes the narrative but also adds a level of transcendence (and material for further conjecture) that Fitzgerald had always intended his novel to achieve: as Fitzgerald observed, 'That's the whole burden of this novel—the loss of those illusions that give such colour to the world that you don't care whether things are true or false as long as they partake of the magical glory.'[45]

The characters in *The Great Gatsby* are presented in as fragmented and sketchy a manner as the narrative. Fitzgerald admitted, 'You are right about Gatsby being blurred and patchy. I never at any one time saw him clear myself—for he started as one man I knew and then changed into myself—the amalgam was never complete in my mind.'[46] That Gatsby retains some mystery until the end is essential to the narrative; the revelation of his 'greatness' must come through Nick Carraway's words after he has sorted out the events of that summer. Because the meaning of Gatsby's quest and his invention of a new identity to achieve his dream are the core of the novel, a more naturalistic approach would distract the reader from those concerns. Thus, Gatsby himself embodies not only the Horatio Alger myth of success (although Gatsby's wealth is far more than any Alger hero ever achieved), but all of the stories of self-made men that dotted the history of American expansion in the late nineteenth century.[47] He is on the one hand a variation of the log-cabin boy who, after an early education at the feet of a genuine relic of that expansion, pioneer-debauchee Dan Cody, rises to unparalleled wealth and power, and on the other, a modern racketeer moving easily between bootleggers and gangsters like Meyer Wolfsheim and apparently respectable but deeply corrupt Wall Street brokers. Gatsby has created himself, literally patched himself together out of popular ideas and books about self-improvement and success that he encountered during his difficult journey from youth to manhood. His attempt to link his background to Nick's—he says that he is the son of wealthy parents from the Middle West, educated at Oxford as part of a family tradition—is in fact, as critics have noted, less interesting than his real background, with its echoes of those hardy pioneers who set out to conquer the frontier. Yet by the end, perhaps because, like Nick, the reader has had to reconstruct Gatsby, almost like a jigsaw puzzle, he becomes the most distinct individual in the novel.[48]

Tom and Daisy are representatives of their world, yet they are more clearly depicted than Gatsby and Nick. Tom is powerful and corrupt; his affair with Myrtle Wilson is just one of many he has conducted during the five years he has been married to Daisy. His fascination with contemporary discussions of race—his determination to preserve Nordic purity—is as much a reflection of his absorption of fragments of ideas that he has plucked from public discussion as is Gatsby's piecemeal creation of his history. Like others in the novel, Tom 'drifts', seeking, like each of the characters, some elusive moment of happiness—for him, it is a wistful search for 'the dramatic turbulence of some irrecoverable football game' (Ch. I). By the end of the novel Tom comes to symbolize the impenetrable wall of an older moneyed class from which Gatsby is barred.

Daisy Buchanan is less clear in physical outline than Tom, but because she represents so much to Gatsby, Fitzgerald delineates her by associations—with wealth, excitement, mystery, romance. It is Daisy's voice that fills the novel, a thrilling voice of promise, possibility, unexpected joy; for Nick it is an indiscreet voice, but for Gatsby, as we later learn, 'Her voice is full of money' (Ch. VII). Does Daisy love Gatsby? Or does she love the idea of Gatsby's faithful adoration? Gatsby, after all, has given her back her own youth (her dream?), and she knows that in an instant she might lose it should some new party guest, 'some authentically radiant young girl . . . with one fresh glance at Gatsby . . . blot out those five years of unwavering devotion' (Ch. VI). Does she use Gatsby to retaliate against Tom's infidelities? These are tangential questions, for Daisy's response to the events at the end is, for Nick, and for the reader who shares Nick's judgment of Gatsby, a betrayal. In recent years, some critics have found sympathy for Daisy as an emotionally thwarted woman and a mistreated wife, but that view falters against the symbolic weight Fitzgerald gives her in relation to the story of Gatsby which is, of course, at the centre of the novel.

Myrtle Wilson is defined by her coarse voice, by her sensuality, and by her own dreams (in their own way as vital as Gatsby's), which derive from scandal magazines, popular novels, and advertisements. She dreams too, of being a wealthy matron (the decor of the apartment Tom provides for her is a comic pastiche of tapestry and portraits that mocks her efforts to appear upper-class). She married George Wilson because she thought he was a 'gentleman', whatever that word means to Myrtle; she looks forward to becoming Mrs Tom Buchanan and, like so many other Americans in the new consumer culture of the 1920s, to going shopping. Myrtle's affair with Tom is a travesty of Gatsby's love for Daisy. When she met Tom, she thought over and over, 'You can't live forever' (Ch. II), but Gatsby's love partakes of eternity.

Jordan Baker, whom Nick describes as a hard, limited person, plays an important role in the novel. She shares in the corruption of the era, and she is essential in two other respects: when Nick becomes caught by the contagion of Gatsby's dream, he allows himself to pretend that Jordan can provide him with a taste of that romantic wonder; also, having known Daisy when they were both girls in Louisville, she offers in flashback an accurate observer's account of Daisy's romance with Gatsby, and of Daisy's marriage to Tom Buchanan. In contrast to all of the fragmentary knowledge, gossip, and innuendo throughout the novel, Jordan's recollection is notably straightforward and unadorned, quite in character with her personality and situation—although she has been identified by Nick as a cheat, she would have no reason to lie about Daisy and Gatsby. Her narrative also reveals a dimension to Jordan that Nick has not perceived: her own susceptibility to romance which has made the memory unforgettable.

George Wilson is a reflection of his environment—one of the 'ash-gray' men who inhabit the valley of ashes that lies between West Egg and New York City, over which brood the enormous eyes of Dr T. J. Eckleburg. He embodies the pervasive sense of drift and exhaustion that exists beside the raw vitality of the new age, most vividly embodied in his wife, Myrtle.

Several minor figures dart through the novel—they come and go like all of the guests at Gatsby's parties: Klipspringer, Owl-Eyes, Myrtle's sister Catherine, and Meyer Wolfsheim. But the character who tells us about Gatsby, Nick Carraway, has remained for many commentators an ambiguous presence in the novel.[49] Some have questioned his sexual preferences, while others have noted his snobbery, his inability to make a commitment, and even his honesty. But the novel is Nick's story as well as Gatsby's. Nick tells us at the outset that he has been wounded by the events of that summer, that his unaffected scorn for Gatsby changed to admiration, and the congenitally uncommitted Nick ultimately commits himself totally to Gatsby. Not only does he tell Gatsby that he's 'worth the whole damn bunch put together' (Ch. VIII), but he also rescues Gatsby from obscurity and wholesale neglect. And he takes complete charge of Gatsby's affairs when nobody else comes forward. The novel thus is the story of two men: Gatsby, who pursues his incorruptible dream, and Nick Carraway, who for much of the way does not clearly see or understand what is happening, a confusion shared by the reader. But Nick too has a dream; however amorphous it may be, and the novel is about Nick's discovery and ultimately our discovery of the meaning of Gatsby's story, which is nothing less than the meaning of American democracy, individualism, and heroism.

Even the early reviewers of the novel praised Fitzgerald's style, but few recognized the difficulty of separating style from meaning. Fitzgerald felt that the closest literary analogy to *Gatsby* was poetry; he tried and succeeded, as in poetry, in making the imagery and symbolism convey the many ideas that readers over the past seventy years have discovered embedded in the text. The language in the novel, which Fitzgerald described as 'blankets of excellent prose',[50] follows a pattern of incremental repetition; as Milton Stern has demonstrated,[51] Fitzgerald uses various flowers that attain symbolic significance through repetition. Daisy's name immediately suggests the motif of flowers. The rose suggests the appeal (rosiness) of the world of the very rich, and the colour is associated throughout the text with the possession of wealth. Further, Nick seems to Daisy 'an absolute rose' (Ch. I). The rose is ultimately linked to Gatsby's rose-coloured dream, and leads us to consider—as all such symbolic allusions ultimately do—the meaning of that dream.

The novel abounds in colours, which form a narrative connection, from for example, the green light at the end of Daisy's dock, to the 'fresh green breast of the new world' (Ch. IX), the two passages ultimately linking Gatsby's dream with that of the Dutch sailors who first touched the shores of the New World. Jackson R. Bryer has traced the way recurrent patterns of language achieve specific objectives: 'They are marvellously descriptive and evocative . . . they are often so original and witty that they surprise and capture the reader's attention . . . and they metaphorically encapsulate or suggest in microcosmic form the meanings of the novel as a whole.'[52]

As Bryer indicates, Fitzgerald's use of colour is often jarring when linked with the objects described. He notes other small elements of style including recurring ambivalent descriptive phrases or oxymorons which suggest the ambiguities at the heart of the novel, like Jordan Baker's 'charming, discontented face' (Ch. I). Another repeated pattern is the linking of nouns with unusual adjectives, like 'triumphant hat-boxes' (Ch. I), and the frequent incongruity of subject and verb, like the wreck of the car which 'crouched' (Ch. II) in Wilson's garage.[53] There is also a vocabulary of impermanence and evanescence; words like 'whisperings', 'drift', 'restlessness', 'innuendoes', 'murmurings', that reflect the insecurity of the era, the social changes that prevent individuals from finding meaning or moral order in a disordered home, city, nation, and finally, universe. Conversely, the word 'vitality' appears frequently, suggesting the struggle between energy and desiccation as embodied in Gatsby and Myrtle Wilson on the one hand, and the Buchanans on the other.

There are 450 words related to time, as we would expect in a novel whose main character wants nothing less than to bring back the past, to preserve a golden moment from five years earlier that for him symbolizes eternity. Yet these time words do not create an orderly chronology, but rather suggest the difficulty of locating any place, action, or individual within a specific moment. The guest list, from a timetable dated 5 July 1922, locates those who came to Gatsby's party in space and time, but they all blur as Nick struggles to remember them, even 'a prince of something whom we called Duke and whose name, if I ever knew it, I have forgotten' (Ch. IV). The guest list itself evolves out of and concludes on a note of anonymity that suggests the movement of Gatsby's own life and destiny: from the unknown James Gatz, to his metamorphosis into the notorious Jay Gatsby, to his mythic resurrection in Nick's vision of the nameless Dutch sailors. The pattern of naming, from anonymity, to identification, to higher eternal anonymity serves to reinforce the novel's broad implications: Gatsby's story is more than the tale of one man; it is our nation's and beyond that, Everyman's.[54]

Other stylistic patterns reinforce the difficulty of perception: what is the meaning of the panoply of persons and events Fitzgerald has so richly described? The language is so filled with indefiniteness, complications, and subjectivity, that we are left looking for a way to place it all in perspective. Yet the prose is so controlled and rhythmic—Nick's soaring language at the end is the ultimate triumph of style—that it succeeds in imparting definition to the life and dream of the great Gatsby.

Finally, what is the meaning of *The Great Gatsby*? Like the narrative patterns, the characters, the language and style, the meaning is embedded in the text, yet remains elusive. Perhaps that is why so many readers are drawn back to the book, for no one reading can possibly provide the solutions to all of the mysteries, or arrive at one statement that might encompass all of the ideas that have been raised. The novel is a story about America as it developed after the Civil War, when the promise of the new world was invested in the often ruthless settlement of the frontier; it is, after all, a story about East and West, not simply Wall Street and Nick's bracing Middle West, but also the dream of the first settlers for whom the New World flowered. It is a dream that clashes inevitably with the forces of the new technology, and the rapacity that fuelled the nation's expansion, destroying the gifts of nature in the process.

It is about one man whose sense of romantic possibility (which he shares with those who first stepped on America's shores) resides in the unattainable woman who symbolizes the beauty that wealth preserves and protects, a beauty that, for Gatsby, represents all of the possibilities of this life and of eternal life. His quest for Daisy is no less than the search for destiny, for the very meaning of human existence: 'He knew that when he kissed this girl and forever wed his unutterable visions to her perishable breath, his mind would never romp again like the mind of God. . . . Then he kissed her. At his lips' touch she blossomed for him like a flower and the incarnation was complete' (Ch. VI). It is in this passage that the echo of religion from a dim, half-forgotten past resides. Gatsby must recapture this moment, for he has embodied his spiritual vision in the material world—in Daisy Buchanan whose voice suggests to him an eternal life inextricably associated with money. But Gatsby is not one of the true descendants of Victorian debauchery, like Dan Cody, but rather, a young man whose ideas have come piecemeal throughout his life, from the stories of success a boy would pick up from the Alger books and from Benjamin Franklin's rules for self-improvement (including 'The Way to Wealth'), as well as from the hard realities of his own youth.

Gatsby is also about the creation of a self in a new world in which personal identity resides in the perception of others. Fitzgerald's emphasis on vision, introduced by the brooding eyes of Dr Eckleburg and, for example, in the numerous impressions of Gatsby's house as it appears to Nick, to Daisy, and to Mr Gatz, suggests how dependent the sense of the outer world is on how others see it. Thus Gatsby would have to create a new identity—James Gatz becoming Jay Gatsby—simply in order for this new self to exist in a world whose outlines he clearly understands, but whose depths he never fathoms. His construction of a new identity is frail; his reunion with Daisy is inseparable from his idea of self, but it is smashed by Tom Buchanan's derisive dismissal of 'Mr Nobody from Nowhere' (Ch. VII). Again, Fitzgerald touches on a theme that haunted American writers as dissimilar as

Henry James and Theodore Dreiser: in a society without an old established class structure, where the idea of a privileged class comes from British models, how does an individual compete with the descendants of 'old money' (which might have come from such enterprises as the wholesale hardware business belonging to Nick's family) who invent a royal ancestry to fit into a class system that the wealth from nineteenth-century expansion created? 'Family' is a key word in the novel, as it was in the early twentieth century: as Berman notes, 'Even in advertisements it generally means the combination of race, class and especially religion.'[55] So that when Tom Buchanan defends 'family life and family institutions', seeking to stave off the threat of 'intermarriage between black and white' (Ch. VII), he is doing no less than defending the identity of that privileged class against wealthy *arrivistes* like Gatsby and the *habitués* of West Egg.

Through the development of Nick Carraway, the novel becomes a search for moral order. The young man who prided himself on suspending moral judgemnts has by the end provided judgments of Gatsby and of the Buchanans and, above all, has defended loyalty and friendship, which seem no longer to exist in his world. His faithfulness to Gatsby's dream is itself a bulwark against the dissolution of moral order that defines his world. Tirelessly, Nick performs the trivial tasks that nothing less than simple humanity demands—and in so doing, defends an idea of morality which has been swept away by tides of change. However much we have questioned Nick's involvement in the events of that summer, he emerges as a new kind of hero. He has cleaned up the mess made by the Buchanans, and has salvaged Gatsby's dream for the reader to consider.

The last passages of the novel contain Nick's, and Fitzgerald's, final words on the meaning of Gatsby's life (the charged prose lifts it above the first-person narrative pattern of the rest of the book, with perhaps the exception of the last paragraph of Nick's opening remarks when he describes Gatsby's extraordinary gift for hope). For Gatsby's dream at the end is the dream of Everyman: of the Dutch sailors who first set foot on the new world—and by extension of all of the American Adams who searched for freedom and democracy in the frontier. It is also the dream of those young people caught between two worlds, the one scarcely dead, the other driven by raw energy yet inexorably drifting toward death. It is for all of us a yearning for more time, perhaps for that 'orgastic future' (Ch. IX), and a wistful regret for what has been lost. At the end, despite the powerful image of loss, we share Gatsby's romantic hope; like him, we are beating against the current. Surely that image of the individual pursuing his destiny, however fruitless that pursuit may prove, is the greatness of Gatsby, and perhaps of us all.

From "Introduction," *The Great Gatsby*, by F. Scott Fitzgerald (New York: Oxford University Press, 1998): vii-xxxv. Copyright © 1998 by Oxford University Press. Reprinted by permission of Oxford University Press, Inc.

Notes

1. *F. Scott Fitzgerald: A Life in Letters*, ed. Matthew J. Bruccoli (New York: Scribner's, 1994), 80.

2. Fitzgerald had misgivings about the title. He used *Among the Ash Heaps and Millionaires* for a time, and later *Trimalchio in West Egg*, *Gold-hatted Gatsby*, *Trimalchio*, and *The High-Bouncing Lover*. Shortly before publication, Fitzgerald wired Perkins trying to change the title to *Under the Red, White and Blue*, but it was too late for the change. Trimalchio was a particular favourite because Fitzgerald saw similarities between Gatsby's parties and Trimalchio's lavish entertainment in the Roman novel *Satyricon* by Petronius (d. AD 66).

3. *The Letters of F. Scott Fitzgerald*, ed. Andrew Turnbull (New York: Scribner's, 1963), 79.

4. Letter to Maxwell Perkins, 20 May 1940. *Dear Scott/Dear Max: The Fitzgerald–Perkins Correspondence*, ed. John Kuehl and Jackson R. Bryer (New York: Scribner's, 1971), 261. Spelling errors in Fitzgerald's letters have not been corrected for this edition.

5. Introduction to Modern Library edition of *The Great Gatsby*, repr. in Matthew J. Bruccoli and Jackson R. Bryer (eds.), *F. Scott Fitzgerald in His Own Time: A Miscellany* (Kent, Oh.: Kent State University Press, 1971), 156.

6. *Letters of F. Scott Fitzgerald*, 113.

7. Letter to Maxwell Perkins, June 1922; *Dear Scott/Dear Max*, 60.

8. Letter to Maxwell Perkins, mid-July 1922; *Correspondence of F. Scott Fitzger-*

ald, ed. Matthew J. Bruccoli and Margaret M. Duggan with Susan Walker (New York: Random House, 1980), 112.

9. Letter to Maxwell Perkins, 10 Sept. 1924; *Correspondence of F. Scott Fitzgerald*, 146; letter to Thomas Boyd, May 1924, 141.

10. Letter to Maxwell Perkins, before 16 Apr. 1924; *Letters of F. Scott Fitzgerald*, 163.

11. *Dear Scott/Dear Max*, 82–5; Matthew J. Bruccoli, Introduction, *New Essays On The Great Gatsby* (New York: Cambridge University Press, 1985), 1–2. Bruccoli states; '*Gatsby* achieved its greatness in proof.'

12. See Matthew J. Bruccoli, *Apparatus for F. Scott Fitzgerald's The Great Gatsby* [*Under the Red, White and Blue*] (Columbia: University of South Carolina Press, 1974) for a full description of the changes from holograph manuscript to published novel. There are no surviving typescript pages of *The Great Gatsby*, except for some insets on galleys. The holograph first draft of the novel is at Princeton University Library, a set of the unrevised first proofs is in the Bruccoli Collection, and Fitzgerald's duplicate set of marked, reworked proofs is also at the Princeton University Library. The unrevised proofs in the Bruccoli Collection approximate Fitzgerald's final revised typescript, with Perkins's corrections and publisher's styling added. How much typescript Fitzgerald submitted before receiving the unrevised proofs is not known. For a full discussion of Fitzgerald's process of revision, see *The Great Gatsby*, ed. Matthew J. Bruccoli (Cambridge and New York: Cambridge University Press, 1991), pp. ix–xx, xxv–lv.

13. In Jackson B. Bryer (ed.), *The Critical Reputation of F. Scott Fitzgerald: A Bibliographical Study* (Hamden, Conn.: Archon, 1967), 64.

14. See Bryer, *Critical Reputation of F. Scott Fitzgerald*, 59–70, for excerpts from contemporary American and British reviews of the novel.

15. Gilbert Seldes, 'Spring Flight', *The Dial*, 79 (Aug. 1925), 162.

16. F. Scott Fitzgerald, *The Crack-Up*, ed. Edmund Wilson (New York: New Directions, 1945), 308–10.

17. Letter to Maxwell Perkins, 1 May 1925; *Dear Scott/Dear Max*, 105. The cover was created by Francis Cugat, who worked in Hollywood as an art designer. Against a dark blue background, a woman's eyes stare out at us; looking closely, we can see a reclining nude female figure on the iris of each eye. A green teardrop falls from one eye, and far below, the lights of a carnival appear before the backdrop of the city's skyline. Because the drawing was finished before the book was completed, we may conjecture on the effect it might have had on Fitzgerald's picture of the eyes of Dr T. J. Eckleburg. See Charles Scribner III, 'Celestial Eyes—from Metamorphosis to Masterpiece', *Princeton University Library Chronicle*, 53 (Winter 1992), 140–55, for a full discussion of the Cugat artwork.

18. *Correspondence of F. Scott Fitzgerald*, 239.

19. Letter to Fitzgerald, autumn 1936; *Correspondence of F. Scott Fitzgerald*, 459.

20. 'Not Wholly "Lost"', *New York Times*, 24 Dec. 1940; 'Notes and Comments', *New Yorker*, 4 Jan. 1941; in Bruccoli and Bryer, *F. Scott Fitzgerald in His Own Time*, 470, 474.

21. Ronald Berman, *The Great Gatsby and Fitzgerald's World of Ideas* (Tuscaloosa and London: University of Alabama Press, 1997), 18.

22. See Frederick James Smith, 'Fitzgerald, Flappers and Fame', in Matthew J. Bruccoli, Scottie Fitzgerald Smith, and Joan P. Kerr (eds.), *The Romantic Egoists* (New York: Charles Scribner's Sons, 1974), 79. Despite Fitzgerald's assertion, we should remember that when interviewed, he often took a strongly iconoclastic position, dictated in part by his awareness of his public role as anointed spokesman for the Jazz Age.

23. Berman, *The Great Gatsby and Fitzgerald's World of Ideas*, 32.

24. See Jay Martin, *Harvests of Change: American Literature 1865–1914* (Englewood Cliffs, NJ: Prentice-Hall, 1967), 1–24, for an account of those changes which affected the writers of the period before World War I.

25. James Fullarton Muirhead, *America, the Land of Contrasts: A Briton's View of His American Kin* (London and New York, 1898), 22; quoted in Martin, *Harvests of Change*, 23.

26. Martin, *Harvests of Change*, 11.

27. See Richard Lehan, *The Great Gatsby: The Limits of Wonder* (Boston: Twayne, 1990), 1–10, for a thorough discussion of the historical background of the novel.

28. Richard Lehan explores Fitzgerald's connection with these two Long Island polo players, and correctly assesses Fitzgerald's attitude toward the war (*The Great Gatsby: The Limits of Wonder*, 5).

29. F. Scott Fitzgerald, 'Echoes of the Jazz Age', in *The Crack-Up*, 13.

30. See Eliot Asinof, *Eight Men Out* (New York: Holt Rinehart & Winston, 1963) for a full account of the episode.

31. See my article 'From Griffith's Girls to "*Daddy's Girl*"', *Twentieth Century Literature*, 26 (F. Scott Fitzgerald Issue, Summer 1980), 189–221, for a discussion of D. W. Griffith's influence on Fitzgerald during the early years of the movies.

32. See Leo Katcher, *The Big Bankroll* (New York: Harper, 1959) for an account of the Rosenthal case.

33. Letter to Cecilia Delihant Taylor, after Oct. 1922; *F. Scott Fitzgerald: A Life in Letters*, 63.

34. F. Scott Fitzgerald, 'Echoes of the Jazz Age', in *The Crack-Up*, 21.

35. For a full discussion of influences on Fitzgerald, see Robert Roulston, 'Something Borrowed, Something New: A Discussion of Literary Influences on *The Great Gatsby*' in Scott Donaldson (ed.), *Critical Essays on F. Scott Fitzgerald's The Great Gatsby* (Boston: G. K. Hall, 1984), 55–64.

36. Richard Lehan, 'F. Scott Fitzgerald and Romantic Destiny', *Twentieth Century Literature*, 26 (F. Scott Fitzgerald Issue, 1980), 140.

37. Bruccoli and Bryer, *F. Scott Fitzgerald in His Own Time*, 156.

38. *F. Scott Fitzgerald: A Life in Letters*, 100–1. See also Matthew J. Bruccoli, '"An Instance of Apparent Plagiarism"', *Princeton University Library Chronicle*, 40 (Spring 1978), 171–8.

39. *F. Scott Fitzgerald: A Life in Letters*, 341–2.

40. Letter to Beatrice Dance, 11 Oct. 1938; *Correspondence of F. Scott Fitzgerald*, 517.

41. Letter to Corey Ford, July 1937; *Letters of F. Scott Fitzgerald*, 551.

42. Berman, *The Great Gatsby and Fitzgerald's World of Ideas*, 25.

43. Lehan, *The Great Gatsby: The Limits of Wonder*, 127.

44. Ronald Berman, *The Great Gatsby and Modern Times* (Urbana and Chicago: University of Illinois Press, 1994), 43–4, discusses Fitzgerald's repeated use of the word 'drift' to describe characters' movements.

45. Letter to Ludlow Fowler, Aug. 1924; *Correspondence of F. Scott Fitzgerald*, 145.

46. Letter to John Peale Bishop, 9 Aug. 1925; *Letters of F. Scott Fitzgerald*, 358.

47. Estimates of the sales of Alger books vary from 100 million to 400 million. The name of Horatio Alger (1832–99), author of over 100 titles, became synonymous with the achievement of the young American boy rising from rags to riches.

48. See Berman, *The Great Gatsby and Fitzgerald's World of Ideas*, 131–54, for a discussion of the issues and ideas from the late nineteenth and early twentieth centuries that Gatsby would have absorbed.

49. For a summary of the problems critics have found with Nick Carraway, see Scott Donaldson, 'The Trouble with Nick', in *Critical Essays on The Great Gatsby*, 131–9.

50. Letter to Edmund Wilson, spring 1925; *Letters of F. Scott Fitzgerald*, 342.

51. Milton R. Stern, *The Golden Moment: The Novels of F. Scott Fitzgerald* (Urbana: University of Illinois Press, 1970), 280–8.

52. Jackson R. Bryer, 'Style as Meaning in *The Great Gatsby*: Notes Toward a New Approach', in Donaldson (ed.), *Critical Essays on The Great Gatsby*, 124.

53. Ibid. 124–7.

54. See my essay, 'Gatsby's Guest List and Fitzgerald's Technique of Naming', *Fitzgerald/Hemingway Annual*, 4 (1972), 99–112, for a discussion of the guest list.

55. *The Great Gatsby and Fitzgerald's World of Ideas*, 39.

The Great Gatsby:
Fitzgerald's Opulent Synthesis (1925)_____

Robert Roulston and Helen H. Roulston

Fitzgerald did not care much for the title of his most perfect book. When returning the proofs in January 1925 from Rome, Fitzgerald indicated to Maxwell Perkins that he preferred to call the work *Trimalchio* and felt that the title finally chosen was unsatisfactory because of a lack of emphasis in the work, "even ironically," on the greatness of Jay Gatsby.[1] Fitzgerald's doubts persisted. In March he still favored *Trimalchio* but was considering reverting to an earlier choice, *Gold-Hatted Gatsby*. Just as the novel was on the verge of publication, he proposed yet another title, *Under the Red, White and Blue*.[2] Some of the other possibilities Fitzgerald was considering have certain advantages over the title that finally appeared on the cover. *Under the Red, White and Blue*, for example, places clearer emphasis on the all-important theme of Gatsby as an exemplar and victim of the American Dream; *Trimalchio* and *On The Road to West Egg* more pointedly conjure up Gatsby's pursuit of wealth and glamour.

Yet the title finally chosen, with its apparent contradiction, splendidly conveys the quality that most gives *The Great Gatsby* its peculiar magic. That quality is not its irony, its tragedy, its realism, its fantasy, its wit, its poetry, its compassion, its satire, its narrative adroitness, its sharp characterizations, but its marvelous inclusion of all these attributes along with numerous others that often seem barely compatible with the rest. No less remarkable is the combination of a richness of texture and profusion of detail with masterly compression.

Fitzgerald's previously cited letter to Roger Burlingame suggests what may have contributed to the multiple vision pervading nearly every level of *Gatsby*—the pervasive feeling of wanting "to be back somewhere."[3] Indications are that Fitzgerald's own nostalgia operated on two tiers, with the Midwest and New York both being its objects. He began work on *Gatsby* at Great Neck, but under financial duress he set the project aside in late 1923 and produced a spate of stories for large-circulation magazines. After paying off his most pressing debts, he set off for Europe with Zelda in April of the following year, later settling on the Riviera and in June renting a villa in Saint Raphael. There he wrote most of *Gatsby* but added some final touches in Italy after receiving the proofs from Scribner's. As a matter of fact, he soon had an excellent reason for wanting to be "back somewhere." While he was working on his book, Zelda was becoming involved with a French aviator, Edouard Jozan. Fitzgerald thus found himself in the anomalous situation of writing a novel in which the hero is trying to win another man's wife, while the latter man, in turn, is having an affair with the wife of a poor garage owner. The narrator recoils in disgust and returns to the moral certainties of his home in the Midwest. Yet for all Nick Carraway's animadversions against the corruptness of the East, Fitzgerald invests New York with genuine glamour and excitement, suggesting that he was already looking back on his life there almost as wistfully as upon his earlier experiences in Minnesota.

At the center of this complex and subtle work is a plot that seems simplicity itself. A poor young man named James Gatz, from North Dakota, changes his name to Jay Gatsby, becomes an army officer, and at a dance in Louisville meets and falls in love with a local belle, Daisy Fay. Daisy marries a man of her own class, wealthy Tom Buchanan from Chicago. Determined to win her back, Gatsby amasses a fortune through various criminal enterprises, buys a huge mansion across the bay from the Buchanans' estate on Long Island and almost succeeds in inducing her to leave Tom. Eventually, though, her resolve collapses, and she stays with her husband. Thereafter, through a dizzying series of enough twists to sustain the narrative lines of half a dozen stories in the *Saturday Evening Post*, Fitzgerald manages to have Daisy, while behind the wheel of Gatsby's automobile, accidentally kill Tom's mistress, Myrtle Wilson. Myrtle's husband, George, suspects first Tom, then Gatsby. Fitzgerald finally brings everything to a bloody catastrophe by having the deranged George Wilson shoot Gatsby in Gatsby's own swimming pool.

Not only are the basic boy-meets-girl, loses-girl story and the clever plotting reminiscent of Fitzgerald's *Post* fiction. Here too are the themes and narrative situations that had sustained him for the last half dozen years: rich girl–poor boy (and vice versa), North versus South, Midwest versus East Coast, the Horatio Alger motif,[4] the weakling who turns on his victimizers, the outsider harried by his social or economic superiors, the loss of illusions, a longing for the past, sexual jealousy. The hero is even a variant on one of Fitzgerald's very earliest favorite types, the gentleman burglar. All these strands, though, are woven into a fabric of stunning richness. In fact, Fitzgerald's multiple vision pervades every level, from the smallest stylistic touches to the overall structure.

One of the most conspicuous peculiarities of Fitzgerald's prose is his fondness for oxymorons, those phrases combining incongruous elements. Nowhere are they more striking than in *Gatsby*. Gatsby's gangster mentor, Meyer Wolfsheim,[5] for instance, eats with "ferocious delicacy," and Gatsby himself pursues a vision of "meretricious beauty" and of "ineffable gaudiness" and perceives "the unreality of reality." Even when modifiers do not exactly cancel out their nouns, the juxtaposition is often startling, as when Fitzgerald refers to Wolfsheim's "tragic nose," the "cheerful snobbery" of Daisy's milieu in Louisville, or—in a touch of synesthesia—the "frothy odor" of a beverage. Then there are the "adventitious authority" of the detective at the scene of Myrtle Wilson's death and the "racy pasquinade" the press will make of the whole episode.

In such phrases Fitzgerald is not merely being clever. He is doing in miniature what he does stylistically throughout the novel. In an interview for an episode on Fitzgerald in the television series, *Biography*, the Canadian author and acquaintance of both Fitzgerald and Ernest Hemingway, Morley Callaghan, contrasted the styles of the two writers. Hemingway's language, Callaghan contended, is much closer to the American vernacular, whereas Fitzgerald's is more literary and traditional. Most would probably assent to Callaghan's distinction. But anyone who carefully compares the opening sentences of Hemingway's *The Sun Also Rises* with those of *Gatsby* should notice something strange. Nick Carraway, Fitzgerald's narrator, says: "In my younger and more vulnerable years my father gave me some advice that I've been turning over in my mind ever since" (*GG*, 5). Now "younger and more vulnerable" may be somewhat literary, but "turning over" is not, nor is the contraction "I've." Neither are "haven't" and "you've" in the second sentence, nor are "didn't" and we've" in the third. Jake Barnes, Nick's counterpart in Hemingway's first novel, uses no contractions throughout the opening pages, even when the colloquial stance seems to cry out for them, as in the second sentence, which begins "Do not think that I am very much impressed" (5). Would Jake really have said "do not" and "I am" rather than "don't" and "I'm"? Now everybody knows that Hemingway's ear for the rhythms of language was one of the marvels of the modern world. Jake's more formal usage here certainly makes his delivery appropriately staccato and hard-boiled.

The fact, though, is that Fitzgerald's greater blend of formal and informal usage at the outset of *Gatsby* allows him the widest possible stylistic latitude, and he proceeds to take full advantage of the opportunities thus afforded. Nick, therefore, is able, with little sense of disjuncture, to descant in a conversational manner, as if confiding to the reader over a glass of ale, and suddenly shift to blazing lyrical passages when recounting some particular enthusiasm or emotional crisis. In a recent review of a volume of stories by Fitzgerald, Jay McInerney commented upon Fitzgerald's repeated use of an old-fashioned way of addressing the reader in a manner reminiscent of Thackeray. The repeated echoes of Thackeray should hardly be surprising. Fitzgerald more than once stressed his debt to the English novelist and in 1934 pointed out in a letter to John Jamieson that, though he had little familiarity with French authors during his formative years, he had read Thackeray "over and over."[6]

Since most critics seem more intrigued by the structural, symbolic, and thematic aspects of *Gatsby* than by its style, the influence of

Thackeray has received less attention than the apparent impact of Conrad and Spengler, or even of Wharton and Eliot. Thackeray, though, is a looming presence no less than another of Fitzgerald's idols, John Keats, albeit the aura of the latter is less pervasive in *Gatsby* than it is in *Tender Is the Night*. At any rate, Nick can switch from being a Thackeray-like raconteur to prose poet and back again without losing his recognizable voice or his coherence as a character. Indeed, as Nick tells his tale, he achieves his considerable linguistic variety without lapsing into the eclecticism that mars some of Fitzgerald's earlier writings. Gatsby, for instance, contains nothing like the outright mimicry of Oscar Wilde that intrudes in *This Side of Paradise* or the stylistic mannerisms of H. L. Mencken in "May Day," "The Diamond as Big as the Ritz," and *The Beautiful and Damned*. Thus Nick, the calm reporter of incidents, without stepping out of character, can give vent to a lyrical outburst when contemplating Long Island Sound from the veranda of the Buchanans: "Slowly the white wings of the boat moved against the blue cool limit of the sky. Ahead lay the scalloped ocean and the abounding blessed isles" (124). Most splendid of all is the concluding barrage of prose that fuses Gatsby's dream of success with the vision of an unspoiled American continent greeting the first Dutch mariners.

Another important dichotomy involves the different ways in which Fitzgerald depicts Long Island and Manhattan. Although both locales emerge vividly from the page, nearly everything east of the Queensboro Bridge is distorted by a thick layer of symbolism. In Manhattan everything is not merely sharp but usually almost literally accurate, with thoroughfares and buildings given their actual names. Tom's love nest, for instance, is specified as being on West 158th Street, and Nick first encounters Meyer Wolfsheim in a cellar restaurant on Forty-second Street. Nick usually dines at the Yale Club and often strolls afterward "down Madison Avenue past the old Murray Hill Hotel, and over Thirty-third Street to the Pennsylvania Station" (61). Nick in Manhattan may enjoy reveries about romantic women, but those reveries transpire on bustling Fifth Avenue, and Wolfsheim's unromantic office is on frenzied Broadway. When the main characters assemble in town, it is not in some vague fictive venue, but in the Plaza Hotel, which Tom specifies as being on the south side of Central Park.

Now all this is quite remote from the manner in which Fitzgerald renames and even reinvents sites on Long Island, in the process investing them with symbolic resonances more reminiscent of Hawthorne than of Dreiser. The Valley of the Ashes is indubitably modeled on the city dump Fitzgerald passed many times, traveling between Manhattan and Great Neck; but Fitzgerald's portentous designation—along with imagery suggestive of Eliot's *The Waste Land* and the huge fading eyes of T. J. Eckleburg—convert a commonplace eyesore into a vast metaphor of modern desolation and futility, personified by its feckless denizen, George Wilson. Something similar occurs with Great Neck when it is refashioned into West Egg. To be sure, among Fitzgerald's neighbors were scores of show business types, shady entrepreneurs, and no doubt some out-and-out crooks. But the opposition between it and the communities across Manhasset Bay were by no means as stark as the contrast between Nick's and Gatsby's unfashionable neighborhood and the posh East Egg. After all, if Gatsby had lived near the real-life party giver, Herbert Bayard Swope, and had stared out across the bay, instead of seeing the green light on Daisy's dock, he might have observed Eddie Cantor strolling along the shore, while the Astors and the Sloanes were over on the other side of the peninsula.

In this matter, as in so many others in Gatsby, the contrast is not absolute. Manhattan has its own aura of magic, for Nick at least; and Long Island is rendered with enough specificity to give it an abundance of verisimilitude. Nevertheless, Manhattan—where Wolfsheim reigns and Tom carries on his squalid amour—is a land of where Gatsby's romantic vision starts to crack at the Plaza under the blows of Tom's hard malice. Long Island has been the realm of those dark twins—the grand dreams nurtured in West Egg and the nightmares of the Valley of Ashes where Myrtle Wilson's death sets into motion the sequence of events that destroy Gatsby.

Just as the language of *Gatsby* is varied yet cohesive, so the portraits of the characters, from minor ones up to Gatsby himself, are complex and frequently ambiguous. Even in sometimes perfunctory magazine pieces, Fitzgerald would use incongruous characterization as a kind of trick, evidently realizing that unexpected behavior makes a character both more interesting and more lifelike. Some calculated inconsistencies in *Gatsby* are of this nature. Thus Meyer Wolfsheim's whistling "The Rosary" before Nick vainly tries to persuade him to come to Gatsby's funeral, is a ludicrous, vivid departure from stereotype. It is also, however, one of several manifestations of the sentimentality that makes Wolfsheim's predatory criminality, symbolized by his cuff links made of human molars, all the more sinister. Indeed, nearly all the important characters are, in terms of behavior, what an oxymoron is in terms of language—walking and talking sets of opposites. Jordan Baker, the golfer who lies and who cheats, is an unsporting sportswoman. George Wilson is a wimpish murderer. Myrtle Wilson's flashy, trashy sister behaves with "a surprising amount of character" at the inquest (171).

The most significantly ambivalent are the four major characters. Carraway is a gullible skeptic and a biased objectivist. As a result, his accounts of Tom and Daisy Buchanan and of Jay Gatsby, in particular, are downright prismatic. Nick's profession of "unaffected scorn" for everything that Gatsby represents, is all but negated in the very same paragraph by a veritable paean to Gatsby's "heightened sensitivity to the promises of life" and to Gatsby's "extraordinary gift for hope" and "romantic readiness." After describing his last meeting with Gatsby, Nick comments that he "disapproved of him from beginning to end." Yet his final words to Gatsby have been, "You're worth the whole damn bunch put together." The "bunch" alluded to are the "rotten crowd" consisting mainly of Tom, Daisy, and Jordan (162). As for Nick himself, he modestly asserts that he is "one of the few honest people" he knows (64). But when Jordan, at their last meeting, tells him that she had made a "wrong guess" when she first regarded him as "an honest straightforward person," he can only lamely assent: "I'm five years too old to lie to myself and call it honor." Throughout their relationship, his behavior has been so calculating, and his perception of her is generally so negative, that it is difficult to believe his final assertion that he is "half in love with her" (186). In fact, he seems to have been using her quite as much as earlier he had used the girl from the accounting department in the brokerage office where he worked, only to break off the affair because her brother had begun eyeing him with suspicion.

The point is not that Nick is a scoundrel, a fool, or a liar. It is rather that, just as his diction can shift from Ring Lardner–like colloquialisms, such as "whole rotten bunch," to flights of Keatsean poesy, so he can see the merits of people he dislikes and defects of those he likes, and behave with perfectly normal inconsistency. He can both love and condemn, hate and forgive, just as he can contemplate a panorama from the window of Tom and Myrtle's trysting place on the upper West Side of Manhattan and exclaim: "I was within and without, simultaneously enchanted and repelled by the inexhaustible variety of life" (40).

The result of this illusion of evenhandedness is that the reader trusts Nick and, more important, likes him, much as the reader of *Huckleberry Finn* likes Mark Twain's equally inconsistent narrator-hero. Nick is ingratiating, witty, self-deprecating, and, whenever Fitzgerald wants him to be, stupendously eloquent. Nick cajoles one into assent, again like Huck Finn, by his charm and by his all-too-human failings as much as by his virtues. He says he has been drunk only twice in his life, then proceeds to give a half-comic, half-nightmarish account of one of those two times. He can priggishly rebuff Gatsby's offer of an "opportunity to pick up a little money," on the grounds that "the offer was obviously and tactlessly for a service to be rendered" (88). Nick can then proceed to render exactly the same service gratis by, in effect, becoming Gatsby's pimp when he arranges a tête-à-tête between Gatsby and Nick's own distant cousin, Daisy. By this point, however, Nick has depicted Daisy's husband as so odious that the reader believes Tom, a flagrant and compulsive adulterer, richly deserves being cuckolded. So persuasive is Nick that readers as acute as Henry Dan Piper and Milton R. Stern are willing to accept his moral judgments with few reservations.[7] Such reservations are expressed, though, by Robert W. Stallman and John F. Callahan.[8] The reality of this matter, as with so much else about this novel, is complex. Nick both is and is not a spokesman for his creator. He does and does not resemble Fitzgerald himself. The events depicted do and do not support Nick's conclusions.

Perhaps nowhere else does Nick editorialize so insistently as when denigrating his bête noire, Tom Buchanan. In an article published in the late 1970s, I (Robert Roulston) argue that Tom is a comic villain rather than the monstrous embodiment of pure evil that many critics have found him. There I also point out that, despite Nick's unrelenting hostility, Tom embodies many of Fitzgerald's own traits and even expresses some of Fitzgerald's own most cherished beliefs. In other words, if Fitzgerald had wanted to say of a character in Gatsby what Flaubert said of Emma Bovary—"Madame Bovary c'est moi"—he could quite as aptly have chosen Tom as Nick or even Gatsby. Alone of the major characters, Tom drinks heavily. In fact Fitzgerald specifically indicates that Gatsby, Daisy, and Nick drink little. Tom, on the other hand, is constantly asking about liquor, ordering it, and swilling it. Tom, moreover, is the only one to have been involved in Fitzgerald's favorite college activity, football. This former end at Yale, indeed, has achieved what the undersized Scott Fitzgerald had been able only to yearn for, gridiron glory. Also Tom possesses something else Fitzgerald envied, great wealth. Tom's tastes, moreover, are certainly closer to Fitzgerald's than are those of Gatsby, with his flashy pink suits, his bogus French villa, his vulgar car, which Tom sneeringly calls a circus wagon. Tom drives a modest roadster, lives in a proper upper-class Georgian mansion, and knows a phony police dog when a street peddler tries foisting one on him and Myrtle. Of course, by presenting Tom as a brute, a bully, a snob, a bigot, and a dunce, Fitzgerald is simultaneously making Tom both a scapegoat, who shares some of his creator's defects, and a Halloween figure in a plutocrat's mask who can be gleefully mocked.

Yet one should resist assuming that, when he dismisses Tom's rantings about miscegenation and the collapse of moral norms as "impassioned gibberish," Nick is wholly speaking for Fitzgerald. Tom's alarms over "The Rise of the Colored Empires" and "intermarriage between black and white" may be stated in the most fatuous possible manner (17, 137). Nevertheless, Tom alone of the major characters, is expressing exactly the sort of apprehensions Fitzgerald gave vent to a few years earlier in the previously noted letter from Europe to Edmund Wilson, when Fitzgerald fulminated against "the Negroid strain" he believed to be defiling the Nordic races of the Old World.[9] To be sure, Fitzgerald was too sophisticated to give much credence to the kind of crude racist tracts Tom Buchanan cited, such as the one by "this fellow Goddard," an apparent reference to Theodore Lothrop Stoddard's *The Rising Tide of Color*.[10] Tom, however, is the only character to exhibit more than a trace of the kind of musing Fitzgerald claimed to be indulging in during the summer of 1924 when he was supposedly under the spell of Oswald Spengler. Whether Fitzgerald had actually read Spengler—an unlikely occurrence, as Sklar observes, in view of Fitzgerald's inability to read German and the lack of an English translation at the time—Gatsby does present a picture of a civilization in disarray.[11]

If Fitzgerald did not read Spengler, he probably read about him, as Richard Lehan and Dalton Gross contend, and unquestionably read *The Waste Land* of T. S. Eliot, who was familiar with Spengler and whose poem depicts exactly the kind of cultural breakdown that was a frequent theme in Fitzgerald's writings, from the 1917 undergraduate story, "Sentiment—and the Use of Rouge" to the uncompleted final novel, *The Last Tycoon*. Nick Carraway, however, has little to say directly about the matter. To be sure, he depicts the collapse of norms—of debutantes being debauched at wild parties, of casual adulteries, of socialites consorting with criminals, of blacks being driven about by a white chauffeur. But he is seldom especially incensed, at least not enough to comment even to the extent that he does upon Jordan's cheating at golf and Wolfsheim's "play[ing] with the faith of fifty million people" by rigging the World Series (78).

Jordan and Daisy have even less to say on such matters. It is only Tom who sees himself standing on "the last barricade of civilization." One of his very first utterances, in fact, is "Civilization's going to pieces" (17). Tom alone is given to apocalyptic reflections, as when he blurts out in the sweltering salon of his house—"I read somewhere that the sun's getting hotter every year. . . . or wait a minute—it's just the opposite—the sun's getting colder every year" (124). In his obtuseness, Tom has succinctly given utterance to the still-reigning twin theories as to the cosmic cataclysms most likely to befall the planet. Just as Gatsby emerges as a noble crook, so Buchanan is a kind of wise fool and a knavish moralist—a buffoonish Oswald Spengler and tongue-tied T. S. Eliot. For all his repugnance, Nick shakes Tom's hand at their last encounter. In part this action is a recognition that Tom is a kind of innocent—"I felt suddenly as though I were talking to a child." But Nick also realizes that Tom believes that his behavior to Gatsby was "entirely justified" (188). Aside from Nick's own complicity—after all, he knows the true circumstances behind the deaths of Myrtle and Gatsby but has remained silent—he does have a kind of kinship with Tom, both legally and socially. Daisy is a relative, and Nick's own background is closer to Tom's than to Gatsby's.

Whatever ambivalence exists in Nick's presentation of Tom, nothing is unclear about the delineation of him. Many readers probably share Maxwell Perkins's response to him: "I would know Tom Buchanan if I met him on the street and would avoid him."[12] Readers would be less likely to recognize the other two main characters, in part because Nick envelops them in a romantic haze. Thus, whereas we know that Tom is a "sturdy straw haired man of thirty" with "gruff husky tenor," with "two shining arrogant eyes," and a way of "leaning aggressively forward," Daisy and Gatsby are described less precisely

(11). Daisy is dark, petite, but otherwise is delineated in rather general terms. One of her attributes, however, seems to preoccupy Nick to the point of obsession—her voice. He describes it variously as "low" and "thrilling," and as "glowing and singing" (13, 19). Jordan suspects Daisy may have had amorous dalliances, mainly because "there's something in that voice of hers" (82). Later Nick responds to the "exhilarating ripple" in her voice, but when he calls it "indiscreet," Gatsby instantly defines it in such a way as to lead to a veritable epiphany for Nick. "Her voice is full of money," Gatsby asserts. And Nick responds tremulously: "That was it. . . . It was full of money—that was the inexhaustible charm that rose and fell in it" (127).

Perhaps nowhere, not even while at their last meeting when Nick tells Gatsby that Gatsby is worth more than all the others, are the two men in more perfect accord. Nick here becomes Gatsby's complete double. For all the abyss between their social and educational backgrounds, this parvenu and former roustabout from North Dakota and Nick, the Ivy League alumnus with patrician forebears and scion of a moderately "well-to-do" Midwestern family, are one in their awe of the kind of style and manner only a lifetime of great wealth can confer (7). Here Fitzgerald, the outside-insider, after having split himself in two, in effect, by creating this pair of outwardly dissimilar characters, unites them. A few pages later, though, he will expose the ugly side of precisely the kind of wealth and social status of which both men are in awe. All along Daisy, in spite of the vague charm of her voice, has been revealed by her behavior as spoiled, shallow, selfish, and affected. Despite Fitzgerald's having assigned to her some of Zelda's mannerisms and even some of Zelda's actual statements,[13] Daisy has little of Zelda's formidable personality. Daisy's dark hair and her wealthy background, indeed, make her more like Fitzgerald's first great love, Ginevra King, than like Zelda, to whom the novel is dedicated. The meeting between Gatsby and Daisy at a dance in Louisville, however, is similar to the first meeting between Scott and Zelda in Montgomery, while Fitzgerald was stationed at nearby Camp Sheridan. In a sense

Gatsby's attempt to win back Daisy is a variant of Fitzgerald's own pursuit of a second golden girl, after his first had rejected him. And for a while events in Fitzgerald's own courtship seemed about to follow the earlier pattern, for Zelda too, after agreeing to marry Scott, broke off their engagement, only to relent after *This Side of Paradise* was accepted.

If Nick and Gatsby are never so akin as when they agree on the nature of Daisy's voice, they are never so at odds as when they comment on the relationship of past and present. And their disagreement embodies one of the major dichotomies in the novel, and perhaps in Fitzgerald's entire outlook. After Nick tells Gatsby he "can't repeat the past," Gatsby instantly rejoins: "Why of course you can!" (116).

At that point, Nick and Gatsby seem at an impasse. Their disagreement reflects a rift deep within Fitzgerald's own character, his manic-depressive alternations between sanguine expectations and bleak disappointments. In *This Side of Paradise*, the rift had found expression in Amory Blaine's up-and-down pattern of behavior, as he rushed from one enthusiasm to another and into and out of infatuations and love affairs, often disillusioned, but never crushed. In *Gatsby* Fitzgerald deftly cleaved apart those conflicting tendencies, giving to Jay Gatsby the "extraordinary gift for hope" and the "romantic readiness" that the more saturnine Nick can envy but only sporadically attain (6). Nick, to be sure, can burst into paeans about the magic of Manhattan and the coziness of prairie life. But his cool, calculating liaison with Jordan Baker, his cautious appraisal of the charms of Daisy Buchanan, his tendency to blend into a group—whether it be with the vulgarians at Tom and Myrtle's love nest on 158th Street, the carousers at Gatsby's parties, or with the Buchanans at dinner at their fashionable estate in East Egg—are all as far removed from Gatsby's relentless pursuit of wealth and of Daisy as they are distant from Fitzgerald's own bibulous antics that by the mid-1920s were already getting him into brawls and into police courts.

But for all the differences between them, Nick and Gatsby are spiritual twins, bound together by their Midwestern backgrounds, their service in the same Third Division in the war, their age, their tendency to perceive themselves as outsiders, and especially by their entrancement with wealth. Indeed, both men are mesmerized by wealth. Only someone with such a regard for riches would refer, as Nick does, to the Buchanans as drifting to where people are "rich together" or would believe a street peddler to bear an "absurd resemblance to John D. Rockefeller" (10, 31). And only someone who reveres wealth could so persistently seek it and so extravagantly flaunt it as Gatsby does.

Let us take Fitzgerald at his word that in the novel he did not place any emphasis even ironically on the greatness of Gatsby. But, explaining to Perkins why he did not let Tom Buchanan—"the best character I've ever done"—"dominate the book," Fitzgerald wrote: "Gatsby sticks in my heart."[14] In the same letter, Fitzgerald also agreed with Perkins that Gatsby and Daisy were both too vaguely depicted; but he promised to do something about the problem, at least in regard to Gatsby, before returning the proofs from Rome. Although Fitzgerald did add some details about Gatsby's business dealings and about his personal life, even in the final version Gatsby remains the least fully delineated important character in the book. Nick describes Gatsby as "an elegant young rough-neck, a year or two over thirty" (53), and that is about all Fitzgerald has to say on the subject, as opposed to the graphic details given about even such minor characters as Chester McKee, Meyer Wolfsheim, and Myrtle's sister. As noted previously, Daisy is also enveloped in a romantic haze, in part to express Gatsby's idealized vision of her, a vision that even Nick cannot completely escape.

Gatsby, however, is different. Just as he remains an isolated figure at his own parties—and a total outsider when Nick, Daisy, Tom, and Jordan share reminiscences in their suite at the Plaza—so he is odd man out in the book that bears his name in the title, despite Fitzgerald's misgivings. Among all the bric-a-brac of realism surrounding him, Gatsby remains as mythic a figure as James Fenimore Cooper's Natty

Bumppo. To be sure, even Cooper may have been too literary for Gatsby's tastes, for as the man with owl-eyed glasses at Gatsby's party points out to Nick, the pages of the books in Gatsby's Gothic library are uncut. But when Gatsby's father, Henry C. Gatz, brings a treasured memento to his son's funeral, it is a pulp-fiction equivalent of Cooper, "a ragged old copy of" *Hopalong Cassidy.* The schedule inside the back cover, with its list of resolutions, one of which is to "read one improving book or magazine a week," suggests that one of those books was probably by Benjamin Franklin, who was given to exactly the sort of schemes for self-improvement young James Gatz was devising for himself (181–82).

Thus if Gatsby is not great, he represents some great as well as some terrible things. Perhaps inspired by Kurtz's pamphlet in Joseph Conrad's *Heart of Darkness* with its ghastly genocidal postscript, "exterminate all the brutes," Fitzgerald with this stroke invests his hero with the whole burden of the frontier tradition and of the American belief in success.[15] Fitzgerald, of course, had already associated Gatsby with westward expansion by making Gatsby a protégé of the mining tycoon, Dan Cody (with obvious allusions to Daniel Boone and Buffalo Bill Cody). Also Cody's debauchery and premature senility represent the decline of frontier vigor, just as Gatsby's criminality makes Gatsby's career a perversion of the Benjamin Franklin-Abraham Lincoln type of success story. These two themes come together at the end, where Gatsby, gazing at the green light at the end of Daisy's dock, is identified with Dutch sailors off the primal coast of the "green breast of the new world" (189).

Yet if Gatsby here and elsewhere is a symbol, he is never only a symbol. His pink suit, his repeated use of the phrase *old sport*, his collection of monogrammed shirts, and his presentation of himself as an Oxford man all individualize him enough to keep him from being a mere type, something Fitzgerald was astute enough to avoid. In creating Gatsby, Fitzgerald fused bits of actual people—among them the party-giving neighbor at Great Neck, Herbert Bayard Swope; a boastful bootlegger Fitzgerald had encountered; the stock swindler in the well-publicized Fuller Magee case; and, not least, F. Scott Fitzgerald himself. As we observed in our chapter on *This Side of Paradise*, the hero of that book is not, like Joseph Conrad's Lord Jim, "one of us." Neither is Gatsby, who more accurately could be called all of us. He is the great American Everyman, a real Yankee Doodle Dandy, who instead of riding to London on a pony, rides to a grandiose imitation of "some Hôtel de Ville in Normandy" (9) in a huge gaudy cream-colored automobile, presenting himself as an Oxford alumnus on the basis of a few weeks at the English university in a special program for veterans.

Thus Gatsby is the supreme set of contradictions in this work teeming with them. He is sinister and naive, violent and soft-hearted, both a child of an American backwater and a would-be British aristocrat, an idealist and a predator, stylish and vulgar, tragic and clownish, glamorous and banal in his efforts to recreate himself and his milieu according to a "Platonic image of himself." If Gatsby is surely grand, "a regular Belasco" (104, 50),[16] he comes close to fulfilling Fitzgerald's own definition of genius: "The ability to put into effect whatever is in your mind."[17] Gatsby's "resourcefulness of movement" is "peculiarly American" (68), as is his blend of megalomania and vulgar ostentation that leads him to contrive a fantasy land as bizarre as Disney World, the Trump Tower, and William Randolph Hearst's San Simeon. No wonder Fitzgerald considered calling this book *Under the Red, White and Blue*!

Only a structure as fragmented as that of *The Great Gatsby* could accommodate appropriately such characters and such divergent themes. And only a style so luminous could make such a tangled account seem not only lucid but inevitable. The flashbacks, the stories within the larger story scattered throughout, ought to make *Gatsby* as groping as the novels of Fitzgerald's professed model, Joseph Conrad. Moreover, Carraway himself intrudes at various points, filling in exposition in a manner that ought to break the flow of the narrative. The action, furthermore, often proceeds by short vignettes that seem like scenes in a drama, yet never obtrusively so like the stretches of pure dialogue in *This Side of Paradise* and *The Beautiful and Damned*. Perhaps his recent writing of *The Vegetable* had given Fitzgerald a surer sense of dramatic pacing, despite the failure of the play. Perhaps the deft addition of comments by Nick Carraway and sharp impressionistic bits of description flesh out the badinage of the characters. Whatever the reason, the scenes, despite their brevity, seem neither rushed nor forced, as they, much like Nick's asides and digressions, illuminate character and themes. For example, the banter between Miss Baedeker and Doctor Civet at Gatsby's final party, where Civet reproaches her for drinking so much and she rejoins that she would not let him operate on her with his shaking hands, becomes a synecdoche for the squalor of the entire gathering, which explains Daisy's distaste not just for that particular event, but for West Egg. That distaste, in turn, foreshadows and motivates her rejection of Gatsby in the next chapter.

Thus the novel that Fitzgerald polished up in France in the summer of 1924, with a few later refinements on the proofs, would have enough facets to rival one of Braddock Washington's gems in "The Diamond as Big as the Ritz." Viewed from one perspective, the book is a novel of manners realistically scrutinizing American class distinctions. From another angle, *Gatsby* is a romantic fantasy abounding in lyricism and symbolism. Biting satire alternates with lush impressionistic descriptions that in turn lead into briskly narrated scenes. Colloquial dialogue, prose equivalents of Keats, nostalgia, suspense, violence, snippets of popular songs of the era, and verbal snapshots of clothing styles and automobiles of the time: all are there. So too are glimmerings of personal experiences, some going back as far as Fitzgerald's childhood in Minnesota and others as recent as Zelda's infidelity that summer in France. Despite its diversity *Gatsby* coheres with a diamond-like integrity. The novel, in fact, is a synthesis of all that is best in what he had written, as well as of much of what he had read, up to the mid-1920s. So completely had he assimilated borrowings from Conrad, Spengler, Eliot, Thackeray, and the numerous other writers who are alleged to have influenced him that Fitzgerald could accurately say, to a much greater degree than he could have said of his first two novels, that *Gatsby* is unlike anything he had ever read before.[18] *Gatsby* has no equivalents of the counterfeit bon mots of Wilde and Shaw in *This Side of Paradise* or the wholesale mimicking of Norris and Mencken in *The Beautiful and Damned.*

No less important, *Gatsby* combines the skilled compression of the best of Fitzgerald's popular-magazine fiction, the innovativeness and trenchancy of his best *Smart Set* pieces, and the lyricism and ambitiousness of his two previous novels. It is mercifully free, however, of the pretentiousness that mars some of his earlier efforts. Instead of pontificating on the imperiled state of Western culture, he lets the egregious Tom Buchanan comment fatuously on the collapse of civilization and relies upon the authenticity of the narrative to demonstrate just how far Buchanan's apprehensions are valid.

No one could legitimately say of Fitzgerald, as T. S. Eliot said of Henry James, that he had a mind too fine to be violated by an idea. Fitzgerald's mind was violated again and again—first by Wells and Shaw, then by Mencken, Nietzsche, Spengler, and Marx. Yet somehow, he was astute enough to trust his own perceptions and narrative skills more than half-assimilated abstractions. If *The Great Gatsby* is a lament for a passing civilization, it is no less a paean to his own waning youth and to the scenes of its pleasures and failures. Paradoxically, this novel by a self-proclaimed romantic egotist has a classic clarity and symmetry rare in American fiction including much of Fitzgerald's. Here, as in none of his other works, his finest qualities are in near-perfect equipoise. The youthful artist who once offered to hurl himself from a Paris window in homage to the reigning god of high art, James Joyce, in *Gatsby* formed a comfortable partnership with the clever young man who had learned how to propitiate the awesome deity of popular-magazine fiction, George Horace Lorimer of the *Saturday Evening Post*. Never again would the two be in such complete accord.

From *The Winding Road to West Egg: The Artistic Development of F. Scott Fitzgerald* (Lewisburg, PA: Bucknell University Press, 1995): 155-169. Copyright © 1995 by Bucknell University Press. Reprinted by permission of Bucknell University Press.

Notes

1. Fitzgerald, *Letters*, 177.

2. Fitzgerald, *Correspondence*, 153.

3. Fitzgerald, *Letters*, 479.

4. For a good discussion of the Horatio Alger motif, see Scharnorst, "Scribbling Upward," 26–35.

5. In the original edition, as well as the authorized text edited by Bruccoli and cited throughout this study, the name is spelled "Wolfshiem."

6. Fitzgerald, *Letters*, 509.

7. Piper, *F. Scott Fitzgerald. A Critical Portrait*, 107; Stern, *The Golden Moment*, 196.

8. Stallman, "Gatsby and the Hole in Time," 2–16; Callaghan, "Interview," in *The Other Side of Paradise*.

9. Fitzgerald, *Letters*, 326.

10. For discussions of Stoddard's impact on Fitzgerald, see Stallman ("Gatsby and the Hole in Time," 2–12) and Turlish ("*The Rising Tide of Color,*" 442–44).

11. Fitzgerald wrote to Perkins on 6 June 1940: "Did you ever read Spengler—specifically including the second volume? I read him the same summer I was writing *The Great Gatsby* and I don't think I ever quite recovered from him" (*Letters*, 289–90). Despite Sklar's caveat about Fitzgerald's inability to read German in 1924 when Spengler's work was not yet available in English (*F. Scott Fitzgerald: The Last Laocoön*, 135), Lehan in particular provides a convincing rebuttal, demonstrating Fitzgerald's familiarity with Spengler's main points and confirms conclusions argued back in 1955 by Robert W. Stallman (Lehan, *F. Scott Fitzgerald and the Craft of Fiction*).

12. Fitzgerald and Perkins, *Dear Scott/Dear Max*, 83.

13. After Scotty's birth, Zelda said the words Fitzgerald attributes to Daisy about Daisy's daughter: "I hope its [sic] beautiful and a fool—a beautiful little fool" (Bruccoli, *Some Sort of Epic Grandeur*, 160).

14. Fitzgerald, *Letters*, 173.

15. The question of Conrad's influence on Fitzgerald is almost as vexing as the question of Spengler's impact. As in the case with Spengler, Fitzgerald himself noted the influence, claiming in a 1925 letter to Mencken that in *Gatsby* he was an "imitator" of the older author, adding in parenthesis: "God! I've learned a lot from him" (*Letters*, 482). In 1955, Robert W. Stallman ("Conrad and *The Great Gatsby*" 5–11) cited parallels between *Nostromo*, *Lord Jim*, and *Heart of Darkness*. Sklar minimized some of these parallels by contending that before *Gatsby* Fitzgerald knew only *Nostromo*, "Youth," *A Mirror of the Sun*, *The Nigger of the Narcissus*, and *Victory* (*F. Scott Fitz-*

gerald: The Last Laocoön, 152). Fitzgerald's reference to *Lord Jim*, however, in a 1923 review of Sherwood Anderson and an allusion to *Heart of Darkness* in the 1920 story "The Offshore Pirate" indicate some familiarity with both works. Moreover, most of the parallels cited by Stallman and others, especially Long, seem too striking to be fortuitous (*The Achieving of "The Great Gatsby,"* 85–96).

16. David Belasco (1859–1931) was a flamboyant American theatrical actor, playwright, director, and producer—a sumptuous showman who loved lavish staging and stage machinery to astound his audiences, a Cecil B. De Mille or Steven Spielberg of the legitimate stage. Belasco is perhaps best known today as the author of the plays on which Giacomo Puccini based his operas *Madama Butterfly* and *La Fanciulla del West* (*The Girl of the Golden West*).

17. Fitzgerald, *The Crack-Up*, 123.

18. Fitzgerald, *Correspondence*, 146.

The Craft of Revision:
*The Great Gatsby*_____

Kenneth E. Eble

"With the aid you've given me," Fitzgerald wrote Maxwell Perkins in December, 1924, "I can make *Gatsby* perfect."[1] Fitzgerald had sent the manuscript of the novel to Scribner's in late October, but the novel achieved its final form only after extensive revisions Fitzgerald made in the next four months. The pencil draft and the much revised galley proofs now in the Fitzgerald collection at Princeton library show how thoroughly and expertly Fitzgerald practiced the craft of revision.[2]

I

The pencil draft both reveals and masks Fitzgerald's struggles. The manuscript affords a complete first version, but the pages are not numbered serially from beginning to end, nor are the chapters and sections of chapters all tied together. There are three segments (one a copy of a previous draft) designated "Chapter III," two marked "Chapter VI." The amount of revising varies widely from page to page and chapter to chapter; the beginning and end are comparatively clean, the middle most cluttered. Fitzgerald's clear, regular hand, however, imposes its own sense of order throughout the text. For all the revisions, the script goes about its business with a straightness of line, a regularity of letter that approaches formal elegance. When he is striking out for the first time, the writing tends to be large, seldom exceeding eight words per line or twenty-five lines per page. When he is copying or reworking from a previous draft, the writing becomes compressed—but never crabbed—and gets half again as much on a page.

An admirer of Fitzgerald—of good writing, for that matter—reads the draft with a constant sense of personal involvement, a sensation of small satisfied longings as the right word gets fixed in place, a feeling of strain when the draft version hasn't yet found its perfection of phrase, and a nagging sense throughout of how precariously the writer dangles between the almost and the attained. "All good writing," Fitzgerald wrote his daughter, "is *swimming under water* and holding your breath."[3]

At the beginning of the draft, there appears to have been little gasping for air. There at the outset, virtually as published, is that fine set piece which establishes the tone of the novel with the creation of Nick Carraway and his heightened sense of the fundamental decencies. As one reads the first chapter, however, the satisfaction of seeing the right beginning firmly established soon changes to surprise. The last page of the novel—"gradually I became aware of the old island here that flowered once for Dutch sailors' eyes—a fresh, green breast of the new world."[4]—was originally written as the conclusion of Chapter I. Some time before the draft went into the submission copy, Fitzgerald recognized that the passage was too good for a mere chapter ending, too definitive of the larger purposes of the book, to remain there. By the time the pencil draft was finished, that memorable paragraph had been put into its permanent place, had fixed the image of man holding his breath in the presence of the continent, "face to face for the last time in history with something commensurate to his capacity for wonder."

The three paragraphs which come immediately after, the last paragraphs of the novel, grew out of one long fluid sentence which was originally the final sentence of Chapter I in the draft: "And as I sat there brooding on the old unknown world I too held my breath and waited, until I could feel the motion of America as it turned through the hours—my own blue lawn and the tall incandescent city on the water and beyond that, the dark fields of the republic rolling on under the night." Fitzgerald expanded this suggestion into a full paragraph, crossed out the first attempt, and then rewrote it into three paragraphs on the final page of the draft. There, almost as it appears in the novel, is the green light on Daisy's dock ("green glimmer" in the draft), the orgiastic future (written "orgastic"),[5] and that ultimate sentence, "So we beat on, a boat [changed to "boats"] against the current, borne back ceaselessly into the past." So the draft ends, the last lines written in a "bold, swooping hand," as Fitzgerald described Gatsby's signature, a kind of autograph for the completed work.

The green light (there were originally two) came into the novel at the time of Daisy's meeting with Gatsby. "If it wasn't for the mist," he tells her, "we could see your house across the bay. You always have two green lights that burn all night at the end of your dock." Fitzgerald not only made the green light a central image of the final paragraph, but he went back to the end of the first chapter and added it there: "Involuntarily I glanced seaward—and distinguished nothing except a single green light, minute and far away, that might have been the end of a dock" (pp. 21–22).

II

Throughout the pencil draft, Fitzgerald made numerous revisions which bring out his chief traits as a reviser: he seldom threw anything good away, and he fussed endlessly at getting right things in the right places. The two parties at Gatsby's house, interesting as illustrations of Fitzgerald's mastery of the "scenic method," are equally interesting as examples of how he worked.

The purpose of the first party as it appears in the draft (Chapter III in the book) was chiefly that of creating the proper atmosphere. Though Gatsby makes his first appearance in this section, it is Gatsby's world that most glitters before our eyes. The eight servants (there were only seven in the draft), the five crates (only three in the draft) of oranges and lemons, the caterers spreading the canvas, the musicians gathering, the Rolls-Royce carrying party-goers from the city, are the kind of atmospherics Fitzgerald could always do well. The party itself as it unfolds in the draft reveals a number of intentions that Fitzgerald abandoned as he saw the possibilities of making the party vital to the grander design of the novel.

Originally, whether from strong feelings or in response to his readers' expectations, he took pains to bring out the wild and shocking lives being lived by many of Gatsby's guests. Drug addiction was apparently commonplace, and even more sinister vices were hinted at. A good deal of undergraduate party chatter was also cut from the draft. What a reader of the novel now remembers is what Fitzgerald brought into sharp relief by cutting out the distracting embellishments. "The Jazz History of the World" by Vladimir Tostoff (it was "Leo Epstien" [*sic*] originally; Fitzgerald deleted a number of "Jewish" remarks from the draft) was described in full. When Fitzgerald saw the galleys he called the whole episode "rotten" and reduced the page-and-a-half description to a single clause: "The nature of Mr. Tostoff's composition eluded me . . . ." (p. 50). By the time the party scene had been cut and reworked, almost all that remained was the introduction of Gatsby's physical presence into the novel and the splendid scene of Owl Eyes in Gatsby's high Gothic library.

Among the many excisions in this party scene, one seemed far too good to throw away. In the draft, it began when Jordan Baker exchanges a barbed remark with another girl:

> "You've dyed your hair since then," remarked Miss Baker and I started but the girls had moved casually on and were talking to an elaborate orchid of a woman who sat in state under a white plum tree.
>
> "Do you see who that is?" demanded Jordan Baker interestedly. [I use Fitzgerald's spelling here and elsewhere in quoting from the draft.]
>
> Suddenly I did see, with the peculiar unreal feeling which accompanies the recognition of a hitherto ghostly celebrity of the movies.
>
> "The man with her is her director," she continued. "He's just been married."
>
> "To her?"
>
> "No."
>
> She laughed. The director was bending over his pupil so eagerly that his chin and her metallic black hair were almost in juxtaposition.
>
> "I hope he doesn't slip," she added. "And spoil her hair."

It was still twilight but there was already a moon, produced no doubt like the turkey and the salad out of a caterer's basket. With her hard, slender golden arm drawn through mine we descended the steps. . . .

It is a fine scene, and the girl with the dyed hair, the moon, and the caterer's basket can be found on page 43 of the novel, so smoothly joined together that no one could suspect, much less mourn, the disappearance of that "elaborate orchid" of a woman. But, of course, she did not disappear. The scene was merely transported to the second party where the actress defined the second party as Owl Eyes defined the first:

"Perhaps you know that lady," Gatsby indicated a gorgeous, scarcely human orchid of a woman who sat in state under a white-plum tree. Tom and Daisy stared, with the particularly unreal feeling that accompanies the recognition of a hitherto ghostly celebrity of the movies.
"She's lovely," said Daisy.
"The man bending over her is her director." (p. 106)

Two pages later, at the end of the second party, we see her again:

It was like that. Almost the last thing I remember was standing with Daisy and watching the moving-picture director and his Star. They were still under the white-plum tree and their faces were touching except for a pale, thin ray of moonlight between. It occurred to me that he had been very slowly bending toward her all evening to attain this proximity, and even while I watched I saw him stoop one ultimate degree and kiss at her cheek.
"I like her," said Daisy. "I think she's lovely."
But the rest offended her. . . . (p. 108)

One can almost see the writer's mind in action here. The scene was first created, almost certainly, from the rightness of having a "ghostly celebrity of the movies" at the party. It first served merely as scenery and as a way of hinting at the moral laxity of Gatsby's guests. The need to compress and focus probably brought Fitzgerald to consider cutting it out entirely though it was obviously too good to throw away. By that time, perhaps, the second party scene had been written, another possibility had been opened up. Maybe at once, maybe slowly, Fitzgerald recognized that the scene could be used to capture Daisy's essential aloofness which was to defy even Gatsby's ardor. It may well be that this developed and practiced ability to use everything for its maximum effect, to strike no note, so to speak, without anticipating all its vibrations, is what separates Fitzgerald's work in *The Great Gatsby* from his earlier writing, what makes it seem such a leap from his first novels.

Among the many lessons Fitzgerald applied between the rough draft and the finished novel was that of cutting and setting his diamonds so that they caught up and cast back a multitude of lights. In so doing, he found it unnecessary to have an authorial voice gloss a scene. The brilliance floods in upon the reader; there is no necessity for Nick Carraway to say, as he did at one point in the pencil draft: "I told myself that I was studying it all like a philosopher, a sociologist, that there was a unity here that I could grasp after or would be able to grasp in a minute, a new facet, elemental and profound." The distance Fitzgerald traveled from *This Side of Paradise* and *The Beautiful and Damned* to *The Great Gatsby* is in the rewriting of the novel. There the sociologist and philosopher were at last controlled and the writer assumed full command.

III

Rewriting was important to Fitzgerald because, like many other good writers, he had to see his material assume its form—not in the *idea* of a character or a situation—but in the way character and situation and all the rest got down on paper. Once set down, they began to shape everything else in the novel, began to raise the endless questions of emphasis, balance, direction, unity, impact.

The whole of Chapter II in the finished novel (Chapter III in the draft) is an illustration of how the material took on its final form. That chapter begins with Dr. T. J. Eckleburg's eyes brooding over the ash heaps and culminates in the quarrel in Myrtle's apartment where "making a short deft movement, Tom Buchanan broke her nose with his open hand." Arthur Mizener first pointed out that the powerful symbol introduced in this chapter—Dr. Eckleburg's eyes—was the result of Fitzgerald's seeing a dust jacket portraying Daisy's eyes brooding over an amusement park world. "For Christ's sake," he wrote to Perkins, "don't give anyone that jacket you're saving for me. I've written it into the book."[6] The pencil draft indicates that the chapter—marked Chapter III in the manuscript—was written at a different period of time from that of the earlier chapters. The consecutive numbering of the first sixty-two pages of the novel (the first two chapters) shows that for a long time Fitzgerald intended Chapter II as it now stands in the novel to be the third chapter.

In substance, the chapter remained much the same in the finished novel as it was in the draft. But, in addition to moving the chapter forward, Fitzgerald transposed to the next chapter a four-page section at the end describing Nick's activities later in the summer. Summing up Nick's character at the end of the third chapter gave more point to his concluding remark: "I am one of the few honest ["decent" in the draft] people that I have ever known" (p. 60). Bringing the Eckleburg chapter forward meant that the reader could never travel to or from Gatsby's house without traversing the valley of ashes. And ending the second chapter where it now ends meant that the reader could never get to Gatsby's blue gardens where "men and girls came and went like moths among the whisperings and the champagne and the stars" without waking up waiting for a four o'clock train in Penn Station.

But putting a brilliant chapter in place was only part of the task Fitzgerald could see needed to be done once the material was down on paper. Within that chapter, Fitzgerald's pencil was busily doing its vital work. The substance was all there: Tom and Myrtle and Nick going up to New York, the buying of the dog, the drinking in the apartment, the vapid conversations between the McKees and sister Catherine and Myrtle, the final violence. But some little things were hot. The gray old man with the basket of dogs did not look like John D. Rockefeller until Fitzgerald penciled it in between lines; the mongrel "undoubtedly had Airedale blood" until Fitzgerald made it "an Airedale concerned in it somewhere"; and finally, the pastoral image of Fifth Avenue on a summer Sunday—"I wouldn't have been surprised to see a great flock of white sheep turn the corner"—this didn't arrive until the galleys.

IV

The appearances of Gatsby, as might be expected, are among the most worked-over sections in the draft. Even when the manuscript was submitted, the characterization was not quite satisfactory, either to Fitzgerald or to Maxwell Perkins. The "old sport" phrase which fixes Gatsby as precisely as his gorgeous pink rag of a suit is to be found in only one section of the pencil draft, though it must have been incorporated fully into his speech before Fitzgerald sent off the manuscript. "Couldn't you add one or two characteristics like the use of that phrase 'old sport'—not verbal, but physical ones, perhaps," Perkins suggested.[7] Fitzgerald chose the most elusive of physical characteristics— Gatsby's smile. How he worked it up into a powerfully suggestive bit of characterization can be seen by comparing the pencil draft and the final copy. Gatsby is telling Nick about his experiences during the war:

Rough Draft	*Final Version*
"I was promoted to be a major / and every Allied government gave me a decoration— / even ~~But~~ Montenegro little Montenegro down on the Adriatic / Sea!"	"I was promoted to be a major, and every Allied government gave me a decoration—even Montenegro, little Montenegro down on the Adriatic Sea!"
~~He lifted up the w~~ Little	Little Montenegro! He lifted up

Montenegro! He lifted up the
them
words / and nodded at ~~it~~ with a
faint smile. My incredulity had /
had turned to fascination now;
~~Gatsby was no longer a~~ it was /
~~person he was a magazine I had~~
~~picked up on the casually train~~
like
~~and I was~~ reading the climaxes of
only
all the stories / ~~it contained~~ in a
magazine.

the words and nodded at them—with his smile. The smile comprehended Montenegro's troubled history and sympathized with the brave struggles of the Montenegrin people. It appreciated fully the chain of national circumstances which had elicited this tribute from Montenegro's warm little heart. My incredulity was submerged in fascination now; it was like skimming hastily through a dozen magazines. (pp. 66–67)

The smile is described in even fuller detail in a substantial addition to galley 15 (page 48 of the novel). One can virtually see Fitzgerald striking upon the smile as a characteristic which could give Gatsby substance without destroying his necessary insubstantiality.

Gatsby is revised, not so much into a real person as into a mythical one; what he *is* is not allowed to distract the reader from what he stands for. Without emphasizing the particulars of Gatsby's past, Fitzgerald wanted to place him more squarely before the reader.[8] Many of the further changes made in the galley proofs were directed toward that end. In the first five chapters of the galleys, the changes are the expected ones: routine corrections, happy changes in wording or phrasing, a few deletions, some additions. But at Chapter VI the galley proofs become fat with whole paragraphs and pages pasted in. Whole galleys are crossed out as the easiest way to make the extensive changes Fitzgerald felt were necessary. Throughout this section, he cut passages, tightened dialogue, reduced explicit statements in order to heighten the evocative power of his prose.

The major structural change brought the true story of Gatsby's past out of Chapter VIII and placed it at the beginning of Chapter VI. Chapter V, the meeting between Gatsby and Daisy, was already at the precise center of the novel.[9] That scene is the most static in the book. For a moment, after the confusion of the meeting, the rain, and his own doubts, Gatsby holds past and present together. The revision of Chapter VI, as if to prolong this scene in the reader's mind, leaves the narrative, shifts the scene to the reporter inquiring about Gatsby, and fills in Gatsby's real past. "I take advantage of this short halt," Nick Carraway says, "while Gatsby, so to speak, caught his breath" (p. 102). The deliberate pause illustrates the care with which the novel is constructed. The Gatsby of his self-created present is contrasted with the Gatsby of his real past, and the moment prolonged before the narrative moves on. The rest of Chapter VI focuses on the first moment of disillusion, Gatsby's peculiar establishment seen through Daisy's eyes.

The rewriting so extensive in this chapter is as important as the shifting of material. The draft at this point has five different sets of numbers, and these pieces are fitted only loosely together. The Gatsby who finally emerges from the rewritten galleys answers the criticisms made by Maxwell Perkins and, more important, satisfies Fitzgerald's own critical sense. "ACTION IS CHARACTER," Fitzgerald wrote in his notes for *The Last Tycoon*. His revisions of dialogue, through which the novel often makes its vital disclosures and confrontations, shows his adherence to that precept. The truth of Gatsby's connection with Oxford was originally revealed to Nick Carraway in a somewhat flat, overly detailed conversation in which Gatsby tries to define his feeling for Daisy. Most of that conversation was cut out and the Oxford material worked into the taut dialogue between Tom Buchanan and Gatsby in the Plaza Hotel which prefaces the sweep of the story to its final action.[10]

In the draft, Gatsby reveals his sentimentality directly; he even sings a poor song he had composed as a boy. In the novel, a long passage of this sort is swept away, a good deal of the dialogue is put into exposition, and the effect is preserved by Nick's comment at the end:

"Through all he said, even through his appalling sentimentality . . ." (p. 112). In the draft, Gatsby carefully explains to Nick why he cannot run away. "'I've got to,' he announced with conviction, 'that's what I've got to do—live the past over again.'" Substance and dialogue are cleared away here, but the key idea is kept, held for a better place, and then shaped supremely right, as a climactic statement in a later talk with Nick: "'Can't repeat the past?' he cried incredulously. 'Why of course you can!'" (p. 111). In the draft, much of Gatsby's story is told in dialogue as he talks to Nick. It permits him to talk too much, to say, for example: "'Jay Gatsby!' he cried suddenly in a ringing voice. 'There goes the great Jay Gatsby! That's what people are going to say—wait and see.'" In the novel even the allusion to the title is excised. Gatsby's past is compressed into three pages of swift exposition punctuated by the images of his Platonic self, of his serving "a vast, vulgar, and meretricious beauty," and of Dan Cody and "the savage violence of the frontier brothel and saloon" from which he had come. Finally, in the draft, the undercurrent of passion and heat and boredom which sweeps all of them to the showdown in the Plaza is almost lost. Instead of going directly to the Plaza that fierce afternoon, they all went out to the Polo Grounds and sat through a ball game.

Of the changes in substance in this section—and in the novel—the most interesting is the dropping of a passage in which Gatsby reveals to Nick that Daisy wants them to run away. Daisy, elsewhere in the draft, reveals the same intentions. Perhaps Fitzgerald felt this shifted too much responsibility upon Daisy and made Gatsby more passive than he already was. Or perhaps his cutting here was part of a general intention of making Daisy less guilty of any chargeable wrong. Earlier in the draft, Fitzgerald removed a number of references to a previous romance between Daisy and Nick, and at other points he excised uncomplimentary remarks. The result may be contrary to expectation— that a writer ordinarily reworks to more sharply delineate a character— but it was not contrary to Fitzgerald's extraordinary intention. Daisy moves away from actuality into an idea existing in Gatsby's mind and ultimately to a kind of abstract beauty corrupted and corrupting in taking on material form.

V

After Chapter VI and the first part of Chapter VII, to judge both from the draft and the galleys, the writing seemed to go easier. The description of the accident with its tense climax—"her left breast was swinging loose like a flap"—is in the novel almost exactly as in the pencil draft. "I want Myrtle Wilson's breast ripped off"—he wrote to Perkins, "it's exactly the thing, I think, and I don't want to chop up the good scenes by too much tinkering."[11] Wilson and his vengeance needed little reworking, and though the funeral scene is improved in small ways, as is the conversation with Gatsby's father, no great changes occur here. The last ten pages, the epilogue in which Nick decides to go back West, are much the same, too.

In these last pages, as in the rest of the manuscript, one can only guess at how much writing preceded the version Fitzgerald kept as the pencil draft. "What I cut out of it both physically and emotionally," he wrote later, "would make another novel!"[12] The differences in hand, in numbering of pages, in the paper and pencils used, suggest that much had preceded that draft. Few of the pages have the look of Fitzgerald's hand putting first thoughts to paper, and fewer still—except those obviously recopied—are free of the revision in word and line which shows the craftsman at work.

These marks of Fitzgerald at work, the revelation they give of his ear and his eye and his mind forcing language to do more than it will willingly do, run all through the manuscript.

The best way of summarizing what Fitzgerald did in shaping *The Great Gatsby* from pencil draft to galley to book is to take him at his word in the introduction he wrote in 1934 for the Modern Library edition of the novel. "I had just re-read Conrad's preface to *The Nigger*, and I had recently been kidded half haywire by critics who felt that my material was such as to preclude all dealing with mature persons in a mature world. But, my God! it was my material, and it was all I had to deal with." What he did with it was what Conrad called for in his Preface, fashioned a work which carried "its justification in every line," and which "through an unremitting, never-discouraged care for the shape and ring of sentences" aspired to "the magic suggestiveness of music."

From *American Literature* 36, no. 3 (November, 1964): 315-326. Copyright © 1964 by Duke University Press. Reprinted by permission of Duke University Press.

Notes

1. *The Letters of F. Scott Fitzgerald*, ed. Andrew Turnbull (New York, 1963), p. 172.

2. This study is based on an examination of the original pencil draft and the galley proofs in the Fitzgerald collection in the Princeton Library and subsequent work with a microfilm copy of this material. I am indebted to the University of Utah Research Fund for a grant which enabled me to study the materials at Princeton, to Alexander P. Clark, curator of manuscripts, for his indispensable help in making this material available, and to Mr. Ivan Von Auw and the Fitzgerald estate for permission to use this material.

3. *The Crack-Up*, p. 304.

4. All citations hereafter are from the Scribner Library edition of *The Great Gatsby*.

5. Arthur Mizener points out that Fitzgerald corrected the spelling from "orgastic" to "orgiastic" in his own copy of the book (*The Far Side of Paradise*, Boston, 1951, p. 336, n. 22). Yet Fitzgerald's letter to Maxwell Perkins, January 24, 1925, defends the original term: "'Orgastic' is the adjective for 'orgasm' and it expresses exactly the intended ecstasy. It's not a bit dirty" (*Letters*, p. 175). The word appears as "orgiastic" in most editions of the novel, including the current Scribner's printings.

6. *The Far Side of Paradise*, p. 170. The entire letter is to be found in *Letters*, pp. 165–167.

7. *Editor to Author: The Letters of Maxwell E. Perkins*, ed. John Hall Wheelock (New York, 1950), p. 39.

8. Fitzgerald wrote in response to Perkins's criticism: "His [Gatsby's] vagueness I can repair by *making more pointed*—this doesn't sound good but wait and see. It'll make him clear." In a subsequent letter, he wrote: ". . . Gatsby sticks in my heart. I had him for awhile, then lost him, and now I know I have him again" (*Letters*, pp. 170, 173).

9. Fitzgerald called this chapter his "favorite of all" ("To Maxwell Perkins," circa Dec. 1, 1924, *Letters*, p. 170).

10. Mizener points out that Fitzgerald was revising almost up to the day of publication. The revision of this section came some time around February 18, 1925, when Fitzgerald cabled Maxwell Perkins: "Hold Up Galley Forty For Big Change" (*The Far Side of Paradise*, p. 164; p. 335, n. 63). Fitzgerald returned the proofs about February 18th. In a letter to Perkins, he listed what he had done: "1) I've brought Gatsby to life. 2) I've accounted for his money. 3) I've fixed up the two weak chapters (VI and VII). 4) I've improved his first party. 5) I've broken up his long narrative in Chapter VIII" (*Letters*, p. 177).

11. *Letters*, p. 175.

12. Introduction to Modern Library edition of *The Great Gatsby* (New York, 1934), p. x.

CRITICAL READINGS

"A World Complete In Itself":
Gatsby's Elegiac Narration _____

Dan Coleman

The only *general* attribute of projected romance . . . is the fact [that it deals with] experience disengaged, disembroiled, disencumbered, exempt from the conditions that we usually know to attach to it. . . . The balloon of experience is in fact of course tied to the earth, and under that necessity we swing, thanks to a rope of remarkable length, in the more or less commodious car of the imagination; but it is by the rope we know where we are, and from the moment that cable is cut we are at large and unrelated. . . . The art of the romancer is, 'for the fun of it,' insidiously to cut the cable, to cut it without our detecting him.—Henry James, preface to *The American*

[I]n my new novel I'm thrown directly on purely creative work—not trashy imaginings as in my stories but the sustained imagination of a sincere and yet radiant world.—F. Scott Fitzgerald, letter to Maxwell Perkins[1]

Nick Carraway begins his story by describing how it will end. "Gatsby turned out all right," he explains, ". . . it is what preyed on Gatsby, what foul dust floated in the wake of his dreams that temporarily closed out my interest in the abortive sorrows and short-winded elations of men" (6–7). By insisting from his narrative's outset on its hero's happy ending, Nick sets for himself an essentially elegiac ambition: to ensure that his readers come to the last page of the novel convinced that Gatsby is "something gorgeous" (6). At the same time, the clarity with which Nick defines his narrative's end invites us to consider the rest of his story as a means, to study the functions of its form, to consider how—and how well—*Gatsby*'s parts cooperate or conflict with the achievement of its whole. By taking our bearings from Nick's clearly articulated purpose, we might steer clear of the twin perils described by Roman Jakobson in his critique of "linguist[s] deaf to the poetic function of language and . . . literary scholar[s] indifferent to linguistic problems" (377). That is to say: the *telos* by which Nick tries so intently to organize his narrative offers us an excellent opportunity to explore how a novel's formal structures create its aesthetic effects.

However, the attempt to identify Nick's elegiac ambition with Gatsby's informing design poses serious problems: neither Nick's sense of Gatsby's happy ending nor his ability to persuade us of it turns out to be as sure and stable as at first they seem. Returned to its context, Nick's affirmation of Gatsby's ultimate success suggests his underlying uncertainty; within the speech in which it occurs, the clear note of Nick's assertion begins to quaver:

> [T]here was something gorgeous about [Gatsby] . . . a romantic readiness such as I have never found in any other person and which it is not likely I shall ever find again. No—Gatsby turned out all right at the end; it is what preyed on Gatsby, what foul dust floated in the wake of his dreams that temporarily closed out my interest in the abortive sorrows and short-winded elations of men. (6–7)

The sentence that ends by insisting on Gatsby's distinction from the corruption which surrounded him, begins by responding to a question that hasn't been asked (*No—Gatsby turned out all right at the end*). Nick's triumphant declaration of his hero's happy ending must overcome his own equivocation; it is not simply an *assertion* but an *answer*. Although ostensibly alone, Nick protests as if defending his claim against another speaker. "To whom," we might wonder, "is Nick saying 'No'?"

It might be that Nick responds to a silent part of himself, a skeptical inner voice so forceful that Nick must deny it "aloud." If so, Nick's "No" reveals the sense in which this narrator's *commitment* to making his hero turn out all right cannot be separated from his *uncertainty* about whether or not Gatsby really did. From this perspective, the same tension exposed by the content of Nick's closing speech—i.e., Nick's immense admiration for a man who "represented everything for which [he has] an unaffected scorn"—shows up in its dialogic form, through the crack in Nick's narrative voice (7).[2]

Drawn back-and-forth between fascination and skepticism, Nick's story is simultaneously an elegiac fiction that aims to make sure that everything turns out all right—and a "history of the summer" that tries to make sense of what really happened (10). In this respect, the ambivalence of Nick's narrative is matched by the precariousness of his narratorial authority. Because he is not only the ostensible writer of this story but a character within it, Nick lacks a privileged position outside the fiction's frame. Unlike a more powerful author, Nick cannot ensure that any apparent competition with his own Last Word is really just a game whose outcome has been decided ahead of time, a fight rigged from the start. Since Nick's narrative voice can never completely transcend that plane on which the other characters speak—nor silence that skepticism in himself which whispers against any simple faith in his hero—Nick's control of the narrative is always uncertain and his ability to bring Gatsby to a happy ending is always in doubt. Any power Nick may possess to make Gatsby turn out all right is not given but accomplished; any ring of authority his words may achieve will never be pure but, instead, always colored by his struggle to achieve it. The history of the summer, then, is also the history of Nick's attempts as a narrator to find a voice with which he can conjure around his hero "a world complete in itself" where "even Gatsby could happen" (110, 73).

(Recon)figuring the Facts: Metaphoric Worlds

With this uncertain "sense of an ending" before his eyes, Nick opens his story by identifying its origin: "and the history of the summer really begins on the evening I drove over there to have dinner with the Tom Buchanans" (10).[3] However, Nick's description of "the white palaces of fashionable East Egg glitter[ing] along the water" seems less the material of history than the stuff that fairy tales are made of (10). Unable or unwilling to draw clearly those boundaries which distinguish the Actual from the Imaginary, Nick's narrative begins by creating an uneasy commerce between the two.

Compelled by Tom into the living room of his fashionable East Egg mansion, Nick enters a "bright, rosy-colored space" in which

> The only completely stationary object . . . was an enormous couch on which two young women were buoyed up as though upon an anchored balloon. They were both in white and their dresses were rippling and fluttering as if they had just been blown back in after a short flight around the house. I must have stood for a few moments listening to the whip and snap of the curtains and the groan of a picture on the wall. Then there was a boom as Tom Buchanan shut the rear windows and the caught wind died out about the room and the curtains and the rugs and the two young women ballooned slowly to the floor. (12)

The conceit of the balloon, which begins with a simile's qualifications (*as if, as though*), moves through the collocation created by the "whip and snap of the curtains" and the hyperbolic "groan of a picture on the wall" to end by almost escaping its figurative tethers. Over the course of Nick's description, the balloon-like couch becomes a couch-balloon that settles—like any real balloon would—*because* the wind which suspended it has died out. That is to say: a metaphor which is initially, obviously impossible (we know that couches can't really float) and clearly subordinated to the reality it describes (i.e., as the image is supposed to help us understand the sense in which the couch "floats") ultimately becomes entirely plausible, existing independently in that strange new world the metaphor makes. In other words, this passage takes its readers from a "realistic" place where a simile can fancifully compare a couch to a balloon, to a world in which there really are couch-balloons—a magical universe furnished with facts entirely alien to ours, but regulated by wholly familiar laws of cause and effect. Nick's description reverses the usual literal–figurative hierarchy; his fantastic trope momentarily warps reality around it.

Like "the fresh grass outside that seemed to grow a little way into the house," Nick's metaphor crosses that boundary which separates the ordinary from the fantastic, warping the novel's world by means well-described by Dorothy Mack (12). "Metaphoring," she argues, "is . . . more than *saying* something; it is fabricating another 'reality.' In choosing to extend the scope of a particular presupposition to a particular topic, the speaker *imposes* a way of seeing, feeling, connecting, and judging; he forces his unique and momentary 'world-creating' and 'contrary-to-fact' perspective on the hearer" (84). Along similar lines, Samuel Levin has suggested that most readers, when faced by a metaphor that misrepresents what they know to be true of the world, typically revise their construal of the literal meaning of the words (e.g., "her lips are not *really* roses, but red in the way that roses are"). Readers have, however, another option: instead of treating their ideas of the world as stable and the metaphor's meaning as changeable, they can "[take] the metaphoric expression literally and [accept] the epistemological consequences that ensue" (*Metaphoric Worlds* 4):

[Al]though preternatural states of affairs cannot be conceived as actually existing, the possibility of their existing can be conceived *of*: We can form a *conception* of what the world would have to be like were it in fact to comprise such states of affairs. . . . If we read in a poem "the sky is angry," we conceive of a world in which the sky might be angry; in the same way, the wind might be hungry, the stars happy, and so on. The usual process of construal is simply inverted; instead of constructing an interpretation that consists with conditions in the actual world, we construct one that conforms to the actual language of the utterance. In consequence what emerges as metaphoric is not the language in which the poem is expressed, but the world that language has caused us to project. We have projected ourselves into a metaphoric world. ("Language 121")

This world where language is taken literally is one in which Nick's narrative invites us to spend much of our readerly time. Throughout the novel, the transformative effects of Nick's metaphors are reinforced by his habit of changing similes which compare A and B into metaphors which equate A and B—or even into substitutions by means of which A takes the place of B. This tendency to take rhetorical figures "seriously" marks Nick's narrative from its beginning; within the scope of a single page in the first chapter, Jordan is transformed—like the couch that briefly "becomes" a balloon—from someone whose chin is "raised a little as if she were balancing something on it" into "the balancing girl." At the same time, the "something" that Jordan seemed to Nick to be balancing—which initially exists only hypothetically as an analogy that Nick draws for his readers ("her chin [was] raised a little *as if* she were balancing something on it")[4]—becomes an actual presence within that story-world shared by Nick and the novel's other characters: "the object she was balancing had obviously tottered a little and given her something of a fright" (13).

The process of "taking literally" by which *Gatsby*'s metaphors disrupt our readerly expectations is insightfully analyzed by Leonard Podis. "[M]ost of Nick's markedly anti-realistic metaphors," he argues, ". . . take place in the contexts of what seem to be nearly surreal excursions. The metaphors usually occur in clusters, such that the experiences which are being set forth attain almost visionary status" (64). In the clusters that Podis analyzes, a series of "non-rational" metaphors pile one upon the next until their accumulation of incredible claims begins to outweigh the reader's sense of the novel's realism. Nick's description of Gatsby's ultimate vision exemplifies this overwhelming:

He must have looked up at an unfamiliar sky through frightening leaves and shivered as he found what a grotesque thing a rose is and how raw the sunlight was upon the scarcely created grass. A new world, material without being real, where poor ghosts, breathing dreams like air, drifted fortuitously about . . . like that ashen, fantastic figure gliding toward him through the amorphous trees. (quoted in Podis 63)

"The epithets employed here," Podis argues, "'unfamiliar sky,' 'frightening leaves,' 'grotesque . . . rose,' 'raw sunlight,' and 'scarcely created grass'—are all metaphorical in that the adjectives are to a degree . . . incompatible with the nouns they modify" (63–64). While not "radically" non-rational, Podis contends, these "semantic clashes" begin to "challenge our ability to conceptualize them rationally" (69, 64). Not, however, until the second half of the passage does Nick's mix of metaphors start to disturb his readers' sense of the basic continuity between the reality represented within the novel and the one they're used to. Though spelled out clearly, the analogy which asks us to imagine ghosts "breathing dreams like air" makes no ordinary sense; dreams have no qualities in common with the stuff we breathe: "None of the presuppositions which come attached to the term 'dreams' will match up with the specifications of the metaphor. The only alternative [left to the reader] is to create new suppositions about 'dreams,' suppositions which involve a highly subjective way of seeing" (64). Nick's report of a "figure gliding . . . through the trees" creates similar kinds of difficulties for readers trying to construe it: "The presuppositions attached to 'gliding' will allow the word to be applied to a person on a dance floor, but the stretching of vision to connect this action with a gunman stalking his human target produces a bizarre, distorted effect" (64).

However, Podis's illuminating study fails to account for the full range of powers exercised by Gatsby's metaphors. A more complete analysis would also shed light on how these figures can "work together" not only *cumulatively*, but *cooperatively*. Podis's explanation of how Nick's weird descriptions can add up to "cause everyday reality to disintegrate into an amorphous other-world" overlooks the ways in which they can also cause the novel's fantastic reality to hold together (64). For example: while the premises underlying Nick's description of Daisy and Jordan's couch-balloon are indeed "other-worldly," the logic which informs this other-world is both familiar and coherent. In the same way, there is an internal consistency that binds together Nick's early description of the novel's landscape, and makes it seem not so unreasonable that there should be "a pair of enormous eggs" in "the great wet barnyard of Long Island Sound" (9).[5]

"Eggs" is attracted to "barnyards" by the same force that binds together the figure underlying the image of gentle ballooning which runs beneath Nick's description of Daisy and Jordan on the couch. As W. J. Harvey explains, "buoyed" and "anchored" continue a nautical theme which begins in the preceding paragraph's Homeric allusion (*wine-colored rug*) and extends into the "rippling and fluttering" of the women's dresses, the "whip and snap of the curtains" and the "groan of a picture on the wall."[6] Thematically interrelated, all of these words are part of the same linguistic "collocation," a term nicely explained by Ronald Carter as "the company habitually kept by a word" (159).[7] Like a conversation between paranoiacs whose perspectives are warped in exactly the same way (or alternatively: like the crazy banter that bounces between the guests around the Mad Hatter's tea table) the visions of the world presented by *Gatsby*'s fantastic metaphors grow compelling by their consensus. And the more successfully they collude together, the more likely we are as readers to take their common fantasy for granted, to consider a couch floating like a balloon or a lawn running like a horse as not particularly unusual. That is to say: Nick's metaphorical networks, while often "anti-realistic," are not always "non-rational." The "surreal excursions" on which Nick's metaphors invite his readers may take them to a place whose "unreality" is made coherent by the mutually corroborating claims of the metaphors which constitute it (*Gatsby* 105).

Recalcitrant Railroads, Ash Men, and the Eyes of T. J. Eckleburg: Animate Landscapes in the Valley of Ashes

Indeed, those fantastic worlds created within Nick's extended metaphors threaten at times to take over the novel's reality altogether:

About half way between West Egg and New York the motor-road hastily joins the railroad and runs beside it for a quarter of a mile so as to shrink away from a certain desolate area of land. This is a valley of ashes—a fantastic farm where ashes grow like wheat into ridges and hills and grotesque gardens, where ashes take the forms of houses and chimneys and rising smoke and finally, with a transcendent effort, of men who move dimly and already crumbling through the powdery air. . . .

But above the grey land and the spasms of bleak dust which drift endlessly over it, you perceive, after a moment, the eyes of Doctor T. J. Eckleburg. The eyes of Dr. T. J. Eckleburg are blue and gigantic—their retinas are one yard high. They look out of no face but, instead, from a pair of enormous yellow spectacles which pass over a nonexistent nose. (27)

From an opening that locates the Valley in relation to at least one real place, Nick's description moves through mild personification into unconstrained animism. Not content with the subdued anthropomorphism of a road which "hastily joins the railroad . . . so as to shrink away" from the waste land, the narrative literalizes the landscape's previously figurative personality, endowing it with not merely the power to act like human beings, but the unqualified ability to become them.[8]

While surveying this allusion-turned-landscape, the reader is instructed with almost hypnotic repetition: "You perceive, after a moment, the eyes of Dr. T. J. Eckleburg. The eyes of Dr. T. J. Eckleburg are blue." Described with the precision of a driver's license (eyes: blue; retinas: one yard high) and assigned a flatly declarative agency (*They look out of no face*), these eyes maintain their fantastically independent existence until at least the passage's end, when their impossible size and facelessness begin to resolve into a realistic explanation: "Evidently some wild wag of an oculist set them there to fatten his practice" (28).

However, the extrapolated optician has left town by the time of the story's telling, and only his sign remains to "brood on over the solemn dumping ground"—an inscrutable spirit above a vast abyss of ashes which delivers forth men only by the most transcendent figural effort. With its referent dead or moved away, the billboard has become a floating signifier; disconnected from the author of its meaning, it lies open to infinite interpretation:

> "God sees everything," repeated Wilson.
> "That's an advertisement," Michaelis assured him. (167)

Like this *oculist absconditus* who is simultaneously the advertisement's referent and its creator, Nick is both subject and author of a signifier which must exist without his being there to guarantee its significance (i.e., that Gatsby turned out all right at the end). From this perspective, Nick's first-person narration might be understood as an attempt to put some semblance of authorial presence behind his sign.

Gatsby's Bodily Double: Myrtle Wilson's Graphic Realism

The cable-cutting fantasy of the Valley, however, is brought sharply down to earth by Tom Buchanan's mistress, whose vivid "incarnation" brings into the novel an insistent facticity dynamically opposed to Gatsby's unutterable visions. From the moment of her descent from the rooms which Nick imagines as "sumptuous and romantic apartments . . . concealed overhead," Myrtle's "thickish figure" "block[s] out the light" in "the shadow of a garage." "Walking through her husband as if he were a ghost," Myrtle smolders in the midst of an otherwise burntout landscape, the only presence in the Valley substantial enough to escape the overhanging veil of ashes (29–30). Whereas our first sight of Gatsby tells us little more than what his posture suggests to Nick's faraway perspective (a glimpse of arms stretched trembling toward a green light distant over dark water), Myrtle is immediately given to us fully realized in all her bodily magnificence—"[carrying] her surplus flesh sensuously" in a "spotted dress of dark blue crêpe-de-chine";

shaking hands, wetting her lips, commanding her husband and her lover. In sharpening this contrast, the novel sketches out the meanness of James Gatz's life only after it has shown us the grandeur of Gatsby's, while ensuring that the barren circumstances which drive Myrtle's ambition are the first thing we learn about her. Immediately defined by her context—her husband, sister and friends; her history; the way she decorates her house—Myrtle is bound into the physical world around her; Gatsby, on the other hand, is given to us "at large and unrelated" in a way that leaves him much freer to slip from the realistic and into the allegorical. Nonetheless, Myrtle's sharp sense of purpose draws her close to Gatsby; she too is a "[boat] against the current" (189). Balanced on the intensity of their common desire to escape their respective origins, the novel's motion might be figured as a rocking back-and-forth between the concrete realism of Myrtle's story and the indefinite fantasy of Gatsby's.

From Myrtle's perspective deep in the ashes of the wasteland, Tom Buchanan represents the possibility of escape, the power to acquire all the goods on "the list of things [she's] got to get. A massage and a wave and a collar for the dog and one of those cute little ash trays where you touch a spring, and a wreath with a black silk bow for mother's grave that'll last all summer" (41). The most precisely described location in the novel, all the rooms in Myrtle's apartment are small, and her living room is "crowded to the doors with a set of tapestried furniture entirely too large for it so that to move about was to stumble continually over scenes of ladies swinging in the gardens of Versailles" (33).[9] Filled with the kind of "realistic" detail otherwise absent from Nick's descriptions—an "over-enlarged photograph, apparently [of] a hen sitting on a blurred rock," "old copies of 'Town Tattle'" lying on the table, Catherine's "solid sticky bob of red hair," "the remains of the spot of dried lather" adhering to Mr. McKee's cheek, a dog biscuit "decompos[ing] apathetically in [a] saucer of milk"—Myrtle's apartment, unlike every other setting in the story, is rendered with a graphic specificity a set designer could accurately reproduce (33, 34, 41).

Speech, too, gains an almost physical presence at Myrtle's party. Whereas the ineffable thrill of Daisy's voice leaves behind both words and the world to which they might refer ("I had to follow the sound of [Daisy's voice] for a moment, up and down, with my ear alone before any words came through"), Myrtle's speech bears her body with it: "Myrtle pulled her chair close to mine and suddenly her warm breath poured over me" (90, 40). At the same time, conversation undergoes a similar incarnation, sinking from the ethereal brilliance of Daisy and Jordan's intricate banter to the dull vulgarity of Myrtle's ultra-mundane exchange with her sister and Mrs. McKee:

> "I had a woman up here last week to look at my feet and when she gave me the bill you'd of thought she had my appendicitus [sic] out."
> "What was the name of the woman?" asked Mrs. McKee.
> "Mrs. Eberhardt. She goes around looking at people's feet in their own homes."
> "I like your dress," remarked Mrs. McKee. "I think it's adorable." (35)

So insipid that it soon prompts Tom to yawn "audibly," dialogue in Myrtle's apartment moves gracelessly between clumsy speakers and subjects whose indelicacy (bills, appendicitus, feet) and discontinuity (Mrs. McKee's completely off-topic remark about Myrtle's dress) would never be allowed in to East Egg's elegantly choreographed repartee (36).

This mood of overcrowding and crudeness grows stronger as Nick gets drunker and Myrtle takes up more and more of the space in her apartment: "Her laughter, her gestures, her assertions became more violently affected moment by moment and as she expanded the room grew smaller around her until she seemed to be revolving on a noisy, creaking pivot through the smoky air" (35). At Myrtle's party, the gears show; the splendor which momentarily vanishes from Gatsby's face to reveal "an elegant young rough-neck . . . whose elaborate formality of speech almost missed being absurd" lies beyond the reach of Myrtle's violent affectations (53). In that strictly tangible world she dominates by the magnificence of her body and the intensity of her desire, Myrtle can accomplish no more than a physical expansion.

Nor does Nick's narration in any way assist Myrtle's transcendence: if it is relatively easy to visualize the balloon to which Daisy and Jordan's couch is compared, it's not at all clear what kind of thing Myrtle is supposed to look like as she spins on her pivot.[10] Still bound to the earth, Myrtle's metaphor fails to achieve the independent intelligibility that distinguishes more viable analogies; the "incoherent failure" of Nick's image draws our attention to the distance between Myrtle's material condition and the possibilities for romance which exist beyond it (188). Lacking Gatsby's theatrical ability to make something spectacular of himself and his world—to transform the fundamental terms of his reality and thereby elude the limits they impose—Myrtle swells to enormous proportions without ever becoming larger-than-life.

Through Nick's deepening haze, Myrtle's party grows increasingly more incomprehensible:

Sitting on Tom's lap Mrs. Wilson called up several people on the telephone; then there were no cigarettes and I went out to buy some at the drug store on the corner. When I came back they had disappeared so I sat down discreetly in the living room and read a chapter of "Simon Called Peter"—either it was terrible stuff or the whiskey distorted things because it didn't make any sense to me. (33–34)

Joined by transitions that obscure causation (*then* there were no cigarettes; *and* I went out; *when* I came back), events seem strangely unrelated; A follows B for no apparent reason. The tenor of the scene soon swings out of the confused and into the chaotic: "People disappeared, reappeared, made plans to go somewhere, and then lost each other, searched for each other, found each other a few feet away" (41). Then Tom breaks Myrtle's nose and Nick leaves a tableau dominated by a "despairing figure on the couch bleeding fluently[11] and trying to spread a copy of 'Town Tattle' over the tapestry scenes of Versailles" (42).

Compelled by Tom to attend Myrtle's party and to abandon an "almost pastoral" vision of the city (complete with the promise of "a great flock of white sheep" waiting around the corner) Nick proves equally unable to excuse himself once he's there (32). "Called . . . back into the room" by the "shrill voice of Mrs. McKee," Nick is denied escape to a sky he imagines as "the blue honey of the Mediterranean" and is drawn again into the fiercely mundane web of Myrtle's parlor (38). Nick would rather be somewhere else:

> I wanted to get out and walk eastward toward the park through the soft twilight but each time I tried to go I became entangled in some wild strident argument which pulled me back, as if with ropes, into my chair. Yet high over the city our line of yellow windows must have contributed their share of human secrecy to the casual watcher in the darkening streets, and I was him too, looking up and wondering. I was within and without, simultaneously enchanted and repelled by the inexhaustible variety of life. (40)

If not simply repelled by what is happening at Myrtle's party, Nick is attracted to the life around him only when imagining his distance from it. For Nick, the furious confusion of Myrtle's party represents a concerted effort to force him to "play a part" in the too-real drama surrounding him (39). As such, it frustrates his attempts to gain the distance a reader—or an author—needs in order to give significant shape to "the inexhaustible variety of life."

Trimalchio's Banquet: A World Complete in Itself

Whereas the chaos of Myrtle's party leaves Nick "entangled" in mundane detail, Gatsby's party offers what Henry James calls an "experience disengaged, disembroiled, disencumbered, [and] exempt from the conditions that we usually know to attach to it." The detachment Nick discovers in his hero—"no one swooned backward on

Gatsby and no French bob touched Gatsby's shoulder and no singing quartets were formed with Gatsby's head for one link"—is the same isolation which makes possible his party's almost allusive poise: "In his blue gardens men and girls came and went like moths among the whisperings and the stars" (55, 43). Yet, in order for Gatsby's party to happen around Nick-the-character, Nick-the-narrator needs to make it happen. In order for his elegiac ambitions to succeed, Nick must conjure our assent to a "world complete in itself" (110).

If Gatsby's party—assembled every fortnight by "a corps of caterers" out of "canvas" and "colored lights"—resembles nothing so much as a theater set, Nick is simultaneously the most enthusiastic member of its audience and the stage manager responsible for making sure that nobody wonders about the missing fourth wall (44, 43). In order to achieve Gatsby's Belasco-like "triumph" and make credible his magnificent fakery, Nick's narration must work as hard as the caterers and the gardeners put together (50):

> Every Friday five crates of oranges and lemons arrived from a fruiterer in New York—every Monday these same oranges and lemons left his back door in a pyramid of pulpless halves. There was a machine in the kitchen which could extract the juice of two hundred oranges in half an hour, if a little button was pressed two hundred times by a butler's thumb. (43–44)

The butler doesn't press the button; the button is pressed by a butler's thumb: like the magician's other hand, Nick's rhetorical figure diverts our attention from everything about the butler not included in his representative part. This seemingly explicit account of the origins of the juice consumed at Gatsby's party obscures entirely the agency of those responsible for making the fruit arrive as oranges and lemons and leave as empty peels. The button is pressed and unseen mechanisms move and marvelous things happen for no reason we can see; by hiding the connection between effects and their causes, Nick's recurrent use of synecdoche casts over Gatsby's party the spell of inexplicability.

Like a bouncer checking invitations, this exclusive trope keeps out of the party everything that distracts from its essential riot: "A tray of cocktails floated at us through the twilight and we sat down at a table with the two girls in yellow and three men, each one introduced to us as Mr. Mumble" (47). Disconnected from any person carrying them, the drinks can appear without reminding us of the waiter who will walk offstage and into a life of his own as soon as the curtain falls. In the same way, Nick almost entirely obscures the other guests at the table—eliminating all those features that play no part in the effect he's creating—to leave as synecdochical distillates their single aspect of color (*the two girls in yellow*) or peculiarity of speech (*Mr. Mumble*).[12]

Reigning over West Egg is a sense of unreality, a strangeness of tone partially accomplished by the sudden shift of tense by means of which Nick drives his story into the present. After a paragraph which details the preparations for Gatsby's party, Nick swerves without warning into the present perfect: "By seven o'clock the orchestra has arrived," he tells us, without any explanation of how the band—or the narrative—got there (44). Gatsby's party is filled with things which seem to exist only in the present:

> The last swimmers have come in from the beach now and are dressing upstairs; the cars from New York are parked five deep in the drive, and already the halls and salons and verandas are gaudy with primary colors and hair shorn in strange new ways and shawls beyond the dreams of Castille. (44)

Paratactically arranged to emphasize the simultaneity of its parts, this parade of phenomena leaves no tracks which might lead back to the past from which it came. Everything at Gatsby's party "already" is without any explanation of how it got *to be* that way. There is no chain of causes leading out from the "now" and into an historical background; this is a world of effects only, "a thing that merely *happened*" for no apparent reason: "People were not invited—they went there. They got into automobiles which bore them out to Long Island and somehow they ended up at Gatsby's door" (78, 45). Alone among a crowd of guests perfectly uninterested in even the immediate past—who "accepted Gatsby's hospitality and paid him the subtle tribute of knowing nothing whatever about him"—only the guest called Owl Eyes cares about origins and causes: "Who brought you," he asks Nick and Jordan, ". . . Or did you just come? I was brought. Most people were brought" (65, 50). As we learn later at Gatsby's funeral, Owl Eyes is also the only one besides Nick who cares about Gatsby; in this respect there seems to be a connection between the skeptical fascination and the compassion both he and Nick feel for Gatsby.

Unmarked by the conditions of its creation, Gatsby's party springs "from [its] Platonic conception"; like the "city . . . all built with a wish out of non-olfactory money," Nick's magnificent fabrication floats free from any trace of the smell of sweat (or worse) involved in its construction (104, 73). In this respect, the accomplishment of Gatsby's party exemplifies what Henry James describes as the essential artistic act: "Really, universally, relations stop nowhere, and the exquisite problem of the artist is eternally but to draw, by a geometry of his own, the circle within which they shall happily *appear* to do so."[13]

The Rock of the World and the Fairy's Wing: Escape versus Transformation

No such circle exists around Myrtle's party to obscure its relations to the rest of the world. Whereas Gatsby's revelry transfigures the materials of real life into theater, Myrtle's small rooms are dominated by a strictly representative photography, by pictures whose titles (e.g., "Montauk Point—the Gulls" and "Montauk Point—the Sea") suggest a perfectly literal treatment of their subjects. Indeed, Tom's parody of McKee's style of titling—"George B. Wilson at the Gasoline Pump"—sounds like nothing so much as a newspaper caption (37). Although the guests at Myrtle's party talk a lot about how Mr. McKee might "make something of" his subject matter, he seems largely uninterested in a kind of art that would significantly transform his materials (36). Nick hints at the poverty of McKee's creativity in the simile by which he describes him: "Mr. McKee was asleep on a chair with his fists clenched in his lap, like a photograph of a man of action" (41). In the same way that McKee can *become* a photograph just by coming to rest, he can *make* one by simply holding his subject still. As Robert Emmet Long puts it: "If the role of the artist is to achieve a vision underlying the inchoate material of reality, McKee is an artist *manqué*, who records only surfaces. Of his wife . . . he has taken one hundred twenty-seven photographs, a figure that, in its exactness, emphasizes the hopeless literalness of his mind" (108–9). One might add that the number of photos, by its magnitude, also emphasizes McKee's failure to isolate the essence of his subject in an interpretive portrait. Unable to make artistic value out of the facts he's given, McKee is left trying to record the "inexhaustible variety" of his wife's changing appearance in a potentially infinite series of snapshots. That is to say: this photographer lacks the aesthetic control which keeps an author from slipping into what Roland Barthes calls "a downward spiral into endless detail":

[W]hen discourse is no longer guided and limited by the structural imperatives of the story . . . there is nothing to tell the writer why he should stop descriptive details at one point rather than another: if it was not subject to aesthetic or rhetorical choice, any "seeing" would be inexhaustible by discourse; there would always be some corner, some detail, some nuance of location or colour to add. (14)

Those artistic imperatives which inform Gatsby's party lose their power in a world dominated by indiscriminate "seeing." More than miles separate the chorus girl whose broken sobs smear her make-up into musical notes and Myrtle's sister Catherine, of whose eyebrows Nick says: "[they] had been plucked and then drawn on again at a more rakish angle but the efforts of nature toward the restoration of the old alignment gave a blurred air to her face" (56, 34). In Gatsby's universe, a driver can emerge from a crash not only unscathed but oblivious to the fact that he has shorn a wheel off his car (58–60). At Myrtle's party, where the conditions of nature can be blurred but never overcome, her very real blood will leave lasting stains on unmistakable furniture.

Embedded in a fiercely material condition, Myrtle has no reason to believe in "the unreality of reality, [the] promise that the rock of the world [is] founded securely on a fairy's wing" (105). Like Nick, she knows that "you can't repeat the past" and recognizes more clearly than anything else that "you can't live forever" (116, 40). Unable to make a grail of her unmysterious lover, Myrtle is like Gatsby before he falls for Daisy, wanting no more than to "take what he could and go" (156). Because she cannot imagine changing the world in which she lives, Myrtle longs only to escape it for a better one. By contrast, Gatsby is uninterested in escape as such. The young James Gatz keeps no list of things he's got to get; in its place, he sketches into his copy of *Hopalong Cassidy* a schedule for self-transformation.

Making Gatsby Happen: The Tone of a Narrator's Voice

Yet Gatsby is only partially responsible for filling out his Platonic conception of himself. The well-wrought creation of Nick's visionary longing, Gatsby is as much a man-made self as a self-made man. In order to become the "something gorgeous" the preface promises, Gatsby needs Nick to fill in the gaps and overlook the failures in his "unbroken series of successful gestures." For Gatsby to happen, Nick must write a greenhouse around his hero's delicate greatness and persuade both us and himself to believe in it.

The obstacles Nick must surmount in order to accomplish our sense of Gatsby's gorgeousness become clearest at those moments when he fails to do so. We become sharply aware of the resistance overcome by Nick's most impressive act of cable-cutting—his rendering of the strange magnificence of Gatsby's party—when gravity reasserts itself so forcefully in Daisy's presence:

There were the same people . . . the same many-colored, many-keyed commotion, but I felt an unpleasantness in the air, a pervading harshness that hadn't been there before. Or perhaps I had merely grown used to it, grown to accept West Egg as a world complete in itself, with its own standards and its own great figures . . . and now I was looking at it again, through Daisy's eyes. (110)

By focusing our attention on the incompleteness of Gatsby's world, Daisy's perspective reveals the limitations of those standards on which its radiance depends—the fragility of that environment in which this hero can happen. Daisy's presence at Gatsby's party exposes how ephemeral is that greatness he shares with the protagonist of *Tender is the Night*: "[T]o be included in Dick Diver's world for a while was a remarkable experience. . . . So long as [people] subscribed to it completely, their happiness was his preoccupation, but at the first flicker of doubt as to its all-inclusiveness he evaporated before their eyes" (36).

Looking back, one can see more clearly the effect of Nick's narration earlier in the novel, the part it plays in transforming the "many-keyed commotion" of Gatsby's extravaganza into "something significant, elemental and profound" (51). In themselves, the events which close Gatsby's first party are horrible; yet, when translated through the tissue of Nick's perception, they come across very differently:

I looked around. Most of the remaining women were now having fights with men said to be their husbands. Even Jordan's party, the quartet from East Egg, were rent asunder by dissension. . . .

The reluctance to go home was not confined to wayward men. The hall was at present occupied by two deplorably sober men and their highly indignant wives. . . .

In spite of the wives' agreement that [their husbands'] malevolence was beyond credibility the dispute ended in a short struggle and both wives were lifted kicking into the night. (56–57)

From an incongruous combination of modifiers (e.g., "deplorably so-ber men"), Nick's description rings through a scale of strikingly dis-cordant linguistic registers: the elevation of "malevolence . . . beyond credibility" abuts the journalistic straightforwardness of "the dispute ended in a short struggle" and finally sublimates off as the mock-lyrical "lifted kicking into the night." The facts themselves are brutal; only by ironizing them into playful inconsequence can Nick write a scene of couples fighting into a proper finale to Gatsby's party. In an-other sense, there are no facts; wrapped round in the dense weave of his narrative voice, people and things disappear behind Nick's telling of them.[14]

The same voice is almost silent when Daisy visits Gatsby's party. Like a reporter trying simply to keep track of what he sees, Nick's narratorial role is limited to little more than transcribing directly quoted dialogue. As a result, Nick's power to inflect the events he pre-sents is sharply restricted. A transparent narrator innocently bystanding, Nick does little to distract us from seeing that there's nothing funny in Daisy's offering Tom her "little gold pencil" to take down the address of another woman; the "genial" tone Nick hears in Daisy's voice is not *his* wry irony but *her* cutting sarcasm (112). At the same time, Daisy's cynical acceptance of Tom's flirtation adds an ugliness to his adultery that is less immediate when we see him alone with either Myrtle or Daisy. "I'd enjoyed these same people only two weeks before," Nick tells us. "But what had amused me then turned septic on the air now" (112). The narrative lends no redeeming sparkle to the only exchange we're given between the party regulars:

> "Anything I hate is to get my head stuck in a pool," mumbled Miss Bae-deker. "They almost drowned me once over in New Jersey."
> "Then you ought to leave it alone," countered Doctor Civet.
> "Speak for yourself!" cried Miss Baedeker violently. "Your hand shakes. I wouldn't let you operate on me!" (113)

Though only talk, the dialogue in this scene suggests that having your head stuck in a pool could get you drowned, that the hilarious drunkenness of a doctor might matter in those operating rooms the talk makes real—in that world which lies beyond the edge of Gatsby's perfect lawn, that outside realm whose presence proves the incompleteness of Nick's fantastic one.

How They Turn Out at the End: Deaths Physical and Metaphorical

The air of menace which hangs over Daisy's visit precipitates violently in the scene of the car crash. Having escaped from the rooms in which she has been locked up by her husband, Myrtle runs out into the road, screaming back at George:

> "Beat me!" [Michaelis] heard [Myrtle] cry. "Throw me down and beat me, you dirty little coward!"
>
> A moment later she rushed out into the dusk, waving her hands and shouting; before he could move from his door the business was over.
>
> The "death car," as the newspapers called it, didn't stop; it came out of the gathering darkness, wavered tragically for a moment and then disappeared around the next bend. . . . The other car . . . came to rest a hundred yards beyond, and its driver hurried back to where Myrtle Wilson, her life violently extinguished, knelt in the road and mingled her thick, dark blood with the dust.
>
> Michaelis and this man reached her first but when they had torn open her shirtwaist still damp with perspiration they saw that her left breast was swinging loose like a flap and there was no need to listen for the heart beneath. The mouth was wide open and ripped at the corners as though she had choked a little in giving up the tremendous vitality she had stored so long. (144–45)

As the narrative veers away from Myrtle to Michaelis's view of her, the crash becomes "the business" and the moment of impact is hidden by a shift to the newspaper's even more distant perspective. When we next see Myrtle, it's not immediately clear what happened during the car's tragic wavering; the agency suggested by Myrtle's kneeling and mingling almost overwhelms our sense of her devastation—a fact which has been relegated to a phrase tangential to the line of force drawn from the subject to its predicate ("its driver hurried back to where Myrtle Wilson, *her life violently extinguished*, knelt in the road and mingled her thick, dark blood with the dust").

If left at all confused, however, we are quickly set straight by the next paragraph's brutally direct statement. From the mechanical image of Myrtle's breast "swinging loose like a flap," Michaelis's sweep of vision brings us to "the heart" and "[t]he mouth": impersonal parts that have nothing to do with the woman until now defined by the sensuality with which she carried her "surplus flesh" (29). Only a slamming car could tear away that bodily life no dream could sustain, and once Myrtle is dead, there is absolutely nothing of her left.

If Myrtle after the crash has little in common with Myrtle before it, Gatsby is barely changed by his murder; in this sense, Myrtle's is the only physical death in the novel. The "colossal vitality of his illusion" is inseparable from Gatsby's own vitality; the moment his dream proves impossible is the moment of his own extinction (101). Gatsby's death as a character has nothing to do with the trigger George Wilson pulls; he fades out of the story long before his redundant executioner can accomplish his misguided justice.

Sticks and Stones: Mundane Speech and Body Heat

The day of Gatsby's doom is the kind when train tickets return stained by the sweat of the conductor's hand, when convertibles' seats leave their drivers wishing they'd parked in the shade, when even the butler glistens slightly. Through a noon like a teakettle boiling—"only the hot whistles of the National Biscuit Company broke the simmering hush" (120)—Nick returns to the scene of his history's beginning and enters the Buchanans' living room to discover that everything has changed:

chapter one

The only completely stationary object in the room was an enormous couch on which two young women were buoyed up as though upon an anchored balloon. They were both in white and their dresses were rippling and fluttering as if they had just been blown back in after a short flight around the house. (12)

chapter seven

Daisy and Jordan lay upon an enormous couch, like silver idols, weighing down their own white dresses against the singing breeze of the fan.
"We can't move," they said together. (122)

The words Daisy didn't mean at all when she welcomed Nick in the first chapter—"'I'm p-paralyzed with happiness'"—are here corroborated by the narrative's description (13). Flirt-talk has moved that much closer to fact; metaphor has deflated and fallen back to earth; the women who once floated through the room like balloons are now silver ballast unmoved by the breeze.

At the same time, speech, which began the novel as the ephemeral fluff behind which the Real was obscured, has now gained an almost bodily presence: "'The thing to do is to forget about the heat,'" says Tom. "'You make it ten times worse by crabbing about it'" (133). Overwhelmed by the materiality of her immediate environment—what Italo Calvino calls "the weight, the inertia, the opacity of the world" (4)—Daisy's voice "struggle[s] on through the heat, beating against it, moulding its senselessness into forms" (125). The temperature weighs heavily on that cable-cutting banter which might otherwise have relieved the scene's oppressive mood: "'It's so hot,' [Daisy] complained. 'You go. We'll ride around and meet you after.' With an effort her wit rose faintly, 'We'll meet you on some corner. I'll be the man smoking two cigarettes'" (132). In air so thick that "every extra gesture was an affront to the common store of life," not even the thrill of Daisy's casual fiction can raise conversation above that sensuous experience Nick recalls most vividly, the "sharp physical memory that . . . my underwear kept climbing like a damp snake around my legs and intermittent beads of sweat raced cool across my back" (121, 132–33). No longer able to lift its audience away from the bodies of the novel's characters, language now clings tightly to them.

Wanting "nothing less of Daisy than that she should go to her husband and say, 'I never loved you,'" Gatsby arranges a confrontation with Tom designed to set the stage for his return with Daisy to the life they left five years earlier (116). But Daisy refuses to play the role Gatsby has scripted for her, and our hero proves unable to "'fix everything just the way it was before'" (117). Unwilling to say that she never loved her husband, to "[wipe] out" the three years of their marriage, Daisy leaves Gatsby facing Tom's triumphant insistence that "'there're things between Daisy and me that you'll never know, things that neither of us can ever forget'" (139, 140). Against these "things"—the irrevocable history of a honeymoon in a particular place, the fact of a real daughter—Gatsby has no defense; his fantastic ambitions have run aground on the rock of the world. For Nick's hero, this is the moment of the car's impact: Tom's unrefuted claims, the narrator tells us, "seemed to bite physically into Gatsby," and later we learn that "'Jay Gatsby' had broken up like glass against Tom's hard malice" (140, 155). "Jay Gatsby"—the perfect achievement of James Gatz's carefully scheduled metamorphosis—exists no longer; the man who filled the contours of the name he invented for himself has been translated by Tom into "Mr. Nobody from Nowhere" (137).

The destruction of his defining dream nearly complete, there is not much more of Gatsby's story left to tell. From his first sight of an indistinct neighbor with arms stretched toward a distant green light, Nick has been brought to a vision of Gatsby waiting on Daisy's lawn to make sure she'll be all right, the "sacredness of [his] vigil" reduced to a "watching over nothing" (153). Nick's description of Gatsby's death feels almost like an epilogue:

> There was a faint, barely perceptible movement of the water as the fresh flow from one end urged its way toward the drain at the other. With little ripples that were hardly the shadows of waves, the laden mattress moved irregularly down the pool. A small gust of wind that scarcely corrugated the surface was enough to disturb its accidental course with its accidental burden. The touch of a cluster of leaves revolved it slowly, tracing, like the leg of a compass, a thin red circle in the water.
>
> It was after we started with Gatsby toward the house that the gardener saw Wilson's body a little way off in the grass, and the holocaust was complete. (97, 170)

In a world where motion and matter have been reduced to an absolute minimum and action has been emptied of intent, there is no mention of the corpse Nick has discovered. The mass that warps the mattress lacks the weight to keep its course against the most qualified of currents (so scarce it hardly shadows waves); in the absence of all desire, this ghostly bier spins slowly at the touch of leaves.

As its hero fades and the novel's exhausted plot winds down, the history of Nick's attempt to author a purely creative work rises to a climax. In his account of Gatsby's last moments, Nick's narrative leaves behind the matter-of-fact and enters entirely into the metaphorical: where Myrtle's violent destruction leaves behind a thing out of which her personality has been brutally ripped, all that remains of the man that was Gatsby is a red circle drawn across troubled water. What's left of Gatsby the hero transcends not only the fact of his body but the limitations of physical law altogether: in the real world, the shot that killed a man floating on an air mattress would likely puncture the raft and leave him lying at the bottom of the pool. By his cable-cutting account of Gatsby's death, Nick sets him spinning impossibly through a world disengaged from what we know of how things work—into the only world in which even Gatsby could happen and turn out all right at the end.

From *The Journal of Narrative Technique* 27, no. 2 (Spring 1997): 207-233. Copyright © 1997 by Eastern Michigan University Press. Reprinted by permission of Eastern Michigan University Press.

Notes

1. James 33–34; Fitzgerald, *Life* 67.

2. In this respect, Nick experiences what Mikhail Bakhtin describes as a "full dialogization of consciousness" in which "[t]he other's discourse . . . penetrates the consciousness and speech of the hero" in forms which "would not be appropriate in monologically confident speech" (222).

3. In so doing, Nick designs a narrative like one of Kermode's "end-determined fictions": "Men, like poets, rush 'into the middest,' *in media res*, when they are born; they also die *in mediis rebus*, and to make sense of their span they need fictive concords with origins and ends, such as give meaning to lives and to poems" (6, 7).

4. This parenthetical space within which speakers ask their listeners to visualize a nonexistent comparison (as Nick asks us to imagine a woman balancing an object on her chin) might function like the "asides" in a play. Both rhetorical forms create a space outside the ordinary channels of communication from which characters can speak more directly to their audiences.

5. Nick's surrounding description might reinforce our sense of the rightness of this "world elsewhere": "Twenty miles from the city a pair of enormous eggs, identical in contour and separated only by a courtesy bay, jut out into the most domesticated body of salt water in the Western Hemisphere, the great wet barnyard of Long Island Sound" (9). By hinting at a likeness between "domesticated" inlets and chickens laying eggs for farmers, Nick's unusual choice of words might suggest that both these natural bodies are redefined by the "courtesy" they show toward human beings.

6. To Harvey's acute analysis of how these two images create a "double exposure," I would add that the apparently onomatopoeic description of Tom closing the windows—"Then there was a boom as Tom Buchanan shut the rear windows"—serves not only as the sound of the windows slamming, but as a ship's "boom" as well, thereby closing the collocation of metaphors (95). There are other moments in *Gatsby* when Fitzgerald creates a context that brings out the homonymic potential of words; see, for

example, the description which distinguishes Myrtle from the ashes that surround her: "She smiled slowly and walking through her husband as if he were a ghost shook hands with Tom, looking him *flush* in the eye. Then she *wet* her lips" (my emphasis, 30).

7. "For example," Carter continues, "'busy' [and] 'buzz' have a high probability of co-occurrence with 'bee'; bee in turn regularly co-occurs with words such as 'hive' or 'honey' and less regularly with items such as 'intrepid' or 'transmogrifying'" (159).

8. It's worth noticing the resemblance between the paratactic sentences through which the ashes transmute themselves into people and those syntactic hurdles over which the Buchanans' lawn must leap in its race toward their house:

> The lawn started at the beach and ran toward the front door for a quarter of a mile, jumping over sun-dials and brick walks and burning gardens—finally, when it reached the house drifting up the side in bright vines as though from the momentum of its run. (11)
>
> * * *
>
> where ashes take the forms of houses and chimneys and rising smoke and finally, with a transcendent effort, of men who move dimly and already crumbling through the powdery air.

The parallel sentence shapes shared by these animate terrains might suggest an unlikely consonance between East Egg and the Valley of Ashes. In the basic insincerity behind Daisy's thrilling smiles, the dimly remembered scandal associated with Jordan's sardonic charm, and the cruelty implicit in Tom's lever-like body, there might be ashes already. Within worlds more or less explicitly burnt out, where people lack those dreaming ambitions which could give form to their restlessness, agency diffuses into landscapes which run and leap and shape themselves.

9. The same images of opulence with which Myrtle can only cover her furniture, serve as the models by which Gatsby builds his dream into concrete being; her ungainly aspirations to "scenes . . . of Versailles" are his actual "Marie Antoinette music rooms and Restoration salons" (96).

10. As Podis puts it: "The vehicle used to metaphorize Myrtle . . . comes with no definite presuppositions attached to it, since it has no prior existence in language" (65).

11. Drawn by material ambitions into a relationship that is "just personal," Myrtle expresses herself most articulately in "body-language"; she is rendered "fluent" only by the flow of her blood. Without the narrator on her side to obscure her too-sensual contours, Myrtle lacks the means to tell a story in which she turns out all right at the end. Because she has no one to speak her unutterable visions for her, Myrtle proves finally as perishable as her flesh.

12. For a different approach to Fitzgerald's use of this trope, see Hilton Anderson's discussion of "Synecdoche in *The Great Gatsby*." Basically, Anderson argues that Fitzgerald represents Gatsby by his smile and Daisy by her voice in order to delay his readers' discovery of these characters' more distasteful qualities.

13. Preface to *Roderick Hudson* (5).

14. Fitzgerald recognizes the power of this kind of obscuration in his explanation of

the "tremendous fault" constituted by the novel's lack of "an emotional presentment of Daisy's attitude toward Gatsby after their reunion (and the consequent lack of logic or importance in her throwing him over)": "Everyone has felt this but no one has spotted it because its [sic] concealed beneath elaborate and overlapping blankets of prose" (Letter to H. L. Mencken, *Life* 110).

Works Cited

Bakhtin, Mikhail M. 1984. *Problems of Dostoevsky's Poetics*. Ed. and Trans. by Caryl Emerson. Minnesota: University of Minnesota Press.

Barthes, Roland. 1982. "The Reality Effect." Rpt. in *French Literary Theory Today: A Reader*. Ed. Tzvetan Todorov. Trans. R. Carter. Cambridge University Press.

Carter, Ronald. 1982. "Sociolinguistics and the Integrated English Lesson." In *Linguistics and the Teacher*. Ed. Ronald Carter. Boston: Routledge.

Fitzgerald, F. Scott. 1994. *A Life in Letters*. Ed. Matthew J. Bruccoli. New York: Charles Scribner's Sons.

———. 1992. *The Great Gatsby*. New York: Macmillan.

———. 1996. *Tender is the Night*. New York: Macmillan.

Harvey, W. J. 1968. "Theme and Texture in *The Great Gatsby*." Rpt. in *Twentieth Century Interpretations of* The Great Gatsby. Ed. Ernest H. Lockridge. Englewood Cliffs, New Jersey: Prentice-Hall.

Jakobson, Roman. 1960. "Closing Statement: Linguistics and Poetics." In *Style in Language*. Ed. Thomas A. Sebeok. New York: John Wiley & Sons.

James, Henry. 1934. "Preface." *The American*. Rpt. in *The Art of the Novel*. New York: Charles Scribner's Sons.

———. 1934. "Preface." *Roderick Hudson*. Rpt. in *The Art of the Novel*. New York: Charles Scribner's Sons.

Kermode, Frank. 1966. *The Sense of an Ending*. New York: Oxford University Press.

Levin, Samuel R. 1988. *Metaphoric Worlds: Conceptions of a Romantic Nature*. New Haven: Yale University Press.

———. 1993. "Language, concepts, and world: Three domains of metaphor." In *Metaphor and Thought*, 2nd ed. Ed. Andrew Ortony. Cambridge: Cambridge University Press.

Long, Robert Emmet. 1984. "*The Great Gatsby*—The Intricate Art." Rpt. in *Critical Essays on Fitzgerald's* The Great Gatsby. Ed. Scott Donaldson. Boston: G. K. Hall & Company.

Mack, Dorothy. 1973. "Metaphoring as One Kind of Speech Act." *Meaning: A Common Ground of Linguistics and Literature*. Ed. Don L. F. Nilsen. Cedar Falls: University of Northern Iowa Press.

Podis, Leonard A. 1977. "'The Unreality of Reality': Metaphor in *The Great Gatsby*." *Style* 11: 56–72.

Poirier, Richard. 1966. *A World Elsewhere: The Place of Style in American Literature*. New York: Oxford University Press.

"A Fragment of Lost Words":
Narrative Ellipses in *The Great Gatsby*_____

Matthew J. Bolton

As a great short novel, *The Great Gatsby* gathers force and power not only from what it says, but also from what it chooses not to say. Nick Carraway, Fitzgerald's enigmatic narrator, relates Jay Gatsby's story in a manner that is at once concise and elliptical. These two qualities are not at odds with each other; in fact, the more concise one is, the more one must leave out. Such narrative elisions—the places in the text where Nick omits important information or jumps over some event in Gatsby's life or his own—might draw the reader's attention to the process of selection that is at work in the novel as a whole. Every narrative has elisions. Wolfgang Iser terms these moments "gaps," and argues that differences in interpretations arise from readers filling the narrative's gaps in different ways:

> One text is potentially capable of several different realizations, and no reading can ever exhaust the full potential, for each individual reader will fill in the gaps in his own way, thereby excluding the various other possibilities; as he reads, he will make his own decision as to how the gap is to be filled. (280)

Such gaps are of particular importance in *The Great Gatsby*, for the novel's brevity (180 pages in the Scribner edition) is predicated on its narrator's selectivity, on his readiness to leave some things unsaid. Nick has powers of concentration and elimination that one might more readily associate with the lyric poet than with the novelist. The work of Iser and other narratologists suggests that Nick's process of narrative selection and elision is an essential part of the story he tells. To understand what Nick says about Gatsby and himself, one might study not only Nick's words, but also his elisions, omissions, and silences.

Before turning to the narrative of *The Great Gatsby*, it may be worth defining narratology itself. Narratology might be thought of as an emerging field of study, a critical approach to literature, film, and other media that coalesces around Roland Barthes' writings of the 1960s and Wayne Booth's seminal 1961 study, *The Rhetoric of Fiction*. Yet one could also trace the discussion of narrative elements back to Aristotle's writing on drama, seeing the work of Barthes, Booth, and their contemporaries as continuing a conversation that is several millennia in the making. The early twentieth-century writings of the Russian formalists, notably Vladimir Propp and Mikhail Bakhtin, both of whose work began to appear in English translation in the 1970s, are likewise vital to this conversation. Narratologists also draw on the reflections and theories of English and American novelists, such as E. M. Forster and Henry James. Narratology is therefore a polyglot and heterogeneous school of theory. Its practitioners take a magpie's approach to literary criticism, making use of whatever material serves their needs.

It is appropriate that narratology should be a heterogeneous mode of criticism, for the literary form that is most commonly its subject—the novel—is itself profoundly heterogeneous. The novel is a mixed form, one that, in the hands of a good writer, is pliable, inclusive, and expansive. Its formal elements are so loosely defined as to seem infinitely responsive to the warp and woof of its themes and its subject matter. Its very name speaks of its "newness"; every great novel is a novelty. To see how widely novels vary in structure, one need only compare a collection of novels to a collection of, say, sermons, sonnets, fairy tales, or epics. Narratology may in fact be a response to the heterogeneous nature of the novel; it is an attempt to find a common language for discussing commonalities across radically different novels. The narratologist's focus on literary elements (such as plot or setting), on the representation of time and action, and on the relationships among author, narrator, character, and reader might be seen as an effort to develop a poetics of fiction.

Narratologists of all stripes would make a series of distinctions between author and narrator and between the text of the novel and the world that the text describes. In the case of *The Great Gatsby*, Nick Carraway is not F. Scott Fitzgerald—even if Carraway has at his disposal the full range of Fitzgerald's lyrical powers and even if he, like Fitzgerald, uses those powers to tell Gatsby's story. This distinction between author and character is an elementary one that most students learn by the time they enter high school. The second narratological distinction, on the other hand, is a bit more subtle, requiring that critics settle on some common terms. In the world which Nick Carraway inhabits, a series of events occurred in the summer of 1922—and in the years leading up to that summer—that ultimately led to Jay Gatsby's death. These events, as listed chronologically and causally, might be termed *the story*: Gatsby meets Daisy, loses her to the wealthy Tom Buchanan, resolves to reinvent himself as a wealthy and powerful man, follows her east to Long Island, buys a house across the bay from her, prevails upon Nick to reunite him with Daisy, and so on and so forth. *The story* is the sequence of events in the order in which they occurred in the "real" (albeit fictional) world.

Yet many novels, *Gatsby* among them, do not follow this chronological order. Rather, they represent (notice the literal origin of the word: re-present, to show again) the story according to some other organizing principle. The order in which a given text represents its story might be termed the "narrative discourse." The distinction between story and discourse becomes clear when one thinks of a prototypical mystery novel, where the identity of the murderer and motive for his or her crime—in other words, the events that set the story in motion—are not revealed until the end of the novel. In a similar vein, *The Great Gatsby* does not begin with Gatsby meeting Daisy, but rather with Nick moving to Long Island. Because Nick is the novel's narrator, he presents information on Gatsby in the order in which it was revealed to him. Charles Baxter calls this "the Ishmael Principle," after the narrator of *Moby Dick*, positing: "Gatsby can't tell his story, so Nick Carraway does . . . Gatsby doesn't have the necessary distance on his own situation even to begin to narrate it" (42). Baxter speculates about how un-

---

failingly bland and ridiculous Gatsby's own memoir, were he able to write one, would be. Nick brings to Gatsby's story the right degree of involvement and detachment; he has the poet's ability, as Shelley put it in his "to see life steadily and see it whole."

Yet in order to see Gatsby's story steadily and whole, Nick must exclude from his narrative almost everything that does not speak of Gatsby and his world. He glosses over many of the quotidian details that would have comprised his life and occupied his mind during his time in New York City and on Long Island. The specifics of his bond-office job, the girl from Jersey City whom he dates for awhile, and any number of similar incidents are given only minimal attention. Some novels are omnibus constructions, like the sprawling multi-plot Victorian works that Henry James termed "loose and baggy monsters." A three-volume Dickens or Thackeray novel can expand to incorporate multiple plot lines, incidents, and moods. Fitzgerald's novel, however, functions according to a very different aesthetic. *The Great Gatsby* is a study in concentration of effect and unity of form. Fitzgerald was well aware of the process of selection by which he constructed his novel. Reflecting on his process of composition in a personal letter, he wrote, "in Gatsby I selected the stuff to fit a given mood of 'hauntedness' or whatever you might call it, rejecting in advance in Gatsby, for instance, all the ordinary material of Long Island" (Fitzgerald 1963, 550–51). Seeing life whole requires one to focus wholly on the life one is seeing: Gatsby's, in this case. If a particular aspect of life on Long Island did not fit into this vision, Fitzgerald's narrator would simply omit it.

Yet Nick's narrative selectiveness derives not only from his desire to tell Gatsby's story, but also from his wariness of telling his own. At times, Nick's guardedness makes him what critic Wayne Booth termed "an unreliable narrator." Because he himself is so closely involved with the story he tells, Nick has an interest in leaving gaps between his narrative discourse and the "real" story. This is particularly true when the topic turns to his own biography. Early in the novel, his cousin

Daisy says, "We heard that you were engaged" (19). Nick's response is typically elliptical, after which he tells the reader:

Of course I knew what they were referring to, but I wasn't even vaguely engaged. The fact that gossip had published the banns was one of the reasons I had come East. You can't stop going with an old friend on account of rumors, and on the other hand I had no intention of being rumored into marriage. (19)

This is a marvelously laconic description of a love affair turned sour. Had Daisy not asked after his rumored engagement, it seems likely Nick would not have mentioned it at all. One could argue that Nick recognizes that his failed affair is only tangentially related to the story he tells, and that he therefore relates it in a concise manner. Yet the incident may be more important to Nick than he lets on to his reader. That Nick has fled in the face of rumors that he was to marry a woman raises a host of questions about his own role in the relationship, about his character, and about the set of interests and preoccupations that he brings not only to his budding relationship with Jordan Baker, but to his relationship with Jay Gatsby as well. There is an interplay between his own story and Gatsby's, for both men have come from the Midwest to New York because of women: Nick in flight from one, Gatsby in pursuit of another.

Nick is similarly laconic when talking about his war experience. He mentions it in passing as his excuse for not attending Tom and Daisy's wedding, but it is Gatsby who really introduces Nick's World War I experience into the discourse. His first question to Nick, the two men not having yet been introduced, relates directly to the topic: "'Your face is familiar,' he said, politely, 'Weren't you in the Third Division during the war?'" (47). As with the engagement, it is not at all clear whether the topic of Nick's service would have made its way into the narrative had someone else not introduced it. Though he faithfully records Gatsby's question, Nick summarizes their subsequent conversation:

"We talked for a moment about some wet, gray little villages in France" (47). Aspiring writers are often given the advice to show, not tell. One could imagine the students in a fiction writing workshop objecting to Nick's line as an example of "telling," and suggesting that the author ought to "show" the two veterans discussing their war stories. In not mentioning the specific towns the men talked of and the action they saw, Nick deflates this opening conversation with Gatsby. Of course, this is precisely the effect Nick intends: he is uncomfortable being at the center of the story (or narrative discourse, to be precise), and moves the discourse speedily over the events that illuminate his own story rather than Gatsby's.

Nick is acutely observant and accurate in chronicling the dreams and desires of the people around him, and it is not entirely wrong for him to claim, "Every one suspects himself of at least one of the cardinal virtues, and this is mine: I am one of the few honest people that I have ever known" (59). Yet he is far less scrupulous when it comes to the facts of his own story. Biographical details of his life enter the text only because other characters ask after them. In his conversations with Daisy and Gatsby, Nick finds himself in a narrative double-bind: while he would prefer to omit information about himself, he feels bound faithfully to represent the conversations he has had with his cousin and his neighbor. Nick's strategy, therefore, is to summarize and compress his responses to these questions so as to give them as little space in the discourse as possible. Having seen this process at work twice, the reader ought to begin wondering what else Nick has chosen to omit from his narrative, what else might come to light if only someone were to ask him about it.

One might chalk these omissions up to modesty, were it not for Nick's taking a similar approach when he and Tom come upon the scene of the car accident toward the novel's climax. Nick, who has always been reticent to talk about himself, chooses not to talk to the police or to Wilson of what he knows. Assuming the role of passive witness, he allows Tom to deflect Wilson's suspicions away from himself and onto the owner of the yellow car—Gatsby. Tom lies by omission, saying "That yellow car I was driving this afternoon wasn't mine—do you hear? I haven't seen it all afternoon" (140). In point of fact, Tom has seen the car and knows who was driving it: either Gatsby or Daisy. Tom's insistence that he doesn't own the car is irrelevant. Yet Nick says nothing to naysay Tom's assertion; he simply watches and listens as Tom tells the lie that will eventually lead to Gatsby's murder. Perhaps this should not come as a surprise, for Nick has always seemed to think that he can omit the truth without compromising his basic honesty. Jordan Baker will challenge Nick on these grounds during their last conversation. Rebuffing him for "throwing her over," Jordan says, "I thought you were rather an honest, straightforward person. I thought it was your secret pride" (177). Nick's response, "I'm thirty . . . I'm five years too old to lie to myself and call it honor" (177), is equivocal. Does he mean to deny or confirm her charge? And if breaking off his relationship with Jordan was an act of honesty, then was initiating the relationship in the first place an act of dishonesty?

Other gaps in Nick's narrative may stem not from his unwillingness to talk about himself, but rather from his inability to do so. One such episode comes at the conclusion of the chapter in which Nick has spent the afternoon and evening drinking heavily at the Upper West Side apartment Tom keeps for his mistress, Myrtle. At the end of the evening, Nick rides down in the elevator with Mr. McKee, who invites him to "come to lunch some day":

> "All right," I agreed, "I'll be glad to."
> . . . I was standing beside his bed and he was sitting up between the sheets, clad in his underwear, with a great portfolio in his hands.
> "Beauty and the Beast . . . Loneliness . . . Old Grocery Horse . . . Brook'n Bridge. . ."
> Then I was lying half asleep in the cold lower level of the Pennsylvania Station, staring at the morning *Tribune*, and waiting for the four o'clock train. (38)

To return to Iser's theory of narrative inexhaustibility, how a reader fills in the gap between Nick's conversation in the elevator ("I'll be glad to") and his finding himself in the bedroom of the undressed Mr. McKee (". . . I was standing beside his bed") will make a great deal of difference to one's interpretation not only of this scene but of the novel as a whole. Are Nick's ellipses a form of self-censorship, by which he elides a homosexual encounter—or perhaps only the possibility of one—with McKee? Or do the ellipses mimic the gaps in the memory that can result from drinking too much? Nick would certainly not be the only person in this novel to suffer alcohol-induced blackouts.

In his primer on narrative theory, H. Porter Abbot distinguishes between narrative gaps and narrative cruxes: "In criticism, a crux is an oft-debated element in a work that, depending on how we interpret it, can significantly effect how we interpret the work as a whole" (86). In the case of *The Great Gatsby*, some critics have seen the episode with Mr. McKee as evidence enough that Nick is a homosexual. Such a reading subtly—or not so subtly—shifts Nick's relationship with many of the novel's other characters, particularly Jordan Baker and Jay Gatsby. This interpretation helps explain Nick's horror at finding himself "rumored into marriage," the coolness of his relationship with Jordan, and, of course, the fascination that Gatsby holds for him. To the objection that Nick never declares himself to be gay, one might answer that Nick also does not speak of his rumored engagement or of his war experience. Not identifying himself as gay would be in keeping not only with the general tenor of the times, but also with Nick's typical caginess regarding his personal history.

Yet to conclude that the incident with Mr. McKee establishes Nick's homosexuality would probably be a case of what narratologists call "overreading." Abbot defines overreading as "the act of importing into the text material that is not signified within it" (194). The fact that Nick finds himself in McKee's bedroom is not really enough justification to conclude that Nick has (or is going to have, for notice that there is another narrative gap immediately after the scene with McKee in bed:

"Then I was lying half asleep in the cold lower level of the Pennsylvania Station") any kind of sexual encounter with him. For if Nick's ellipses are a form of self-censorship, then why would he not censor himself more extensively? Why include any mention of being in McKee's apartment at all, if he is in fact at pains to hide from the reader his sexual identity? Perhaps more to the point, Nick's sense of time and of continuity is beginning to fray well before he leaves the apartment. Some two pages earlier, he says "It was nine o'clock—almost immediately afterward I looked at my watch and found it was ten" (36). Later he describes the scene this way: "People disappeared, reappeared, made plans to go somewhere, and then lost each other, searched for each other, found each other a few feet away" (37). While Nick continues to write in the past tense, the repetitive phrasing of the sentence suggests a present-tense, stream-of-consciousness account of the party. Nick's phrasing now (as he narrates events some two years gone) mimics his drunkenness then. Seen in this context, the ellipses that precede Nick's finding himself in McKee's apartment and the abrupt "then" that serves as a transition between the apartment and the train station speak not of self-censorship, but of the hampered perceptions and disjointed memories that drunkenness can produce. These are instances not of Nick exerting control of his narrative, but rather of his losing control of it.

Elsewhere in his narrative, Nick uses ellipses to a different effect. In talking with Jay Gatsby about his plan to marry Daisy, for example, Nick creates the illusion that his present-day conversation has given way to a scene from the past:

> I gathered that he wanted to recover something, some idea of himself perhaps, that had gone into loving Daisy. His life had been confused and disordered since then, but if he could once return to a certain starting place and go over it all slowly, he could find out what that thing was. . .
> . . . One autumn night, five years before, they had been walking down the street when the leaves were falling, and they came to a place where there were no trees and the sidewalk was white with moonlight. (110)

While the voice in the second passage is still Nick's, it is Nick's voice as lent to Gatsby. The third-person pronoun does not change ("he" becomes "they" as Daisy joins Gatsby for a moonlit walk), nor does Nick lose his characteristic lyricism. Yet because the scene is set five years before Nick met Gatsby, Nick himself is effaced; he is no longer a witness, but an amanuensis. Stephen Dedalus, Joyce's young artist, argues that a narrator should be "refined out of existence" (Joyce 2000, 119). Nick approaches such refinement here. Without changing pronouns, Nick changes his relationship to the pronoun. He is not just repeating the story Gatsby told him, but retelling that story by applying some of the techniques of first person narration to a third person passage, as here: "His heart beat faster and faster as Daisy's white face came up to his own. He knew that when he kissed this girl, and forever wed his unutterable visions to her perishable breath, his mind would never romp again like the mind of God" (110). The diction and syntax are Nick's, but they are bent toward recreating and bringing to life an event from Gatsby's life. This is not quite an instance of free indirect discourse, for the "he knew" makes it clear that a narrator is relaying Gatsby's inner thoughts. Nor would it be quite fair to say that the point of view has changed, for Nick is the narrator and Gatsby the character in both the conversation before the ellipses and the imbedded narrative that the ellipses introduce. Perhaps a better term to apply to the passage is one coined by critic Mieke Bal: "focalization." The narrative is focalized or filtered through Gatsby's consciousness, and the effect is to elide the difference between the "I" of the narrator and the "he" of the character, so that the one briefly gives way to the other.

Five years ago, Gatsby kissed Daisy and "wed his unutterable visions to her perishable breath," while in the present day, Nick listens to Gatsby's story and finds some unutterable vision of his own flitting at the edge of his consciousness:

I was reminded of something—an elusive rhythm, a fragment of lost words, that I had heard somewhere a long time ago. For a moment a phrase tried to take shape in my mouth and my lips parted like a dumb man's, as though there was more struggling upon them than a wisp of startled air. But they made no sound, and what I had almost remembered was incommunicable forever. (111)

Here is another of the novel's cruxes, for there is no way to determine just what the phrase is that escapes Nick's mind and fails to issue from his lips. One can assume it would be some kind of epiphany about Gatsby or himself, but there is no way to reconstruct what that epiphany might be. It is loss made manifest, an absence that fills the room and the narrative with its presence. The "fragment of lost words" and "incommunicable . . . phrase" are a bit like the "overwhelming question" that T. S. Eliot's Prufrock refers to but never specifies. Nick might sympathize with Prufrock's complaint that "It is impossible to say just what I mean." Perhaps this incommunicable phrase is a fitting way to conclude a chapter that centers on Gatsby's loss of Daisy. In gaining Daisy, Gatsby gives away "some idea of himself," and when Daisy abandons him for Tom Buchanan she takes that part of him with her (110). Listening to Gatsby's story, Nick experiences a similar sensation of loss. Perhaps in both cases what has been lost is the sense of possibility. Actual women, actual events, and actual words drive out and replace the host of possibilities that once stood as their placeholders. To return to another of Stephen Dedalus's maxims, history is "lodged in the room of the infinite possibilities which it has ousted" (Joyce *Ulysses* 2. 50–1). Just as Gatsby fixes his desire on a single girl, so Nick fixes his narrative discourse on a single chain of events that explains his enigmatic neighbor. He gains a thorough knowledge of Gatsby's life story, but in so doing he loses the sense of manifold possibilities and mystery that his neighbor once held for him. Nick muses, after arranging for Gatsby and Daisy to be reunited, that the light at the end of the Buchanan's dock would no longer hold the "colossal significance" it once did (93). He says, "Now it was again a green light on a dock. His count of enchanted objects had diminished by one" (93). Something of the same effect may be at work for Nick himself, for Gatsby, in telling his story, becomes an ordinary man rather than an enchanted figure of infinite possibility.

At the novel's conclusion, Nick uses ellipses to a different effect, indicating neither time lost to a drunken blackout nor a transition between his own "present tense" narrative and the imbedded narratives of Gatsby's past. In his last encounter with Tom Buchanan, ellipses instead speak to the tension between Nick's impulses toward reflection and narration. A narratologist might take his terms from Aristotle, calling these two elements of the narrative discourse *diegesis* (commentary) and *mimesis* (representation); a layman might term this the distinction between telling and showing. Nick encounters Tom by chance on Fifth Avenue in October. Tom spots him and thrusts out his hand, asking, "What's the matter, Nick? Do you object to shaking hands with me?" Nick tells him he does, and asks Tom whether he told Wilson who owned the yellow car. Tom defends his actions, saying "What if I did tell him? That fellow had it coming . . . He ran over Myrtle like you'd run over a dog and never even stopped his car" (178). Nick knows the truth of the matter—that Daisy, not Gatsby, was driving—yet he chooses not to tell Tom. He muses, "There was nothing I could say, except the one unutterable fact that it wasn't true" (178). Again and again, Nick has chosen to keep silent. He does so again here, perhaps feeling that no facts, no matter how true, could shake Tom's opinion of himself as "entirely justified." He thinks:

> They were careless people, Tom and Daisy—they smashed up things and creatures and then retreated back into their money or their vast carelessness, or whatever it was that kept them together, and let other people clean up the mess they made. . . .
>
> I shook hands with him; it seemed silly not to, for I felt suddenly as though I were talking to a child. (179)

The ellipses that separate these two passages may serve several purposes at once. They show the passage of time, for Nick's realization about Tom and Daisy is not one that came to him months or years later, in writing his account, but rather one that struck him right there on Fifth Avenue on an October afternoon. Thought moves quickly, but it nevertheless moves in time, and some moments must pass while Nick imagines Tom's own sense of self-justification, characterizes Tom and Daisy as "careless people," and decides that he will nevertheless shake Tom's hand. The trailing ellipses indicate these fleeting moments. Fitzgerald—or Nick—has used ellipses this way before. When McKee shows Nick his photographs, for example, each set of ellipses indicates the time in which he turns the page or in some other way draws Nick's attention to a new shot: "Beauty and the Beast . . . Loneliness . . . Old Grocery Horse . . . Brook'n Bridge . . ." (38).

Yet in the final scene with Tom, the ellipses mark more than a passage of time: they indicate an interrupting of the interior monologue to return to a description of external circumstances. There is an abruptness to this transition, as if Nick needs to break off his interior monologue in order both to shake Tom's hand in the "present moment" of the October afternoon and to resume the forward momentum of the story he is narrating some years later. The ellipses indicate that were there time enough to do so, Nick could keep thinking in this same vein, extrapolating out all of the implications of Tom and Daisy's carelessness. Instead he cuts his reverie short, returning to the exigencies of his narrative's plot. He interrupts an instance of diegesis, or telling, in order to return to mimesis, or showing. In shaking Tom's hand, Nick shakes off an interiority that threatens to stall his narrative in its final pages.

Perhaps this breaking off of the interior monologue is explained in part by what Frank Kermode calls "the sense of an ending." The narrative discourse takes on a sort of momentum as it approaches its conclusion. Like a man on his deathbed, a narrator at the end of his story is often gripped by a desire to set his house in order. Nick has his final conversations with Tom, Jordan, Wolfsheim, and the novel's other principal characters. He makes a last visit to Gatsby's mansion. And he tries one last time to draw some conclusions from Gatsby's story:

> Gatsby believed in the green light, the orgastic future that year by year recedes from us. It eluded us then, but that's no matter—to-morrow we will run faster, stretch out our arms farther . . . And one fine morning—
> So we beat on, boats against the current, borne back ceaselessly into the past. (180)

Here Nick uses first a long dash and then a set of ellipses to suggest a breaking away from the present and a reaching out toward a promised, idealized future. Note the shift from "Gatsby" in the first line to the first-person plural "us" and "we" in the second. Nick, his protagonist, and the reader are folded together into a confederacy. The trailing ellipses after "stretch out our arms farther" are falteringly optimistic, the trailing off in midsentence of someone who sees a vision on the horizon. "One fine morning" marks the beginning of the vision itself: the imagined day on which the much-anticipated, orgastic future comes into being. But then a long dash follows, ending this reverie and dashing the dreamer's vision by bringing him back not only to the present, but to a present informed by and drawn back into the past. The novel therefore concludes with Nick caught between an elusive future and an irredeemable past, his narrative voice hovering somewhere between Gatsby and himself, between then and now, between speech and silence.

Works Cited

Abbot, H. Porter. 2002. *The Cambridge Introduction to Narrative.* Cambridge: Cambridge University Press.

Booth, Wayne. 1967. *The Rhetoric of Fiction.* Chicago: University of Chicago Press.

Baxter, Charles. 2007. *The Art of Subtext.* St. Paul, Minn.: Graywolf Press.

Eliot, T. S. 1962. *The Complete Poems and Plays: 1909–1950.* New York: Harcourt, Brace & World.

Fitzgerald, F. Scott. 1925. *The Great Gatsby*. New York: Scribner.
————. 1963. *The Letters of F. Scott Fitzgerald*, edited by Andrew Turnbull. New York: Scribner.
Iser, Wolfgang. 1974. *The Implied Reader: Patterns of Communication in Prose Fiction from Bunyan to Beckett*. Baltimore: Johns Hopkins University Press.
Joyce, James. 2000. *A Portrait of the Artist as a Young Man*. New York: Random House.
————. 1986. *Ulysses*. New York: Random House.

The Great Gatsby and The Obscene Word_____

Barbara Will

I.

In a novel in which language is consistently seen to work against the demands of veracity, at least one formulation in *The Great Gatsby* rings true: Nick Carraway's pronouncement, near the start of the novel, that "Gatsby turned out all right at the end" (Fitzgerald 1999, 6). Jay Gatsby, a figure marked by failure and shadowed by death throughout most of the novel, nevertheless achieves a form of "greatness" in the final paragraphs of his story; it is at this point, in the words of Lionel Trilling, that Gatsby "comes inevitably to stand for America itself" (1963, 17). For it is in the final, lyrical paragraphs of the novel that Gatsby's fate takes on mythic dimensions, becoming an allegory for the course of the American nation and for the struggles and dreams of its citizens. This transformation occurs when the novel's narrator, Nick Carraway, finally perceives what lies beneath the "inessential" surface world of his surroundings: a vital impulse, an originary [sic] American hope. Nick sees Gatsby as the incarnation of this national impulse, this "extraordinary gift for hope," using the same term—"wonder"—to describe Gatsby's desire for Daisy Buchanan and that of the first American colonists gazing at "the fresh green breast of the new world." For Nick, Gatsby's lies, his pretensions, and his corruption are "no matter"; nor is his failure to win back Daisy; what matters is the sustaining belief in the value of striving for a "wondrous" object, not its inevitable disappearance and meaninglessness. And in a significant shift in pronouns of the novel's final sentences, Nick unites Gatsby's effort with a general, if unspecified, national collective: "Gatsby believed in the green light, the orgastic future that year by year recedes before us. It eluded *us* then, but that's no matter— . . . So *we* beat on, boats against the current, borne back ceaselessly into the past" (Fitzgerald 1999, 141; my emphasis). What matters to Gatsby is what matters to "us"; Gatsby's story is "our" story; his fate and the fate of the nation are intertwined. That Gatsby "turned out all right in the end" is thus essential to the novel's vision of a transcendent and collective Americanism.

Yet this ending is in fact at odds with the characterization of Gatsby in the rest of the novel. For if Gatsby ultimately represents a glorified version of "us," then he does so only if we forget that he is for most of the novel a force of corruption: a criminal, a bootlegger, and an adulterer. As critics have often noted, the text stakes its ending on the inevitability of our forgetting everything about Gatsby that has proved troublesome about his character up to this point. What critics have generally overlooked, however, is the fact that the text also self-consciously inscribes this process of forgetting into its own narrative. Appearing to offer two discrepant views of its protagonist, *The Great Gatsby* in fact ultimately challenges its readers to question the terms through which "presence" or "visibility" can be signified.

This, to my mind, is the point of one of the most important yet least critically examined scenes in the novel: the novel's penultimate scene, the transitional scene that immediately precedes the last four paragraphs of the text. It is a scene that begins with Nick Carraway wandering idly down to Long Island Sound past Gatsby's house, killing time on the eve of his return to the mid-west: "On the last night, with my trunk packed and my car sold to the grocer, I went over and looked at that huge incoherent failure of a house once more. On the white steps an obscene word, scrawled by some boy with a piece of brick, stood out clearly in the moonlight and I erased it, drawing my shoe raspingly along the stone" (Fitzgerald 1999, 140). A fleeting, transitory scene; in the next instant, Nick is already down at the shore, "sprawled out on the sand," at which point his epiphany about Gatsby and the green light begins. Yet what this immediate sequence of events implies is that Nick's final epiphany about Gatsby is contingent for its emergence on the act that precedes this epiphany: the repression or erasure of an "obscene word." In order for Gatsby to "turn out all right at the end," to come to "stand for America itself," his link to this word must be erased. Yet by foregrounding the process of this erasure, this "forgetting,"

Critical Insights

Fitzgerald also seems to be problematizing the inevitability of the text's ending: Gatsby "turn[s] out all right" only if we forget, or repress, his obscenity.

While it is easy for a reader to overlook this scene, it requires no real effort to understand why the graffiti scrawled on Gatsby's house would be an obscenity, for the link between Gatsby and the obscene has been repeatedly suggested in the text up to this point: in Nick's reference to Gatsby's "corruption"; in his opening claim that Gatsby "represented everything for which I have an unaffected scorn" (Fitzgerald 1999, 6); in his description of Gatsby's career as "Trimalchio" (88). In this penultimate scene, it is also a link that Fitzgerald frames explicitly in terms of signification, or rather, in terms of what eludes or threatens signification. For by linking Gatsby with an obscene *word*, Fitzgerald appears to be deliberately drawing attention to the etymology of "obscene": as that which is either unrepresentable or beyond the terms of the presentable ("obscene," from the Latin "obscenaeus," meaning both "against the presentable" and "unrepresentable"). Whatever the word scrawled on Gatsby's steps may be, the point is that we cannot know it; it is a word that, precisely in its obscenity, points to a signifying void. Yet as its etymology suggests, the "signifying void" of the obscene can be understood in two ways. On the one hand, the obscene is what eludes representation: it is the unrepresentable, the pre-linguistic, or the anti-linguistic, a force of disruption and implosion, of psychosexual and linguistic shattering. It is similar in process to what Julia Kristeva terms "the abject": that which "draws me toward the place where meaning collapses" (1982, 2). Yet the obscene is also what questions—and thus denaturalizes—the normative thrust of signification. The obscene works against the presentable, as Mary Caputi argues, "in its determined violation of established norms, its eagerness to proclaim from beyond the acceptable, its appeal to the uncanny" (1994, 7). Freud, speaking of "smut," defined it as an "undoing" of repression, while Bakhtin identifies "low" language ("on the stages of local fairs and at buffoon spectacles") as "parodic, and aimed sharply and polemically against the official languages of its given time" (Freud 1957, 101; Bakhtin 1981, 273). In this second sense, the obscene predominantly functions as a threat to the conventional language of narration or the normative discourses of a nation, throwing into question the status of the acceptable or the normal, of the seemingly representable and meaningful, including the political and social hierarchies that sustain "meaning."

As sections two and three of this essay will suggest, both senses of the term "obscene" summarize the life of Jay Gatsby. While Gatsby is a "mystery" for those who attend his parties, he is even more, as Nick Carraway notes, "an elusive rhythm, a fragment of lost words" (Fitzgerald 1999, 87). With his "unutterable visions" that lead to "unutterable depression" and ultimately "incoherent failure," Gatsby is constantly vanishing on the horizon of significance; and this is a problem for characters like Nick and the Buchanans, whose own sense of location in time and social space is very much dependent upon a clear distinction between truth and lies, insiders and outsiders, natives and aliens. Put another way, Gatsby is a figure who problematizes the nature of figuration itself, drawing the text toward an abject void, "toward the place where meaning collapses." But Gatsby is also a figure whose obscenity lies in the challenge he poses to "the presentable," to the natural and the normal—a particularly unsettling idea given not only the text's immediate concerns with the nature of belonging but also the historical moment in which Fitzgerald is writing, an era marked by widespread anxiety about the possible dissolution of the "natural" American in the face of an encroaching "alien menace." As we shall see, such concerns over the nature (and "naturalness") of American identity in the 1920s were shared by Fitzgerald himself, whose own politics at the time of writing *Gatsby* were directed toward immigration restriction and who remained throughout his life suspicious of those who threatened the group to which he felt he belonged, "the old American aristocracy." Given this historical context, Gatsby's indeterminacy and transgressiveness could be said to embody nothing less than the "obscene" fulfillment of Fitzgerald's own suspicions: Gatsby as the threatening figure of the alien, unassimilable to the discourse of political and social Americanism toward which the text is ultimately directed, "unutterable" within the narrative framework that seeks to represent him.

By having Nick erase "the obscene word" from the text as Gatsby's story draws to a close, however, Fitzgerald makes it possible for this story to emerge as the story of America itself. Gatsby the obscene becomes Gatsby the American. Yet while the fact of this transformation is incontestable, its terms remain troubling. Through foregrounding Nick's erasure of the obscene word from Gatsby's house, Fitzgerald deliberately emphasizes the process through which the "whitewashing" of Gatsby's reputation takes place. And as this essay will finally suggest, to emphasize this process is to reveal a central uncertainty, or void, that lies at the heart of the text's final, transcendent vision.

II.

In an early draft of the novel, Nick Carraway makes an interesting observation about Gatsby: "He was provokingly elusive and what he was intrinsically 'like' I'm powerless to say."[1] Nick's crisis of linguistic disempowerment here accompanies the "provokingly elusive" nature of his subject; the problem of Gatsby's "intrinsic likeness" bears wholly on the project of signification. In a character with not enough "likeness" and no apparent "intrinsic" essence, Gatsby is nowhere and everywhere, a "vanishing presence"; and this, as Derrida reminds us, is also the nature of "*différance* . . . which prevents any word, any concept, any major enunciation from coming to summarize and to govern from the theological presence of a center the movement and textual spacing of differences" (1981, 14). If Gatsby—"the man who gives his name to this book"—is meant by Nick to "summarize" and "govern" the work of the text, the meaning and direction of its signifiers, then his "elusiveness" is also what prevents this governance from taking place.

An "elusive rhythm," Gatsby could be said to embody *différance*, if embodiment can be understood as the "being-there of an absen[ce]" or the "disjointure in the very presence of the present" (1994, 6; 25). It is in his fractured and incoherent embodiment, his ever-vanishing "presence," that Gatsby throws into crisis Nick's effort to speak.

"Vanished" is indeed the predominant term in this text, as when at the end of Chapter I Nick first encounters Gatsby, only to find "he had vanished, and I was alone again in the unquiet darkness"; or when, after an awkward meeting with Tom Buchanan, Nick "turned toward Mr. Gatsby but he was no longer there" (Fitzgerald 1999, 59).[2] Gatsby "vanishes" at other key moments in the text: in his failure to appear at his own parties, in his unknowable past and shady business dealings, and in his smile, which "assured you that it had precisely the impression of you that, at your best, you hoped to convey. Precisely at that point it vanished—" (40). As this last sentence suggests, Gatsby even vanishes—literally—from the signifying system of the text itself: the dash, the graphic mark of his unrepresentability, is insistently emphasized whenever he speaks or is spoken about.[3] Although to Nick Gatsby seems at once utterly conventional, utterly knowable—being with him, he notes, was "like skimming hastily through a dozen magazines" (53)—he is also "provokingly elusive," both extending the promise of meaning or presence and "vanishing" at the moment in which that promise leans toward fulfillment. This process is apparent in a number of scenes throughout the novel. Most haunting is Nick's statement following Gatsby's confessional account of his first kiss with Daisy:

> Through all he said, even through his appalling sentimentality, I was reminded of something—an elusive rhythm, a fragment of lost words, that I had heard somewhere a long time ago. For a moment a phrase tried to take shape in my mouth and my lips parted like a dumb man's, as though there was more struggling upon them than a wisp of startled air. But they made no sound and what I had almost remembered was uncommunicable forever. (Fitzgerald 1999, 87)

Nick's effort to speak is here seen to be awakened by Gatsby's own words, with their "elusive rhythm" and nostalgic promise of a return to lost origins; yet memory is also inevitably attended by a failure of articulation ("and what I had almost remembered was uncommunicable forever"). Whoever Gatsby is, whatever he reminds one of, this "presence" ultimately lies outside the limits of the communicable. As in the earlier description of Gatsby's smile, this passage is structured around a contradictory movement (or "disjointure," to recall Derrida) in which presence and appearance pivot into absence and "vanishing" at the precise moment of seeming apprehension. Another such example is found in the party scene of chapter III, which begins with a series of gossipy suppositions about Gatsby's identity by passing partygoers: "'Somebody told me they thought he killed a man once'"; "'it's more that he was a German spy during the war'"; "'he told me once he was an Oxford man.'" With this latter claim, notes Nick, "A dim background started to take shape behind [Gatsby] but at her next remark it faded away" (40). Here, again, the promise of presence or "shape" vanishes at the moment of its emergence; suppositions lead not to truth but to indeterminacy, and who Gatsby is remains just beyond the reach of the "next remark."

Nor is Gatsby's indeterminacy within the text simply an issue of Nick's own notably distorted vision, as the comments of fellow partygoers make clear. While it is true that Nick's perceptions, especially while drunk, contribute exponentially to the idea of Gatsby's elusiveness, other observers also fail to illuminate Gatsby's character. In a crucial (and again, often overlooked) moment during the chapter III party scene, Nick and Jordan encounter a man "with enormous owl-eyed spectacles" sitting in the library of Gatsby's house, who informs them that the books on the shelves are, indeed, "real": "Absolutely real— have pages and everything. I thought they'd be a nice durable cardboard. Matter of fact they're absolutely real. . . . It's a triumph. What thoroughness! What realism! Knew when to stop too—didn't cut the pages. But what do you want? What do you expect?" (Fitzgerald 1999,

37–38). As a figure who, like Doctor T. J. Eckleberg [sic], is linked metonymically in the text to the trope of perception, "Owl Eyes" is presented as one who pierces the façade of social life in the Eggs, exposing—as at Gatsby's funeral—the despair and loneliness that lie underneath the forced gaiety of appearances. In the library scene, Owl Eyes' ability to "expose" is both emphasized and undermined, as the fake-appearing books turn out to be real, yet semi-unreadable. The "realness" of the books signifies presence and meaning; yet their uncut pages underscore the opacity of the text-that-would-be-read. Gatsby, too, is both "really" there and absent, a figure who resists being perceived even by those with "corrected" vision, who voids the signifying process of its meaningful end. "What do you want? What do you expect?" Owl Eyes finally asks himself, Nick, Jordan, and implicitly the reader, calling into question any desire or expectation for knowledge that might attend the experience of "reading" Gatsby.

Hence those few crucial scenes where Gatsby's character promises to be revealed as meaningful and directed toward a significant end invariably prove to be "provokingly elusive." In the famous flashback scene of chapter VI, for example, Nick recalls Gatsby's past as "James Gatz of North Dakota" in order to explain Gatsby's present, portraying his youthful rejection of family and original name as a necessary precondition to his later "glory" as a wealthy, upwardly-mobile adult (Fitzgerald 1999, 76 ff.). Nick's account of Gatsby's adolescent attempts to cast him in a familiar mold: the self-made man, "spr[inging] from his Platonic conception of himself," the spiritual descendent of other hard-working national icons like Horatio Alger or Benjamin Franklin (whose famous "Plan for Self-Examination" would be invoked later in the text in Gatsby's own childhood "Schedule"). Yet the text consistently undermines these seeming "causes" of Gatsby's actions at the very moment of their "revelation." For what this chapter in fact reveals about Gatsby is not so much his identity with an American tradition of hard work and "luck and pluck" but rather his dreaminess, his entrapment in "a universe of ineffable gaudiness," his belief "that the rock of the world was founded securely on a fairy's wing." What motivates Gatsby is not the desire for material betterment ("food and bed") but the evanescent and the intangible; what satisfies him is confirmation of "the unreality of reality." Whatever is, for Gatsby, can be contradicted, "the real" is always "the unreal," and this is troubling both to the descriptive terms and to the larger narrative of American achievement within which Gatsby is meant to emerge as "great." To be sure, to tell the story of a figure trapped in the oxymoronic "unreality of reality" is to tell a modernist story, if modernity, as Jean-François Lyotard suggests, "does not occur without a shattering of belief, without a discovery of the *lack of reality* in reality—a discovery linked to the invention of other realities" (1992, 9). Consistently dreaming beyond the material, social, economic, and temporal boundaries of his surroundings, overturning and reimagining the hierarchies of power and social status that constrain him, Gatsby could be seen as a modernist figure, a deconstructive figure, a figure of *différance*, whose "motivation" is to "shatter . . . belief" and hence "invent . . . [new] realities." Yet *The Great Gatsby* is no *Ulysses*, capturing in the play of signifiers the movement of Gatsby's *"différance"*; however "modernist" Gatsby may be, his character can only be revealed through the moments in which he vanishes from the narrative, through oxymorons, through dashes—all of which point to an unrepresentability at the center of this textual reality.

III.

In a text so haunted by indeterminacy and unrepresentability, what stands out are precisely those efforts that work against "vanishing," that attempt to affirm, make visible, and police boundaries of meaning, identity, community, sexuality, and nation. These are also efforts directed against Gatsby and his elusiveness: efforts either to make sense of Gatsby's character (as in Nick's effort to "reveal" Gatsby's formative past) or to cast him as inherently corrupt and "obscene," as outside the boundaries of sense, propriety, and order, as racially and sexually perverse. These latter efforts are centered in the character of Tom Buchanan, denizen of the isolated town of East Egg, two-timing husband of Daisy, and single-minded adherent to the nativist views of a tome called "The Rise of the Colored Empires," modeled on Lothrop Stoddard's 1920 volume *The Rising Tide of Color Against White World-Supremacy*.[4] For Buchanan, following Stoddard, "The idea is if we don't look out the white race will be—will be utterly submerged," a statement whose characteristic use of the dash emphasizes the anxiety that underwrites American nativism in the 1920s, its sense that the process of Nordic "submersion" by an ever-expanding "colored empire" may already be underway. What the dash in Tom's statement represents is what, for him, would be unspeakable—miscegenation, a process through which "whiteness" and "color" become undifferentiated, through which "race" itself, and the white race in particular, become indeterminate. For Tom, it is Jay Gatsby in particular who represents a mode of racial indeterminacy or "vanishing" that threatens to violate not only the immediate community of East Egg but also the very concept of Americanism itself.

In his recent study of nativism and American literature in the 1920s, Walter Benn Michaels argues that the threat of a disappearing white race constitutes Tom's real concern about Gatsby's union with Daisy; it is the fact that "[f]or Tom . . . Gatsby (né Gatz, with his Wolfsheim [sic] 'gonnegtion') isn't quite white," that sustains his antipathy toward his rival (Michaels 1995, 25).[5] Gatsby's "off-white" status is confirmed earlier in the novel by the comment of Tom's relation-by-marriage Nick Carraway that "I would have accepted without question the information that Gatsby sprang from the swamps of Louisiana or from the lower East Side of New York" (Fitzgerald 1999, 41), a statement that associates Gatsby not with radical otherness but with creole or Jewish difference, both in the 1920s "assigned to the not-fully-white side of the racial spectrum."[6] What most disturbs Tom, and clearly troubles Nick, is not just the fact that Gatsby is a mystery but more that he signals the "vanishing" of whiteness into indeterminacy, and thus threatens the whole economic, discursive, and institutional structure of power supporting the social distinctions and hierarchies at work in *The Great Gatsby*. For Tom (and possibly Nick), whiteness and its attendant privileges—material well-being, entitlement, the feeling of being "safe and proud above the hot struggles of the poor"—is something that must be preserved, safeguarded, barricaded. Thus when Gatsby is most dangerously close to "winning" Daisy, it is not so much his social ambition that threatens Tom as the fact that his pursuit portends "intermarriage between black and white." Gatsby's "obscenity" for Tom lies in the challenge he poses to sexual and racial norms. In exposing Gatsby's link to miscegenation, Tom brings out the deeper social menace against which his own claim to whiteness stands as guardian: "Flushed with his impassioned gibberish he saw himself standing alone on the last barrier of civilization" (101).

That Gatsby is associated with a Jewish crime syndicate, moreover, only redoubles his threatening presence in the text. With his "Wolfsheim 'gonnegtion'" Gatsby seems contaminated by more than just criminality and sexual perversity; for it is the fact of Wolfsheim's crudely stereotyped, animalistic Jewishness that most seems to "taint" Gatsby. The same "taint" is also suggested by Gatsby's layered, problematic name. "Jay Gatsby," of course, is only a WASP fiction adopted by one "James Gatz of North Dakota," yet although the text is directed toward exposing this fiction, the significance of this exposure remains obscure. While the name of "Gatz" is clearly haunted by ethnic, and specifically Jewish, overtones, "Gatz" is also a decidedly ambiguous name. Not *not* Jewish (as opposed to "Gaty," the first version of "Gatz" shown in Fitzgerald's drafts), the name "Gatz" is also not identifiably Jewish (as opposed, for example, to the more common "Katz"). Both Jews and non-Jews have the surname Gatz; moreover, the name "Gatz" sometimes appears as a germanicized alteration of a Yiddish name, "Gets."[7] That Fitzgerald knew of this etymological complexity would not be surprising; as Lottie R. Crim and Neal B. Houston have pointed out, Fitzgerald's use of names in *Gatsby* is remarkably rich and nuanced.[8] By choosing a name, "Gatz," that can generate both Jewish and gentile chains of associations, Fitzgerald seems to be emphasizing once again the way in which his protagonist is always "vanishing" into racial and hence social indeterminacy. Neither identifiably black nor identifiably Jewish, the shifting, obscure, ever-vanishing figure of James Gatz/Jay Gatsby troubles the category of "whiteness," problematizing the force of this category at a moment when such force is of crucial significance.

As Michaels suggests, the specter of a beleaguered whiteness in *The Great Gatsby* needs to be understood in light of the historical moment in which *Gatsby* was written, the early 1920s. This is a moment in which American isolationist fervor is at its peak, a moment in which fears over "the expanded power of the alien" are being openly expressed in political, intellectual, and literary forums. It is a moment marked by the social movement of nativism, with its support of the Johnson-Reed Immigration Act of 1924 and its battle cry "America for the Americans." It is also a moment in which the discourse of "Americanism"—the nativists' privileged term—is linked indubitably to the discourse of whiteness: "Americanism is actually the racial thought of the Nordic race, evolved after a thousand years of experience," writes Clinton Stoddard Burr, author of *America's Race Heritage* (1922).[9] "The great hope of the future here in America lies in the realization that competition of the Nordic with the alien is fatal," warns nativist writer Madison Grant in his 1920 introduction to Lothrop Stoddard's *The Rising Tide of Color*, ". . . In this country we must look to such of our people—our farmers and artisans—as are still of American blood to recognize and meet this danger" (Stoddard 1920, xxxi). Charlotte Perkins Gilman, author and agitator for women's rights, simply worried in 1923, "Is America Too Hospitable?" (Higham 1973, 386, n. 25). For these and other nativists, keeping "American blood" pure—i.e., purely white—in the face of alien expansion was a predominant concern; and one that contributed its ideological part to a host of post-War social measures, from quotas to IQ tests, that were meant to establish and affirm the whiteness or "Nordicism" of the nation.

In *The Great Gatsby* (composed during 1922–24), nativist feeling is clearly exemplified by the views of Tom Buchanan, but also, though more subtly, by the discourse of Nick Carraway, with his "scorn" for the working classes, his stereotyping of immigrants, Jews, and blacks, and his claim to be "descended from the Dukes of Buccleuch"—an aristocratic lineage that, however fictional, is meant to appease any nativist fears about the non-whiteness of the Scottish. Yet while Fitzgerald presents such attempts to shore up whiteness against "alien elements" as "impassioned gibberish," external, biographical evidence suggests that the nativist ideas of Tom and Nick may not be so far from Fitzgerald's own. "Raise the bars of immigration and permit only Scandinavians, Teutons, Anglo Saxons + Celts to enter," Fitzgerald writes in an infamous 1921 letter to Edmund Wilson after a disappointing tourist trip in France and Italy: ". . . My reactions [are] all philistine, anti-socialistic, provincial + racially snobbish. I believe at last in the white man's burden" (1994, 47).[10] Some fifteen years later, in an undated letter from the 1930s to his daughter Scottie lamenting her choice of friends, Fitzgerald reiterates these views:

> Jesus, we're the few remnants of the old American aristocracy that's managed to survive in communicable form—we have the vitality left. And you choose to mix it up with the cheap lower middle class settled on Park Avenue. You know the distinction—and in most of your relations you are wise enough to forget it—but when it comes to falling for a phoney—your instincts should do a better job. All that's rude, tough (in the worst sense), crude and purse proud comes from vermin like the ——'s. (Undated note to Scottie from F. Scott Fitzgerald)[11]

"Mix[ing] it up with the cheap lower middle class," Scottie fails to let her "instincts" create the necessary distinction that would preclude her "falling for a phoney." The "distinction" Fitzgerald refers to is one of class, to be sure, but even more of race—a point made clear by his emphasis on familial "vitality," which directly echoes contemporary nativist discussions of race and degeneracy. Lothrop Stoddard, for one, would differentiate between "Nordics" and "aliens" on the basis of "vitality": "there seems to be no question that the Nordic is far and away the most valuable type; standing, indeed, at the head of the whole human genus" (1920, 162). Yet Stoddard also fears that in the post-War period, "Nordic vitality" has suffered a two-fold blow: decimated by the War, which has left "the men twisted by hereditary deformity or devitalized by hereditary disease . . . at home to propagate the breed," Nordics are also victims of immigrant ambition: "the Nordic native American has been crowded out with amazing rapidity by . . . swarming, prolific aliens, and after two short generations he has in many of our urban areas become almost extinct" (181; 165). Given Fitzgerald's own failure to see action in the War, his lifelong battle with alcoholism, tuberculosis and neurasthenia, and his confession, in the 1930s, "that lack of success of physical sheer power in my life made trouble,"[12] it is somewhat ironic that he would appeal to Scottie on the grounds of their shared claim to familial "vitality." Yet "vitality" is precisely what distinguishes "the old American aristocracy"—or in Stoddard's terms, "the Nordic native American"—from "vermin," and it is the terms of this distinction that Fitzgerald means to emphasize in his letter.

Whether or not Fitzgerald means to emphasize this distinction in *The Great Gatsby* is another matter; beyond his presentation of Tom's ideas as not only hopeless but "pathetic" is the fact that Jay Gatsby is not identifiably Other—like the "modish Negroes" on the Queensboro Bridge or the Greek Michaelis—but simply "not quite white." Yet again, being "not quite" is perhaps Gatsby's most troubling aspect. Located in the liminal space between categories, the space of indeterminacy and *différance*, Gatsby consistently eludes the terms of both national and textual belonging, and it is these terms which, as Fitzgerald explains to his daughter, enable "distinctions" between self and other, white and non-white, American and un-American, to emerge with clarity. To this extent, finally, Gatsby is not only a mystery in the text, a signifier of indeterminacy and unrepresentability; he is also, quite simply, an obscene threat to the national "vitality" of which Tom Buchanan laments the loss, and which *The Great Gatsby* itself purports to celebrate in its final pages.

IV.

When, near the end of his story, Gatsby dies, the event is deemed a "holocaust"—a striking term given his possible link to Jewish origins—yet this is far from the last word that the text provides about the significance of Gatsby's life and death. There is another word closer to the end of the text that seems more nearly to serve as Gatsby's epitaph: an "obscene word, scrawled by some boy with a piece of brick" on the "white steps"of Gatsby's house—a word explicitly framed as a defilement of whiteness, as a mark of impurity.[13] "Jew" or "colored" or "alien" or "Other"—any or all of these terms might appear on Gatsby's steps; but what is perhaps most significant about Nick's reference to "the obscene word" is the illegibility of this word, its location outside or beyond the presentable, its "vanished" status. For it is fitting that the sum of Gatsby's "corruption," his obscurity and indeterminacy, might be expressed by a word that literally cannot be read.[14]

I have attempted, up to this point, to trace both ways in which the figure of Gatsby might be seen as a problem for the signifying project that bears his name. Drawing the reader toward "the place where meaning collapses," Gatsby's "unutterable visions," his evanescent dreams, and his "uncommunicable" presence all point to a narrative and linguistic void that is at odds with the counter effort by Nick and others to make Gatsby into the "governing" presence in the book, into a figure of significance. Moreover, Gatsby's racial indeterminacy, his troubling "off-whiteness," and his link to ethnic criminality further obscure the significance of this figure in a context in which racial difference is seen to be defining and of crucial importance to American identity. Thus it is not surprising that as Gatsby's story draws to a close what was once "provokingly elusive" would come to be figured as "obscene."

What *is* surprising is the way in which the novel finally ends: with Gatsby's obscenity erased as speedily from the text itself as it is from the front steps of his house. After Nick's act of erasure, Gatsby's elusiveness, corruption, and "off-whiteness" are forgotten; in the next moment, a moment in which "vanished trees" appear and the "whispers" of a lost continent become intelligible, a new vision of Gatsby's significance is revealed:

> [A]s the moon rose higher the inessential houses began to melt away until gradually I became aware of the old island here that flowered once for Dutch sailors' eyes—a fresh, green breast of the new world. Its vanished trees, the trees that had made way for Gatsby's house, had once pandered in whispers to the last and greatest of all human dreams; for a transitory enchanted moment man must have held his breath in the presence of this continent, compelled into an aesthetic contemplation he neither understood nor desired, face to face for the last time in history with something commensurate to his capacity for wonder.
>
> And as I sat there, brooding on the old unknown world, I thought of Gatsby's wonder when he first picked out the green light at the end of Daisy's dock. (Fitzgerald 1999, 140–41)

In these famous concluding lines, Nick creates an explicit analogy between the gaze of the Dutch colonists as they first catch sight of the "fresh, green breast of the new world," and Gatsby's vision of the green light at the end of Daisy's dock: Gatsby and the Dutch are joined in contemplative "wonder" as they come face to face with their objects of desire; both represent in their contemplation "the last and greatest of all human dreams." This linkage reverses Gatsby's trajectory toward unrepresentability and recasts his desire in terms of a transcendent national narrative; at this moment, the problem of Gatsby's "intrinsic likeness" disappears, for what Gatsby is "intrinsically 'like'" turns out to be nothing less than "America" itself. If nationalism, as Benedict Anderson writes, "always loom[s] out of an immemorial past and . . . glide[s] into a limitless future" (Bhabha 1990, 1), then the final lines of *Gatsby* establish "America" as eternal mode of human yearning, as a quest narrative that stretches across generations from the Dutch to Gatsby, and hence from the Dutch, to Gatsby, to "us" ("It eluded us then, but that's no matter—tomorrow we will run faster, stretch out our arms farther . . ."). To be sure, this passage is also haunted by another idea of America—an "old island" that precedes the transforming gaze of the colonists and that, like Myrtle's torn and bloody breast, seems momentarily to challenge and render ironic the final, transcendent vision of "the fresh, green breast of the new world." This "old" America, this lost America, reminds us again of Kristeva's notion of the abject: that which threatens meaning, especially in its association with the irreparable loss of the mother's body. Yet abject America is quickly glossed over. What matters here, finally, is the way age, violence, and obscenity—seemingly inevitably—give way before Gatsby's and the colonist's Dream.

But what is perhaps most significant about these concluding paragraphs is their investment not only in resignifying Gatsby but in refiguring the racialist overtones that previously haunted this indeterminacy. By situating Gatsby in a chain of likeness with the "Nordic" Dutch, the text effectively asserts Gatsby's ties to whiteness and "erases" his problematically off-white status, just as it refashions his "uncommunicable" presence as nationally significant. Inasmuch as this ending articulates a triumphalist nationalist credo, it does so in terms that ring with the ideology of nativism. The very figure who represented a threat to the boundaries of linguistic and national meaning is now revealed as the inheritor and guardian of Americanist values, as the natural descendent of the "Teutons, Anglo-Saxons + Celts." Gatsby's problem of being "not quite white" is finally dismissed as so much "foul dust float[ing] in the wake of his dreams" (Fitzgerald 1999, 6).

V.

Jay Gatsby, in other words, "turns out all right at the end"—as Nick Carraway had promised in the opening pages of the novel. This essay has questioned the necessity of that promise, noting the discrepancy between the novel's elegiac conclusion and the larger narrative in which Gatsby figures as troubling and suspect, as liminal and unknowable. Other critics have made similar note of Fitzgerald's desire in his conclusion to move beyond the indeterminate, skeptical, paranoid, and morally relativistic world he chronicles: Gatsby as a sign of his times and of the transcendence of his times. Jeffrey Louis Decker, for one, suggests that the resolution of the novel represents Fitzgerald's "anxious" eagerness to retain "the traditional narrative of virtuous ambitions" despite the bankruptcy of this narrative in a post-War, nativist American society: "In death Gatsby is freed from his venal partnership with immigrant gangsters and remembered within a lineage of northern European explorers," despite the fact that it is precisely Gatsby's connection to immigrant "indeterminacy" that has earlier distinguished him as a threat to Nordic ideology (1997, 78; 97).[15] Chris Fitter writes that the ending of *Gatsby* represents Fitzgerald's "misty melancholia" for a prelapsarian, precapitalist ideal that the text has, up to this point, worked hard to demystify (1998, 14). And Joyce A. Rowe succinctly captures the paradox that "Nick's epilogue . . . keeps alive the very form of that aspiration we have seen issuing in a wasteland of social and moral emptiness" (1988, 103).

As these critiques suggest, Gatsby's final transformation is far from inevitable, but rather "willed" by a Fitzgerald who, as his harshest critic Chris Fitter writes, ultimately prefers "tearful patriotic *frisson*" to any more critical or complex vision of contemporary American culture (1998, 14). Given Fitzgerald's own nativist and isolationist leanings in the 1920s, this assessment seems at least plausible: that *The Great Gatsby*, for all its demystification of American self-definition, might ultimately succumb to a "final reflex of conservative reaction" marked by an essentializing, dehistoricized vision of national belonging (19). Yet to my mind, it is also significant that Fitzgerald deliberately marks the process of this final transformation through Nick's erasure of the "obscene word" on Gatsby's front steps. By calling attention to Nick's act, Fitzgerald seems to be suggesting that the crucial turn in the text—Gatsby's apotheosis into the carrier of the American Dream—takes place by means of the same mechanism of "vanishing" that lies at the heart of his obscene indeterminacy. If the threat of Gatsby in the text lies precisely in the way in which he "vanishes" from categorization and social or racial signification, then Nick's erasure of the obscene word stages a similar process, making the obscene word "vanish" in order to cancel out the obscenity of vanishing. Gatsby is purified by this gesture, but the gesture itself reasserts the primacy of indeterminacy in the text. Put "under erasure" in the Derridean sense, Gatsby's obscenity becomes the absence that allows the text's ultimate presence to emerge: the presence of generations of Nordic American settlers, mythically united for a moment in Nick's transhistorical vision of national essence.

Ironically, the same play of absence and presence is evident in the only two other instances in the text of Fitzgerald's use of the word "obscene." The first use of the term occurs during the party at Myrtle's New York apartment, when in response to a question about her affection for her husband Myrtle lets out a "violent and obscene" answer: an answer that nevertheless remains unrepresented in the text (Fitzgerald 1999, 29). A similar but even more telling use of the term appears in a scene excised from the novel's final version, a scene in which Nick hears a comment Daisy makes to Gatsby at his party:

> "We're together here in your garden, Jay—your beautiful garden," broke out Daisy suddenly. "It doesn't seem possible, does it? I can't believe it's possible. Will you have somebody look up in the encyclopedia and see if it's really true. Look it up under G."
>
> For a moment I thought this was casual chatter—then I realized that she was trying to drown out from us, from herself, a particularly obscene conversation that four women were carrying on at a table just behind. (Fitzgerald 2000, 85)

Although Fitzgerald would delete this passage from *Gatsby*, it clearly prefigures the extant scene in the final version in which Nick erases "the obscene word" from the steps of Gatsby's house. As with the latter, Nick's reference here to "a particularly obscene conversation" is inextricably linked to the problem of Gatsby's signifying status. Daisy's effort to make sense of her present by making Gatsby legible and identifiable, by making him *signify* ("Look it up under G") is reinterpreted by Nick as an effort to repress, "to drown out from us, from herself, a particularly obscene conversation that four women were carrying on at table just behind." Gatsby "turns out all right" in this scene precisely because Nick and the reader cannot hear underneath Daisy's words the "obscene language" that has no place in this text—the language of drunken, sexually liberated women, of criminals, of the working classes, of immigrants and blacks—all threatening, as we have seen, to the elite white social order that both Nick and the Buchanans inhabit. Daisy's act of "whitewashing,"in short, represses Gatsby's link to the obscene in order to reveal him as someone socially significant and unquestionably white. Yet to drown out the obscene, in this instance or in the ultimate conclusion of *Gatsby*, is also, as Fitzgerald himself was well aware, to foreground the power of the obscene to disrupt and undo normative structures of social, national, and linguistic signification. "*We* have the vitality left," claims Fitzgerald to his daughter, but the anxious indeterminacy of his own novel seems to tell another story.

Barbara Will is associate professor of English at Dartmouth College. She is the author of *Gertrude Stein, Modernism, and the Problem of "Genius,"* and is currently at work on a book entitled *Unlikely Collaboration: Gertrude Stein, Bernard Faÿ, and the Vichy Dilemma.*

Notes

Permission to cite from the F. Scott Fitzgerald manuscript collection provided by Princeton University Library and the F. Scott Fitzgerald Literary Trust.

1. Undated note by F. Scott Fitzgerald. From the F. Scott Fitzgerald Archive, Special Collections, Princeton University Library.

2. Gatsby's vanishing during the encounter with Tom in Chapter IV precipitates one of the oddest structural shifts of the narrative, when Nick's narration suddenly gives way to the voice of Jordan Baker narrating the true story of Gatsby and Daisy's past. This is the only place in the novel in which the first-person narration is not controlled by Nick, and seems to impugn Nick's ability to keep his own subject in his sights. Jordan's momentary control over the text at the end of Chapter IV serves briefly to make Gatsby more intelligible, but her voice, no less than Nick's, fails ultimately to "correct" Nick's vision. Jordan remains "incurably dishonest" (Fitzgerald 1995, 63): a "hard, limited person" (84) with her own perceptual blindnesses, as she reveals in the end when she admits that she misread Nick's own honesty.

3. To be sure, the dash—the mark of graphic attenuation or of a "break" in dialogue or thought; the sign of signification in suspension or in the process of hemorrhaging into silence—is also the most prevalent stylistic mark in the text. "What was that word we—," Daisy asks (Fitzgerald 1999, 14), the dash performing stylistically what the question ponders. "I just meant—," George Wilson states (22), as his "voice faded off." Dashes appear throughout most of the narration and dialogue of the novel, as they do in Fitzgerald's writings in general; perhaps only Emily Dickinson, among American writers, is more liberal in her use of the dash (see Crumbley 1997). Yet in *The Great Gatsby*, it is Jay Gatsby who most often "speaks" in dashes: "It's the funniest thing, old sport," he remarks upon finally finding Daisy in his bedroom, "I can't—when I try to—" (72). "And she doesn't understand," he laments later about Daisy, "She used to be able to understand. We'd sit for hours—" (86). "'At least—' He fumbled with a series of beginnings. 'Why, I thought—why, look here, old sport'" (65). Gatsby's speech, as Nick himself notes, struggles awkwardly to mimic the "old euphemisms" of East Egg; his "old sport" and "Oxford man" represent a painstakingly studied insouciance that, according to Nick, "just missed being absurd" (40). Yet in the midst of Gatsby's effort to "certify" his social status in language, to lay claim to the terms of WASP social belonging, the repeated appearance of the dash reminds the reader of the attenuation or failure of Gatsby's effort. Like an obscene word, the dash could be said to work against "the presentable," marking textual moments of effacement, moments in which language simply fades into silence. The literal sign of his indeterminacy in the text, the dash emphasizes Gatsby's absence and presence; it is perhaps telling that Gatsby balances with a "formless grace" on the "dashboard" of his car as he greets Nick one morning (51).

4. In the text, Buchanan alludes carelessly to "'The Rise of the Coloured Empires' by this man Goddard"; according to Matthew Bruccoli, "Fitzgerald did not want to provide the correct title and author" (Fitzgerald 1995, 183). However, it is interesting to speculate about Buchanan's "mistake." "Goddard" may refer to screenwriter and playwright Charles William Goddard, mentioned by Bruccoli as a possible source for the

---

figure of Gatsby himself (see Bruccoli 1981, 184 n.). More likely, Fitzgerald may have been indirectly citing the work of Henry Herbert Goddard, author during the teens and twenties of works on mental deficiency, "the criminal imbecile," and school training of "defective" and "gifted" children. Goddard was a contributor to the same educational series as Lewis Terman, director of the Stanford/Binet IQ tests. Goddard's views on gifted and defective behavior bear a striking resemblance to Lothrop Stoddard's schema of racial types, as well as the latter's claim that the superior "Nordic" races were being actively threatened by a defective "tide" of non-white peoples.

5. Ironically, Tom makes a similar claim about Daisy when he hesitates to include her in his category of "Nordics" ("'This idea is that we're Nordics. I am and you are and you are and—' After an infinitesimal hesitation he included Daisy with a slight nod" [Fitzgerald 1999, 14]). As Michaels points out, whiteness, for Tom, operates through a rigid system of inclusion and exclusion, one threatened by ethnic difference and femininity alike; in order for the category to sustain itself it must exclude anyone who isn't "quite" identifiable.

6. For a discussion of Jewish assimilation in the United States during the first half of the twentieth century, see Brodkin (1998, esp. 103).

7. In a biographical search, "Gatz" appears to be both a Jewish and a Gentile name. As noted, "Gatz" also appears as a germanicized form of the Yiddish "Gets." Thus the reader of *Gatsby* is faced with the possibility that Henry Gatz, father of Jay Gatsby, may already be "passing" as Gentile and is thus much more of a significant prototype for his son's own self-transformation than has previously been acknowledged.

8. The layered complexity of Gatsby's name is consistent with other names in the text that emphasize masquerade and pretense: for example, Mrs. Chrystie, who accompanies Hubert Auerbach to Gatsby's party, "whose name, more than likely, suggests the famous Christie Minstrels of the early nineteenth century. Mrs. Chrystie masquerades as a wife, and while she wears the name of her husband, she pretends to be someone she is not" (Crim and Houston 1989, 83). There is also "the prince of something whom we called Duke" at Gatsby's party (Fitzgerald 1999, 51), as well as the novel *Simon Called Peter* that Myrtle Wilson keeps in her apartment (25). Most telling, for our purposes, is the name "Meyer Wolfshiem," whose odd spelling has rarely been noticed by readers (see Michaels [1995], above), but which represents a marked variant from the German "Wolfsheim." One could argue—as does Edmund Wilson when he "corrects" the text for his 1941 edition (see Bruccoli's "Introduction," Fitzgerald 1995, liv)—that Fitzgerald, a notoriously careless speller, was simply in error in his spelling of "Wolfshiem." However, one could also see this spelling as deliberately emphasizing the same ethnic uncertainty as the name "James Gatz." "Wolfshiem" is a name that sounds and looks "foreign" (and, in this context, "Jewish"), but it does not conform to a Germanic (or German-Jewish) origin. It is a name that troubles, that confuses; a name that masks rather than reveals identity.

9. Clinton Stoddard Burr quoted in Higham (1973, 273), whose work on American nativism offers the most sustained analysis to date of the social and ideological positions adopted by intellectuals of the 1920s.

10. Fitzgerald's youthful correspondence is filled with similar sentiments. In an un-

dated letter to Thomas Boyd, he writes, "All these 'marvellous' places like Majorca turn out to have some one enormous disadvantage—bugs, lepers, Jews, consumptives, or philistines" (F. Scott Fitzgerald Archive, Special Collections, Princeton University Library). For a discussion of how Fitzgerald's attitudes toward ethnic and racial difference changed over the course of his life, see Margolies (1997).

11. Undated note to Scottie from F. Scott Fitzgerald Archive, Special Collections, Princeton University Library. In a letter dated 17 November 1936, Fitzgerald further explicates this typology: "Park Avenue girls are hard, aren't they? Usually the daughters of 'up-and-coming' men and, in a way, the inevitable offspring of that type" (Fitzgerald 1965, 17).

12. Undated note from F. Scott Fitzgerald Archive, Special Collections, Princeton University Library.

13. Ironically, it is a form of whiteness that illuminates this obscenity: Nick first notices the word because it "stood out clearly in the moonlight" (Fitzgerald 1995, 188). Yet while the moon may make visible Gatsby's link to "off-white" obscenity, moonlight also serves the opposite purpose several lines later when it illuminates the "essential" vision of Gatsby and the Dutch explorers that lies underneath the "inessential houses" of Long Island Sound (189). In short, the moon, like the sun and other objects in the firmament—notably, the eyes of Dr. T. J. Eckleburg—is a force of both illumination and obscurity in this text.

14. It is interesting, in this context, to consider the striking parallels between this scene in *Gatsby* and a similar scene in J.D. Salinger's *The Catcher in the Rye*, where Holden Caulfield's fantasy of going West and becoming a deaf-mute, thus rendering himself both unintelligible and uncomprehending, is shattered when he sees an obscenity scrawled on the wall of his sister Phoebe's school. Unlike *Gatsby*, *Catcher* makes this obscenity both literal and visible—"Fuck you"—as if to mock Holden's fantasy of disappearance into indeterminacy. Moreover, *Catcher* emphasizes this shattering by repeatedly restaging Holden's encounter with the obscene word (in the stairwell, in the museum) until he finally is forced to acknowledge that "if I ever die, and they stick me in a cemetery, and I have a tombstone and all, it'll say 'Holden Caulfield' on it, and then what year I was born and what year I died, and then right under that it'll say 'Fuck you'" (1951, 264). Like *Gatsby*, however, the encounter with the obscene word in *Catcher* occurs at precisely the same moment in the text, preceding the novel's final scene of redemption and reconciliation between Holden and Phoebe. To this extent, both texts seem to be emphasizing the transitional necessity of a confrontation with the obscene in their efforts to assert a final, redemptive vision.

15. Michaels makes a related point, focusing on the bond between Tom and Nick that enables this lineage ultimately to emerge: "the differences the novel works to establish between Tom and Nick . . . are in the end—to use Gatsby's phrase—'just personal.' Ironizing Tom's Nordicism, Nick nevertheless extends it" (1995, 41). In its final celebration of a "Nordicist" worldview, Michaels writes, *The Great Gatsby* is "the most obvious example" of a new literary definition of "Americanism" in the 1920s: "Americanism would now be understood as something more than and different from the American citizenship that so many aliens had so easily achieved" (47).

Works Cited

Bakhtin, M. M. 1981. *The Dialogic Imagination*. Trans. Caryl Emerson and Michael Holquist. Austin: University of Texas Press.

Bhabha, Homi K. 1990. "Introduction: Narrating the Nation." In *Nation and Narration*, ed. Homi K. Bhabha. New York: Routledge.

Brodkin, Karen. 1998. *How Jews Became White Folks and What That Says About Race in America*. New York: Rutgers University Press.

Bruccoli, Matthew J. 1981. *Some Sort of Epic Grandeur: The Life of F. Scott Fitzgerald*. New York: Harcourt, Brace.

Caputi, Mary. 1994. *Voluptuous Yearnings: A Feminist Theory of the Obscene*. Lanham, Maryland: Rowman & Littlefield.

Crim, Lottie R., and Neal B. Houston. 1989. "The Catalogue of Names in *The Great Gatsby*." *Re: Arts and Letters* 21:1: 77–92.

Crumbley, Paul. 1997. *Inflections of the Pen: Dash and Voice in Emily Dickinson*. Lexington: University of Kentucky Press.

Decker, Jeffrey Louis. 1997. *Made in America: Self-Styled Success from Horatio Alger to Oprah Winfrey*. Minneapolis: University of Minnesota Press.

Derrida, Jacques. 1981. *Positions*. Trans. Alan Bass. Chicago: University of Chicago Press.

_____. 1994. *Specters of Marx: the State of the Debt, the Work of Mourning, and the New International*. Trans. Peggy Kamuf. New York: Routledge.

Fitter, Chris. 1998. "From the Dream to the Womb: Visionary Impulse and Political Ambivalence in *The Great Gatsby*." *Journal x* 3:1: 1–21.

Fitzgerald, F. Scott. 1965. *Letters to His Daughter*. New York: Scribner.

_____. 1994. *A Life in Letters*. Ed. Matthew J. Bruccoli. New York: Touchstone.

_____. 1995. *The Great Gatsby*. Ed. Matthew J. Bruccoli. 1925. Reprint. New York: Scribner.

_____. 1999. *The Great Gatsby*. Ed. Matthew J. Bruccoli. 1925. Reprint. New York: Cambridge University Press.

_____. 2000. *Trimalchio: An Early Version of The Great Gatsby*. Ed. James L. W. West III. Cambridge: Cambridge University Press.

Freud, Sigmund. 1957. "Jokes and the Unconscious." In *The Standard Edition of the Complete Psychological Works of Sigmund Freud*. Vol. viii, ed. James Strachey. 1905. Reprint. London: The Hogarth Press.

Higham, John. 1973. *Strangers in the Land: Patterns of American Nativism 1860–1925*. New York: Atheneum.

Kristeva, Julia. 1982. *Powers of Horror: An Essay on Abjection*. Trans. Leon S. Roudiez. New York: Columbia University Press.

Lyotard, Jean-François. 1992. *The Postmodern Explained*. Trans. Don Barry, Bernadette Maher, Julian Pefanis, Virginia Spate, and Morgan Thomas. Minneapolis: University of Minnesota Press.

Margolies, Alan. 1997. "The Maturing of F. Scott Fitzgerald." *Twentieth-Century Literature: A Scholarly and Critical Journal* 43:1 (Spring): 75–93.

Michaels, Walter Benn. 1995. *Our America: Nativism, Modernism, and Pluralism.* Durham: Duke University Press.

Rowe, Joyce A. 1988. *Equivocal Endings in Classic American Novels.* Cambridge: Cambridge University Press.

Salinger, J. D. 1951. *The Catcher in the Rye.* Boston: Little, Brown and Co.

Stoddard, Lothrop. 1920. *The Rising Tide of Color Against White World-Supremacy.* With an Introduction by Madison Grant. New York: Scribner's.

Trilling, Lionel. 1963. "F. Scott Fitzgerald." In *F. Scott Fitzgerald: A Collection of Critical Essays*, ed. Arthur Mizener. Englewood Cliffs, N.J.: Prentice-Hall.

Photography and *The Great Gatsby*_____

Lawrence Jay Dessner

The Great Gatsby repeatedly investigates how photography expresses and affects the ways its characters think. Fitzgerald's novel surveys and evaluates many uses of photography and borrows cinematic
techniques for Nick Carraway's narration. In that it is a mode of perception, photography carries implicit philosophic assumptions. Fitzgerald shows us that photography is not merely a means of entertainment, professional or domestic, and a method of documentation, but a
way people who are not self-conscious philosophers reinforce their assumptions about the nature of reality and time.

In its largest perspective, *The Great Gatsby* is a philosophic novel in
which philosophic questions underlie social, political, and psychological concerns. The novel has to do with the disparity between aspiration
and achievement, between the "Dutch sailors'" vision of a "fresh,
green . . . new world" (p. 121)[1] and Nick Carraway's stunned observations of contemporary American life. The "*Great*"-ness of Gatsby is
his remarkable and, in his context inspiring, innocence. He has drunk
deep at the springs of American popular ideology, got, directly or
through modulating transmissions, some of the assumptions that made
potent the legends of Hopalong Cassidy, Buffalo Bill Cody, Horatio
Alger, and the Benjamin Franklin of the *Autobiography*. He has become the quintessential American, the New World's version of the
landed aristocrat—and all through his adherence to the creed of the
self-made man. "The truth," Nick tells us, "was that Jay Gatsby . . .
sprang from his Platonic conception of himself. He was a son of God. . ."
(p. 65). The past, in the Utopian and absolute democracy of Gatsby's
vision, does not matter. History is to him what it was to Henry Ford
(himself an historical version of Fitzgerald's novel): "Bunk."

Photography, in its ability to freeze time—or to run it backwards—
may be a symbolic denial of history, a metaphor of transcendence. So
thoroughly has Gatsby absorbed the idea of freedom from the con-

straints of history, so vital and earnest is his hold on the paradox of the unmoved mover, that he transforms it from a motto into a myth of eternal return to a timeless Eden. Like Bounderby in Dickens's *Hard Times*, Gatsby comes to believe that the past which does not matter did not exist. The pasts he invents for himself are those which claim his purest allegiance, and Daisy's past, her years with Buchanan and the three-year-old toddling and unblinkable evidence and result of history's irreversible flow, are, miraculously, blinked. It is not enough for Daisy to renounce Tom, to wipe the slate clean; she must avow that the slate has never been sullied. Gatsby tells Tom that Daisy "'doesn't love you'" and later even claims that "'she's never loved you.'" Daisy can accept this obliteration of history through a rhetorical ploy: "'Why— how could I love him—possibly?'" But Gatsby wants more than rhetoric, he wants "the truth": "'It doesn't matter any more. Just tell him the truth—that you never loved him—and it's all wiped out forever.'" Here The Power of Positive Thinking is exalted into something more than a psychological method. Daisy knows that her suitor "'want[s] too much,'" that one "'can't help what's past,'" and when Buchanan comes to her aid with hints of particular events of their marital past, "the words seemed to bite physically into Gatsby" (pp. 87–88). Nick had warned his neighbor of that painful possibility: "'I wouldn't ask too much of her. . . . You can't repeat the past.'" To which Gatsby replies, "incredulously," "'Why of course you can!'" (p. 73). In Gatsby's world, things can always be as good as new again—and again. It is nostalgia propelled into a metaphysical principle. It becomes a version of the grand American joke of the used-car driven only by a little old lady, on Sundays, to the nearby church; and even what wear she does inflict on the mechanism, is discounted, not believed in. This mechanical immortality has an analogue in the imagined life made so convincingly real by the marvels of photography. Ageless, forever new, the photographic image incessantly implies that the life it captures is itself subject only to the desires and manipulations of the photographer. And with any "son of God," what the photographer sees is what is. The images he presents reinforce our desires to believe in the ultimate reality of what our needs prompt our imaginations to envisage. The characters in *The Great Gatsby* live in a world of photographic images, and have developed habits of mind, tacit philosophies of ideal existence. The novel itself is a treatment of the concept of time,[2] for it is time's incessant flow that forever separates dream from deed, aspiration from achievement.[3]

The years immediately following World War I were important ones for American photography. New technologies in photography could be turned to civilian use. The Kodak line of inexpensive roll-film cameras, introduced in 1890, improved by advances in chemistry and mechanics, became increasingly simple and sure. By 1920, several manufacturers were offering 16mm motion picture cameras for home use. The first Leica, introduced in 1924, boosted the new vogue for smaller and more versatile cameras which used the 35mm film designed for professional motion pictures. Practitioners and theorists of photographic art—among them Edward Steichen, Alfred Stieglitz, and Edward Weston—made what are now seen as crucial strides in the development of a fine art of photography.[4] The editor of *The American Annual of Photography* had good reason to preface his volume for 1924 with this boast: "Photography has at last reached a position where we can truthfully say it has a place in all our lives, whether we are actively engaged in it or not."[5] The omnipresence of photography in America is accurately portrayed in *The Great Gatsby* and is related to ways in which its characters react to their experience and think about their histories. Nick Carraway, too self-conscious and detached an intelligence to be caught up utterly in Gatsby's dream world, becomes a critic of his defiantly non-historic solipsism and of the habitual faith in the illusions of photography.

For all his protestations to the contrary, Gatsby is a true son of his father, the dismal Gatz from the dismal swamps of Minnesota. The father displays, in his grief, a mixture of awe and "pride," and as that pride increases, and as grief gives place to excitement, "with trembling fingers" he shows Nick a photograph of Gatsby's house, the very house in which they are both standing. Nick had known from the first that

Gatsby's imitation "Hôtel de Ville" lacked the patina and authenticity of age: it is "spanking new under a thin beard of raw ivy" (p. 4). That early assessment is hardly profound, but by the end of the novel, Nick, having fallen under the spell of Gatsby's dream, having found himself Gatsby's survivor and mourner, comes to see that the house, like all the houses that line the Sound, are "inessential" and "melt away gradually" (p. 121). Not the houses but the energies that imagined them are of the essence. The thinness and rawness of Gatsby's ivy is insignificant when one considers the grandeur of his belief, however grotesquely vulgarized, in the power of human aspiration and endeavor. West Egg is a grotesque version, but a version nonetheless of Tennyson's Camelot and of its mythical forebears: "[a] city . . . built / To music, therefore never built at all, / And therefore built for ever."[6] Mr. Gatz senses some of this. The photograph he proffers, showing the signs of much handling and folding, incorporates the essence of his son's dream; the house itself does not: "He pointed out every detail to me eagerly. 'Look there!' [he repeated], and then sought admiration from my eyes." Nick draws the point for us, and not without the sympathy which comes with understanding: "He had shown it so often that I think it was more real to him now than the house itself." Nick noticed that Gatz "seemed reluctant to put away the picture, held it for another minute, lingeringly, before my eyes." The mundane photograph of the great mansion, "cracked in the corners and dirty with many hands" (p. 115), is Gatz's Platonic idea of a house. It is, for him, the timeless, unchanging promise, a well-wrought urn on which the ideal life, stopped and frozen, is eternally lived. It is his version of eternity, of the immortality which is ours through our imaginative victories over time. Photography lends substance to that vision.

There is something ludicrous in the great philosophic weight which Gatz, and Fitzgerald, and now the present writer, assign to this snapshot. But then there is much ludicrous in Nick's admiration for Gatsby—perhaps "love" would not be too strong a word for it—and in Fitzgerald's single, direct valuation of the man: "*Great.*" The snapshot may bear its moral and philosophic weight more gracefully when we notice that the novel has prepared us to see its significance. Just as there are a number of minor automobile accidents before the climactic one which kills Myrtle, the last accident making explicit the meaning of the others, so are there many seemingly trivial references to photographs before this last one of which so much is being made and which is indeed the culmination and explication of the series.

Before turning to the specific references to photography in *The Great Gatsby*, it may be useful to glance at *The Romantic Egoists*,[7] a collection of Fitzgerald memorabilia. The oversize volume is largely an album of domestic photographs, some of them taken, mounted, labeled, and even listed by Scott and Zelda. They are, of course, black-and-white still photographs, utterly unpretentious, poorly lit and composed, and now, redolent of nostalgia. We see Scott at age four in as technically and aesthetically amateurish a photograph as one could imagine. If Henry C. Gatz had snapped his young James, it might have looked like this: a picture that only a parent could be expected to love. Later we have what appears to be Scott and his daughter,[8] both faces obscured in the shadows of their hat brims, posed before the large white columns of a large house. And before that same house we have Scott's "Last photo of father," so the picture is captioned, by hand, in its lower border. Here father and son have removed their hats; "father" holds his towards the lens in what might be taken as a gesture of farewell. *The Romantic Egoists* conveniently and repeatedly demonstrates the large part snapshots played in making and preserving the Fitzgerald family record, their personal pasts. One is tempted to insist that before the days of the Polaroid camera, of high-quality color and high-speed films, before the phenomenon of professional photographic equipment in millions of middle-class households and the explosion of interest in photography as Art, before our days of excellent photographs, in magazines, on television, on color slides, the homely snapshot of Fitzgerald's day, which is Gatsby's day too, mattered a good deal more than we are likely to immediately remember or imagine.

The technological photographic advance whose great impact on the American of the 1920's is well-remembered was the commercial motion picture. As a new business it made new money and new delegates to Gatsby's conventions of the *nouveaux riches*. Nick Carraway—while not the reader of motion-picture magazines that Myrtle Wilson is (p. 17), nor even sympathetic to Jordan Baker's resort to "the movies" in times of great heat and ominous ennui (p. 83)—after properly introducing himself and his situation to his reader, begins his narrative with this: "And so with the sunshine and the great bursts of leaves growing on the trees, just as things grow in fast movies, I had that familiar conviction that life was beginning over again with the summer" (p. 3). "Fast movies" are, no doubt, sequences of time-lapse photography, from rose bud to full flowering, from eggshell to hatched chick, in thirty seconds. The photographic *tour de force* conspires with that of the bursting leaves to press the wistful dream which, in a radically different key, is Gatsby's dream of "beginning over again." A variant on this photographic link with the novel's theme, and further evidence of Nick's familiarity with the techniques of photography and their philosophic tendencies, occurs in his description of Myrtle Wilson as she peers out over her garage apartment: "So engrossed was she that she had no consciousness of being observed, and one emotion after another crept into her face like objects into a slowly developing picture" (p. 83).[9] Photography by its distortion of time is a begetter and sustainer of illusion, but it is also a potential aid to truer seeing, to revelation.

This motif of photography's dual and contradictory possibilities is fleetingly suggested when Nick recalls that he "had seen her [Jordan Baker], or a picture of her, somewhere before" (p. 8). Discovering and coming to grips with the moral identity of Jordan Baker, her true "picture," illusion or revelation, will be part of Nick and the novel's business from now on. But it is with our introduction to Mr. Chester McKee, photographer *extraordinaire*, that the photographic motif comes front and center. Too ignorant to be a scoundrel, too absurdly ineffectual to be taken seriously, we remember him as does Nick as less a photographer than a photograph: "asleep on a chair with his fists clenched in his lap, like a photograph of a man of action" (p. 24). His devotion to the "artistic game" (p. 20), as he calls it, is less disturbing to Nick than the "spot of dried lather" (p. 24) which he wipes from the cheek of the sleeping figure. McKee is so fatuous, Nick's shocked response to him so comic, that we may fail to notice how tenuous is his relationship to the novel's tightly structured plot. McKee leaves the story at the end of Chapter Two and neither returns nor affects the unfolding of the story.

Unlike the generalized guests at Gatsby's parties, McKee is particularized, a character rather than a caricatured name or a briefly embodied joke. He is Myrtle's guest and thus a structural equivalent of Gatsby's party guests, but more important is McKee's function in establishing the photographic theme. The paradoxical nature of photography is noted in the double paradox of the sleeping man who looks like "a photograph of a man of action." Gatsby's dream of recapturing his past relationship with Daisy is prefigured and parodied by McKee's repeated attempts, since his marriage, to capture the ideal essence of his wife on photographic film: he "had photographed her a hundred and twenty-seven times since they had been married" (p. 20). Bungling artist that he is, harridan that *she* is, surely these explain his continued because presumably unsuccessful attempts. McKee's "over-enlarged" photograph of Mrs. Wilson's mother "hovered like an ectoplasm on the wall" and appeared to be "a hen sitting on a blurred rock," although "looked at from a distance . . . the hen resolved itself into a bonnet, and the countenance of a stout old lady beamed down into the room" (pp. 19–20). McKee has evidently overreached himself, sought to make more of his negative, and more of his neighbor's mother, than either could justify. His attempts at self-improvement and timeless idealization of the female through the camera's distorting potential wholly fail. Even without the benefit of McKee's artistry, Myrtle's sister Catherine, in her attempts to improve the countenance Nature gave her, has produced "a *blurred* air to her face" (p. 19, my emphasis). She too, having plucked and redrawn her eyebrows, finds only confusion in her distortion for aesthetic effect. As Myrtle's company, they are both under the influence of Doctor T. J. Eckleburg, that gigantic but sham purveyor of optical improvements.

The novel's social and historical context, the pathos of Gatsby's "factual imitation of some Hôtel de Ville in Normandy" (p. 4), is picked up by the ersatz French old-world elegance of Myrtle's furniture above which, in sole possession of her walls, Mrs. Wilson's mother broods: "The living-room was crowded to the doors with a set of tapestried furniture entirely too large for it, so that to move about was to stumble continually over scenes of ladies swinging in the gardens of Versailles" (p. 19). "Bleeding fluently" from the nose Tom Buchanan has just broken, Myrtle seeks to limit the damage to her pretensions by protecting the tapestried Versailles with, of all things, her copy of *Town Tattle* (p. 25).

Despite his ghastly surroundings, McKee the photographer is a Gatsby who has not "made it," although Buchanan's malicious suggestion that he produce a photograph formally titled "*George B. Wilson at the Gasoline Pump*" (p. 22) sounds a good deal like the sort of aesthetic realism on which successful photographic careers have in fact long been based. McKee has Gatsby's old faith in his chances—in the chances, in this America, for effort to be rewarded. All he needs is a chance: "'If Chester could only get you in that pose,'" Mrs. McKee whines. Her husband takes up her plaintive conditional mode: "'I'd like to. . . .'" "'All I ask is that they should give me a start'" (pp. 20–22). If only I could, if only he would, if only. This is a parodic version of Gatsby's old yearnings, of those dreams which, in their energetic innocence, in the "colossal vitality of his illusion" (p. 63), earned Carraway's fascinated admiration. McKee's aspirations, like his photographs, hardly seem promising, but who is to say that he will not meet his appropriate Dan Cody, his saving "gonnegtion" (p. 46).

Echoing over Chester McKee's self-pitying tale of his as yet unsatisfied dreams is Myrtle Wilson's blunt and bald statement of the spur to such aspirations: "'All I kept thinking about, over and over, was "You can't live forever; you can't live forever"'" (p. 24). Against time's inexorable flow, McKee props not only his mundane ambitions but his aesthetic achievement, his "great portfolio": "'Beauty and the Beast . . . Loneliness . . . Old Grocery Horse . . . Brook'n Bridge'" (p. 25). His "portfolio" is not made up of illicit bonds or of drugstores selling grain alcohol, but it is in its own way, as is Gatsby in his, "great." (Fitzgerald's detailed portrait of McKee tempts us to wonder if he was based on an historic original. Both the titles of McKee's photographs and their extremely soft focus are reminiscent of much of the aesthetic photography of the 1920's.[10] A common criticism from those, like Nick, who disparaged the new "Artistic Photography," was that its results were no more than "fuzzy, blurred pictures."[11])

McKee's photographs are still pictures of aesthetic provenance and so he is not, quite yet anyway, among those makers and sellers of commercial motion pictures who fill Gatsby's gardens. Not yet a fit companion for "Newton Orchid, who controlled Films Par Excellence [yet another Francophile], and Eckhaust and Clyde Cohen and Don S. Schwartze (the son) and Arthur McCarty, all connected with the movies in one way or another" (p. 40). We are to assume, although Nick does not say so, that these movie people owe their status and celebrity to their successful exploitation of the mass instincts for beauty, romance, escape, for a vision—however vulgarized—of perfection and permanence. It is ironic that the pictures that move may capture, hold clear and out of the flow of time, the infinite moments. And ironic also is that this paradox is presented not through any scene from a particular film, but in a prose description of a "moving-picture director and his Star": "They were still under the white-plum tree and their faces were touching except for a pale, thin ray of moonlight between. It occurred to me that he had been very slowly bending toward her all evening to attain this proximity, and even while I watched I saw him stoop one ultimate degree and kiss at her cheek" (p. 71). Nick has applied to these movie people the photographic conceit of the "fast movies" and the "slowly developing picture." The lovers are "still" but so posed and so seen that they suggest an almost infinite suspension of time, a supernally patient and gradual movement.

The Keatsian impulse runs deep in Carraway, and he is moved when he recognizes its manifestations. The imperceptible movement, the change that stands still is a staple of motion picture technique, accomplished by simple technical means: freeze-frame, slow motion, dissolve, fade, etc. Nick has an eye for these. He notes "the eyes of Doctor T. J. Eckleburg, which had just emerged, pale and enormous, from the dissolving night" (p. 107). He thinks of West Egg's "quality of distortion" as if it were "a night scene by El Greco" (p. 118), and, returning to the more modern distortions of photography, has the "inessential houses . . . melt away . . . gradually" (p. 121).

If time can be slowed, distorted, if even the illusion of that possibility can be glimpsed, then Gatsby's absurd insistence that you can "repeat the past" is less utterly absurd. Nick transfers the imagery of the "moving-picture director and his Star" to Gatsby's five-year movement from and then again toward Daisy's lips. He imagines Gatsby thinking that "if he could once return to a certain starting place and go over it all slowly," he could transcend his present confusion. Nick ghost-writes for Gatsby a wildly surrealistic version of his embrace with Daisy, in the old moonlight of Louisville: "His heart beat faster and faster as Daisy's white face came up to his own. He knew that when he kissed this girl . . . his mind would never romp again like the mind of God. So he waited, listening for a moment longer to the tuning-fork that had been struck upon a star. Then he kissed her. At his lips' touch she blossomed for him like a flower and the incarnation was complete" (pp. 73–74). Despite what he calls the "appalling sentimentality" of this telling of Gatsby's story, it reminds Nick "of something—an elusive rhythm, a fragment of lost words," that "uncommunicable forever" as they are, in fact the lost keys to his own lost innocence. Nick is deeply grateful for being inspired to even this elusive and fragmentary epiphany, and will soon acknowledge his debt to Gatsby in language which, in its uncharacteristic verve and diction, reveals something that Nick's propriety usually hides. It is a Gatsby from the right side of the tracks who tells the Gatz Gatsby, "'You're worth the whole damn bunch put together'" (p. 103).

Like his father, Gatsby counts on photographs to validate his problematic history: "'Here's another thing I always carry. A souvenir of Oxford days'" (p. 44). Even more convincing than the engraved medal from Montenegro, "it was a photograph of half a dozen young men in blazers loafing in an archway through which were visible a host of spires. There was Gatsby, looking a little, not much, younger—with a cricket bat in his hand" (p. 44). We expect Nick to respond in the manner of Owl Eyes: "'It's a bona-fide piece of printed matter. It fooled me. This fella's a regular Belasco'" (p. 30). But Nick is capable of deeper belief in the revelations of photography. He sees the picture, and is satisfied: "Then it was all true," he says. "All" in this context includes Gatsby's statement earlier in this conversation: "'I am the son of some wealthy people in the Middle West—all dead now. I was brought up in America but educated at Oxford, because all my ancestors have been educated there for many years. It is a family tradition'" (p. 43). Nick, as he recalls this scene, knows that Gatsby's statement is not true,[12] but the snapshot, at least for the moment, carries great conviction, has the power to suspend disbelief.

On display in Gatsby's room are two additional photographs, a "large" one of Dan Cody—"'He used to be my best friend years ago'" (p. 62)—and a smaller one of Gatsby looking about eighteen and dressed, as was Cody, in "yachting costume." When the paths of these two sailors intersected, James Gatz was reborn as Jay Gatsby. Like Myrtle Wilson who displays a photograph of her mother on her apartment wall, Gatsby exhibits his own "parents." Or if it is true that he "sprang from his Platonic conception of himself," the photographs are of his singular "parent" and his god-father *cum* midwife. The photographs record and preserve the essential myth, the rewriting of history. They can make visible truths which otherwise would be invisible and unknown, and they can present forceful evidence of propositions that are not true, not scientifically or historically true but true to the heart's desire and to its aspiring imagination.

The debate between these kinds of truth began long before the invention and development of photography, but that invention renewed and recast the question.[13] Fitzgerald's use of photography and photographic metaphors in *The Great Gatsby* is an advance over the decision of Delacroix in 1853: "Jusqu'ici, cet art à la machine ne nous a rendu qu'un détestable service: il nous gâte les chefs-d'oeuvre, sans nous satisfaire complètement."[14] The kinds of seeing and the kinds of truth seen and made newly see-able by the camera's new kind of eye can satisfy us completely, although they can also be, like McKee's works, meretricious and banal. In our century, photography does not compete with traditional arts so as to force fiction, or painting, to ape the photograph's needle-sharp accuracy and the completeness of its descriptive record. *The Great Gatsby* can be considered a work of social realism, but its prose style and narrative manner are very far removed from the typical nineteenth-century realists. Fitzgerald gives Nick a richly decorative, metaphoric and imaginative prose style. He has so assimilated photographic ways of seeing that he only rarely names the particular photographic techniques he is borrowing. Their distortions, particularly of time, are unobtrusive because of the large place photography has come to have in our visual consciousness. (One might say that Gatsby's insistence on repeating, even recapturing the past, is the morbidly exaggerated result of seeing too many movies.)

Nick's photographic sensibility can be illustrated from almost any page of the novel:

> He smiled understandingly—much more than understandingly. It was one of those rare smiles with a quality of eternal reassurance in it, that you may come across four or five times in life. It faced—or seemed to face—the whole external world for an instant, and then concentrated on *you* with an irresistible prejudice in your favor. . . . Precisely at that point it vanished— and I was looking at an elegant young roughneck, a year or two over thirty, whose elaborate formality of speech just missed being absurd. (p. 32)

Thackeray or Scott, or even Dickens, could not have written that, nor could their readers have read it in comfort. But the passage could be part of a screenplay. It directs, specifically, the cameraman and the film editor, and we, used to motion pictures, know how to read it and how to recreate the pictures in our minds.

The mind's eye, in another passage, moves with the silky, slow and carefully composed precision of an expert pan and dolly shot: "A wafer of a moon was shining over Gatsby's house, making the night fine as before, and surviving the laughter and the sound of his still glowing garden. A sudden emptiness seemed to flow now from the windows and the great doors, endowing with complete isolation the figure of the host, who stood on the porch, his hand up in a formal gesture of farewell" (p. 37). The naked human eye does not move at that stately pace, nor does it come to rest so imperceptibly and completely. But the eye behind the camera does.

Any photographic technician would know how to put the following kind of distorted time onto film. And none of us would misread it as childish fantasy or metaphysical jest:

> The only completely stationary object in the room was an enormous couch on which two young women were buoyed up as though upon an anchored balloon. They were both in white, and their dresses were rippling and fluttering as if they had just been blown back in after a short flight around the house. . . . Then there was a boom as Tom Buchanan shut the rear windows and the caught wind died out about the room, and the curtains and the rugs and the two young women ballooned slowly to the floor. (p. 6)

An extreme example of the imaginative liberties that photographic technology encourages in the prose writer, like Fitzgerald, is this startling scene of instantaneous change, a jump-cut:

Through the hall of the Buchanans' house blew a faint wind, carrying the sound of the telephone bell out to Gatsby and me as we waited at the door.

"The master's body!" roared the butler into the mouthpiece. "I'm sorry, madame, but we can't furnish it—it's far too hot to touch this noon!"

What he really said was: "Yes . . . Yes . . . I'll see." (p. 76)

One of the more memorable scenes in *The Great Gatsby*, and one Nick calls a "picture," is a distant cousin of the facetious art photograph, "*George B. Wilson at the Gasoline Pump*," a still picture of a mundane subject yet one which reveals, with great impact, a critical insight and the emotional jolt at the discovery of bitter knowledge:

Daisy and Tom were sitting opposite each other at the kitchen table, with a plate of cold fried chicken between them, and two bottles of ale. He was talking intently across the table at her, and in his earnestness his hand had fallen upon and covered her own. . . . They weren't happy, and neither of them had touched the chicken or the ale—and yet they weren't unhappy either. There was an unmistakable air of natural intimacy about the picture, and anybody would have said that they were conspiring together. (p. 97)

The passage could be said to be "Jamesian," comparable to corresponding tableaux in *The Ambassadors* and *The Portrait of a Lady*. The picture seals Gatsby's fate, and Nick's too: his doubts and his hopes are over now. "Jamesian" surely, but just as surely photographic.

Two years after the dismal aftermath of Gatsby's death, Nick remembers "only . . . an endless drill of police and photographers and newspaper men in and out of Gatsby's front door" (p. 109). He retreats to Gatsby's room, upstairs, to search for evidence of the existence of Gatsby's parents, and finds "nothing—only the picture of Dan Cody, a token of forgotten violence, staring down from the wall" (p. 110). Nobody came to the funeral, not even, for Nick's sake, Jordan Baker. There remains one last obligation for Nick, who wants "to leave things in order and not just trust that obliging and indifferent sea to sweep my refuse away" (p. 118). His affair with Jordan is over. He thought he had first seen her in a "picture" (p. 8), a photograph on the sports or social page, but he has come to know her and the moral carelessness of her world. He finds her, here at the end, "dressed to play golf, and I remember thinking she looked like a good illustration, her chin raised a little jauntily, her hair the color of an autumn leaf, her face the same brown tint as the fingerless glove on her knee" (p. 119). The decisive judgment is made before the description of her person and dress: "She looked like a good illustration." For Nick, who knows the potential power of photography, its ways of distorting time in the service of the timeless, who has seen Henry Gatz hold with "trembling fingers," a photograph of a house, and who has come to know the part photographs played in Gatsby's dream-life—to look like an "illustration," however "good," is to fall far short of "Great."

From *Essays in Literature* 6, no. 1 (Spring 1979): 79-89. Copyright © 1979 by Western Illinois University Press. Reprinted by permission of Western Illinois University Press.

Notes

1. F. Scott Fitzgerald, *The Great Gatsby* (New York: Scribner's, [1974]). This is the latest printing of the Scribner Library paperback. It may be distinguished from earlier but still available printings by its length, 121 pages. All subsequent references will be included in the text.

2. This is the emphasis of R. W. Stallman, "Gatsby and the Hole in Time," *Modern Fiction Studies*, 4 (1955), 2–16, and an important aspect of Richard Lehan's reading in *F. Scott Fitzgerald and the Craft of Fiction* (Carbondale: Southern Illinois Univ. Press, 1966), pp. 91–122.

3. This line of interpretation is commonplace today, but early reviewers would have found it as misguided as we now find them. Many superficial appraisals can be seen in Jackson R. Bryer, *The Critical Reputation of F. Scott Fitzgerald: A Bibliographical Study* (Hamden, Conn.: Archon, 1967).

4. The information in this paragraph was derived from "Photography," and "Photographic Art," *Encyclopaedia Britannica*, 1967.

5. Percy Y. Howe, "Preface," *The American Annual of Photography*, 1924, p. 3.

6. *Idylls of the King*, "Gareth and Lynette," ll. 272–74.

7. *The Romantic Egoists*, ed. Matthew J. Bruccoli, Scottie Fitzgerald Smith, and Joan P. Kerr (New York: Scribner's, 1974). See pp. 117, 9.

8. Ibid., p. 165, labeled "March 1929."

9. Stallman, p. 13, refers to this scene as one of the few places in which "the rushing time-flow of the novel gets arrested." He writes of McKee's photography as a "fixing [of] space," p. 10.

10. I have based this generalization on the evidence of the many photographs reproduced in *The American Annual of Photography* from 1920 to 1927. *The Annual* claims that their coverage is broadly representative.

11. Edna Osborne Whitcomb, "Artistic Photography," *The American Annual of Photography*, 1924, p. 172.

12. Nick later says that Gatsby "never told me definitely that his parents were dead" (p. 110). I take this as a lapse on the author's part.

13. For an admirable, brief treatment of this, see Carl Woodring, "Nature and Art in the Nineteenth Century," *PMLA*, 2 (1977), 196–99.

14. Quoted by Woodring, p. 196, from Delacroix's *Journal*, ed. Andree Joubin (Paris: Plon, 1932), II, 59. I translate: "Up to now, this mechanical art has done us only wretched service; it spoils masterpieces for us without satisfying us completely."

Color-Symbolism in *The Great Gatsby*_____

Daniel J. Schneider

The vitality and beauty of F. Scott Fitzgerald's writing are perhaps nowhere more strikingly exhibited than in his handling of the color-symbols in *The Great Gatsby*. We are all familiar with "the green light" at the end of Daisy's dock—that symbol of the "orgiastic future," the limitless promise of the dream Gatsby pursues to its inevitably tragic end; familiar, too, with the ubiquitous yellow—symbol of the money, the crass materialism that corrupts the dream and ultimately destroys it. What apparently has escaped the notice of most readers, however, is both the range of the color-symbols and their complex operation in rendering, at every stage of the action, the central conflict of the work. This article attempts to lay bare the full pattern.

The central conflict of *The Great Gatsby*, announced by Nick in the fourth paragraph of the book, is the conflict between Gatsby's dream and the sordid reality—the foul dust which floats "in the wake of his dreams." Gatsby, Nick tells us, "turned out all right in the end"; the dreamer remains as pure, as inviolable, at bottom, as his dream of a greatness, an attainment "commensurate to [man's] capacity for wonder." What does *not* turn out all right at the end is of course the reality: Gatsby is slain, the enchanted universe is exposed as a world of wholesale corruption and predatory violence, and Nick returns to the Midwest in disgust. As we shall see, the color-symbols render, with a close and delicate discrimination, both the dream and the reality—and these both in their separateness and in their tragic intermingling.

Now the most obvious representation, by means of color, of the novel's basic conflict is the pattern of contrasting lights and darks. Gatsby, Nick tells us, is "like an ecstatic patron of recurrent light." His imagination has created a "universe of ineffable gaudiness," of "a vast, vulgar, and, meretricious beauty"—a world of such stirring vividness that it may be represented now by all the colors of the rainbow (Gatsby's shirts are appropriately "coral and apple-green and lavender and faint orange, with monograms of Indian blue"), now simply by light itself, by glitter, by flash. In his innocence, Gatsby of course sees only the pure light of the grail which he has "committed himself" to follow. The reader, however, sees a great deal more: sees, for example, the grotesque "valley of ashes," "the gray land and the spasms of bleak dust which drift endlessly over it"—the sordid reality lying beneath the fictions of the American dream of limitless Opportunity and Achievement.

If for a time "the whole front" of Gatsby's mansion "catches the light," if the house, "blazing with light" at two o'clock in the morning, "looks like the World's Fair," the reader understands why it comes to be filled with an inexplicable amount of dust everywhere and why "the white steps" are sullied by "an obscene word, scrawled by some boy with a piece of brick." Fair and foul is the intermingling of dream and reality; as Nick observes in Chapter VIII, there is a "gray-turning, gold-turning light" in the mansion, and the moral problem for the young Mid-westerner is to prevent himself from mistaking the glittering appearance for the true state of things.

The light-dark symbolism is employed with great care. It is not accidental, for example, that Daisy and Jordan, when they are introduced to the reader in the first scene of the novel, are dressed in white. In this scene, in which almost all of the color symbols are born, Nick tells us that "the only completely stationary object in the room was an enormous couch on which two young women were buoyed up as though upon an anchored balloon. They were both in white, and their dresses were rippling and fluttering as if they had just been blown back in after a short flight around the house."

White traditionally symbolizes purity, and there is no doubt that Fitzgerald wants to underscore the ironic disparity between the ostensible purity of Daisy and Jordan and their actual corruption. But Fitzgerald is not content with this obvious and facile symbolism. White, in this early appearance in the novel, is strongly associated with airiness, buoyancy, levitation. One is reminded of the statement in Chapter VI that for Gatsby "the rock of the world was founded securely on a fairy's wing." Daisy and Jordan seem about to float off into the air because they are—to both Gatsby and Nick—a bit unreal, like fairies (Daisy's maiden name is Fay); and they are in white because, as we learn in Chapter VII, to wear white is to be "an absolute little dream":

> [Daisy's] face bent into the single wrinkle of the small white neck. "You dream, you. You absolute little dream."
> "Yes," admitted the child calmly. "Aunt Jordan's got on a white dress too."

The white Daisy embodies the vision which Gatsby (who, like Lord Jim, usually wears white suits) seeks to embrace—but which Nick, who discovers the corrupt admixture of dream and reality, rejects in rejecting Jordan. For, except in Gatsby's extravagant imagination, the white does not exist pure: it is invariably stained by the money, the yellow. Daisy is the white flower—with the golden center. If in her virginal beauty she "dressed in white, and had a little white roadster," she is, Nick realizes, "high in a white palace the king's daughter, the golden girl." Her voice is "like money"; she carries a "little gold pencil"; when she visits Gatsby there are "two rows of brass buttons on her dress."

As for the "incurably dishonest" Jordan, she displays a "slender golden arm" and "a golden shoulder"; her fingers are "powdered white over their tan"; the lamp-light shines "bright on . . . the autumn-leaf yellow of her hair." When she enters the hotel with Daisy, both are wearing "small tight hats of metallic cloth"; and when Nick sees them both lying on the couch a second time, they are "like silver idols weighing down their own white dresses against the singing breeze of the fans"—the silver, of course, symbolizing both the dream and the reality, since as the color of the romantic stars and the moon (the first time we observe Gatsby he is gazing up at the "silver pepper of the stars") it is clearly associated with the romantic hope and promise that govern Gatsby's life, and as the color of money it is obviously a symbol of corrupt materialism.

Both Jordan and Daisy are enchanting—but false. And Nick's attitude toward them is identical with his attitude toward life in the East. In the apartment in New York with Tom and Myrtle, he tells us that he is like the "casual watcher in the darkening streets" looking up and wondering" at "our line of yellow windows" in the "long white cake of apartment-houses": "I was within and without, simultaneously enchanted and repelled by the inexhaustible variety of life." Viewed from "without," the windows glow with all the beauty and potency of the Dream; but "within" the apartment, Nick observes only greed, irresponsibility, conspicuous waste: he recognizes that the glow of the windows is that of money, not of enchantment. If, like Gatsby, he has tasted "the incomparable milk of wonder," he discovers that the milk will presently sour: turn yellow.

These conjunctions of white in contexts exhibiting the contrast between the dream and the reality are so numerous that most readers are likely to perceive the symbolic functioning of the colors. The symbolism of blue and red is less obvious.

The first striking reference to blue occurs at the beginning of Chapter II, where Fitzgerald describes the eyes of Doctor T. J. Eckleburg peering out over the Valley of Ashes, "*above* the gray land and the spasms of bleak dust." (italics mine)

> The eyes of Doctor T. J. Eckleburg are blue and gigantic—their retinas are one yard high. They look out of no face, but, instead, from a pair of enormous yellow spectacles which pass over a non-existent nose.

When, later in the novel, Wilson, staring at these same eyes, says, "God sees everything," and Michaelis contradicts him, "That's an advertisement," it is clear that Fitzgerald wants us to view T. J. Eckleburg as a symbol of the corruption of spirit in the Waste Land—as if even God has been violated by materialism and hucksterism—reduced to an advertisement. This might suggest that blue symbolizes a certain ideality; but the meaning of the symbol is not defined until we reach Chapter III, which begins: "There was music from my neighbor's house through the summer nights. In his blue gardens men and women came and went like moths among the whisperings and the champagne and the stars."

The romantic blue is obviously associated with the promise, the dream, that Gatsby has mistaken for reality. Fitzgerald is even more explicit in Chapter VII: "Our eyes lifted over the rose-beds and the hot lawn and the weedy refuse of the dog-days along shore. Slowly the white wings of the boat moved against the blue cool limit of the sky. Ahead lay the scalloped ocean and the abounding blessed isles."

Here blue and white become the symbols of the ultimate bliss, the ideal perfection which Gatsby's parties in the blue gardens seem to promise. If, later on when the parties are over, it is necessary to repair "the ravages of the night before"; if the "five crates of oranges and lemons" that arrive every Friday, leave the back door "in a pyramid of pulpless halves"; if the parties degenerate into ugliness and violence and "a sudden emptiness" falls upon the house—that is, after all, no more than we have already learned to expect: the white and the blue of the dream are inevitably sullied by the yellow. So T. J. Eckleburg's blue eyes are surrounded by yellow spectacles; so the music in the blue gardens is "yellow cocktail music"; so the chauffeur in a uniform of "robin's-egg-blue" turns out to be "one of Wolfsheim's protégés." Gatsby begins his ascent toward Greatness when Dan Cody takes the young man to Duluth and buys him "a blue coat, six pairs of white duck trousers, and a yachting cap." But on the day of his death his clothes change color symbolically—as we shall see after examining the symbolism of red.

The first striking reference to red occurs in Chapter I, where Nick tells us that he "bought a dozen volumes on banking and credit and investment securities, and they stood on my shelf in red and gold like new money from the mint, promising to unfold the shining secrets that Midas and Morgan and Maecenas knew." It is possible that Fitzgerald's choice of red in this context is arbitrary, but a study of the many appearances of the color in the novel, and especially of its appearances in conjunction with yellow and white, suggests strongly that red should be interpreted not merely as image but as symbol. In fact it has, I believe, the same signification as yellow: that is, it may represent either the "ineffable gaudiness" of the dream or the ugliness of the reality.

It stands for the dream because it is one of the glittering colors of Gatsby's romantic universe. We remember that Gatsby describes himself as a collector of jewels, "chiefly rubies," and in Chapter VI Nick remarks ironically: "I saw him opening a chest of rubies to ease, with their crimson-lighted depths, the gnawings of his broken heart." Gatsby's bedazzlement by the crimson rubies is matched by the awed Nick's wonder at what is to him, at the beginning of the novel, the *almost* enchanted world of the Buchanans. Entering this world of the rich, Nick is dazzled by the glowing light, the reds, and the rosiness: he walks "through a high hallway into a bright rosy-colored space"; there is "a rosy-colored porch, open toward the sunset, where four candles flickered on the table in the diminished wind"; the French windows are "glowing . . . with reflected gold"; there is "a half acre of deep, pungent roses"; later on, "the crimson room bloomed with light," and on his way home he observes how "new red gas-pumps sat out in pools of light."

Red, in these passages, is glitter, is enchantment, is dream; but there is another and a more interesting reason for the frequent occurrence of the color. As the color of blood, it is inevitably associated with the violence caused by the human animals who prey upon Gatsby—not merely the Hornbeams and the Blackbucks and Beavers and Ferrets and Wolfsheims, but also the respectable Tom and Daisy, the "careless people" who "smashed up things and creatures and then retreated back into their money or their vast carelessness . . . and let other people clean up the mess they had made." Thus Tom breaks Myrtle's nose and there are "bloody towels upon the bathroom floor." (He is also involved in an accident in which "the girl who was with him," a hotel chambermaid, has her arm broken.) Daisy runs down Myrtle, whose "thick dark blood" mingles with the dust of the Valley of Ashes—the foul dust which floats in the wake of Gatsby's dreams. And Wilson murders Gatsby, whose blood leaves "a thin red circle in the water." The beautiful reds become the color of carnage, and, as Nick tells us, perhaps even Gatsby, discovering the truth about Daisy, would find "what a grotesque thing a rose is."

On the hypothesis that red symbolizes the violent reality as well as the glittering dream, it is not surprising to find that just as yellow is inextricably joined to white, so red is wedded to both white and yellow, to reveal, simultaneously, both the dreamlike enchantment and the actual brutality. Thus it is appropriate that the Buchanans' house is a "cheerful red-and-white Georgian Colonial mansion"; and (though I may be guilty of forcing the symbolism here) I find it significant that Gatsby, when he enters the Buchanan house for the first time, "stood in the center of the crimson carpet and gazed around him with fascinated eyes. Daisy watched him and laughed, her sweet, exciting laugh; a tiny gust of powder rose from her bosom into the air."

Equally appropriate is the fact that Myrtle's sister, one of the careless people who attend Gatsby's parties and who ironically share in the dream, is a "slender worldly girl of about thirty, with a solid, sticky bob of red hair and a complexion powdered milky white." And the red and gold of Nick's dozen books appear again at one of Gatsby's parties—those strange tributes to the Dream which end always in violence—where "one of the girls in yellow was playing the piano, and beside her stood a tall, red-haired young lady from a famous chorus, engaged in song"; the violence occurs only moments later when Nick discovers, in a ditch beside the road, a new coupé shorn of one wheel.

So much for the basic color-symbols, the four primaries. But since, as we have already seen, one of Fitzgerald's techniques is to call attention to the conjunctions of his colors, that tragic and pervasive mingling of dream and reality, we are not surprised to find the writer refining his palette so as to exhibit, in a single word, the wedding of the pure and the corrupt. White and red, for example, may blend to produce pink, the color of the dream stained by violence—or, again, (a simpler interpretation) one of the colors of Gatsby's adolescent universe. In Chapter V, when Daisy excitedly summons Gatsby to observe "a pink and golden billow of foamy clouds above the sea," the pink is obviously part of the picture-postcard Fairyland; but when, after Myrtle's death, Nick, visiting Gatsby in the mansion which contains the "inexplicable amount of dust," sees the dreamer no longer in his customary white but in pink—"His gorgeous pink rag of a suit made a bright spot of color against the white steps"—the suit would seem to be not merely gaudy but blood-stained. Gatsby remains incorruptible, but his house and his clothes reveal the sordidness of the reality. Similarly, in the charged context of events following the murder, it is scarcely surprising to observe, with Nick, the "pink glow from Daisy's room on the second floor" of the Buchanans' house—the glow of enchantment and of blood, of princess and murderess.

Another blending of the primaries is exhibited in Gatsby's car: "I'd seen it. Everybody had seen it. It was a rich cream color, bright with nickel, swollen here and there in its monstrous length with triumphant hat-boxes and supper-boxes and tool boxes, and terraced with a labyrinth of wind-shields that mirrored a dozen suns. . . . With fenders spread like wings we scattered light through half Astoria. . . ."

The glitter of the car is exactly that of the white palaces of East Egg glittering along the water, and like the dresses of Jordan and Daisy, the car possesses a buoyancy, a penchant for levitation. But the white and the shine of the dream fuse inevitably with the yellow of materialism: the car is "a rich cream color." It is only much later, after the slaughter of Myrtle, when the limousine is described as "the death car," that the color of the dream disappears. "It was a yellow car," a witness reports. For the dream is dead, and Daisy's self-seeking has given its unmistakable color to Gatsby's colossal vision.

A similar change of color occurs in the scene in which Nick accompanies Tom and Myrtle to the apartment in New York. Arriving in New York, Myrtle wears a dress of brown muslin—the brown being, of course, a color from the valley of ashes, where among other things one finds "hard brown beetles . . . thudding against the dull light." But when she reaches the apartment she changes into a "dress of cream-colored chiffon, which gave out a continual rustle as she swept about the room." Nick observes that "with the influence of the dress her personality had also undergone a change. The intense vitality that had been so remarkable in the garage was converted into impressive hauteur." She is transformed into the money-stained dream-girl, the Daisy or the Jordan, "high in a white palace, the king's daughter, the golden girl. . . ."

There is, finally, the green light at the end of Daisy's dock, that symbol which Fitzgerald explicitly identifies with "the orgiastic future that year by year recedes before us." Being green, the light summons Gatsby and his fellow Americans to Go Ahead—to "run faster, stretch out our arms farther. . . ." Yet the covert symbolism of the light should by this time be clear: green, as the mixture of yellow and blue, is once again the tragic commingling of dream and reality. Gatsby, seeking the blue, is blind to the sordid yellow. For him the money does not matter, does not exist; it is finally only the white color imagery or the blue color imagery that enchants him. But it is in the pursuit of an adulterated grail that he is destroyed.

First published in *University Review* (now *New Letters*) 31, no. 1, autumn 1964. It is included here with the permission of *New Letters* and the curators of the University of Missouri-Kansas City.

"Herstory" and Daisy Buchanan

Leland S. Person, Jr.

Few critics write about *The Great Gatsby* without discussing Daisy Fay Buchanan; and few, it seems, write about Daisy without entering the unofficial competition of maligning her character. Marius Bewley, for example, refers to Daisy's "vicious emptiness" and her "monstrous moral indifference." To Robert Ornstein she is "criminally amoral," and Alfred Kazin judges her "vulgar and inhuman." Finally, Leslie Fiedler sees Daisy as a "Dark Destroyer," a purveyor of "corruption and death," and the "first notable anti-virgin of our fiction, the proto-type of the blasphemous portraits of the Fair Goddess as bitch in which our twentieth-century fiction abounds."[1] A striking similarity in these negative views of Daisy is their attribution to her of tremendous power over Gatsby and his fate. Equating Daisy with the kind of Circean figures popular in the nineteenth century, the critics tend to accept Gatsby as an essential innocent who "turn[s] out all right at the end."[2] Daisy, on the other hand, becomes the essence of "what preyed on" Gatsby, a part of that "foul dust [that] floated in the wake of his dreams" (p. 2).

Such an easy polarization of characters into Good Boy/Bad Girl, however, arises from a kind of critical double standard and simply belittles the complexity of the novel. Daisy, in fact, is more victim than victimizer: she is victim first of Tom Buchanan's "cruel" power, but then of Gatsby's increasingly depersonalized vision of her. She becomes the unwitting "grail" (p. 149) in Gatsby's adolescent quest to remain ever-faithful to his seventeen-year-old conception of self (p. 99), and even Nick admits that Daisy "tumbled short of his dreams—not through her own fault, but because of the colossal vitality of his illusion. It had gone beyond her, beyond everything" (p. 97). Thus, Daisy's reputed failure of Gatsby is inevitable; no woman, no human being, could ever approximate the platonic ideal he has invented. If she is corrupt by the end of the novel and part of a "conspiratorial" (p. 146) coterie with Tom, that corruption is not so much inherent in her character as it is the progressive result of her treatment by the other characters.

In addition to being a symbol of Gatsby's illusions, Daisy has her own story, her own spokesman in Jordan Baker, even her own dream. Nick, for example, senses a similar "romantic readiness" in Daisy as in Gatsby, and during the famous scene in Gatsby's mansion, Daisy herself expresses the same desire to escape the temporal world. "'I'd like to just get one of those pink clouds,'" she tells Gatsby, "'and put you in it and push you around'" (p. 95). If Daisy fails to measure up to Gatsby's fantasy, therefore, he for his part clearly fails to measure up to hers. At the same time that she exists as the ideal object of Gatsby's quest, in other words, Daisy becomes his female double. She is both anima and Doppelgänger, and *The Great Gatsby* is finally the story of the failure of a mutual dream. The novel describes the death of a romantic vision of America and embodies that theme in the accelerated dissociation—the mutual alienation —of men and women before the materialistic values of modern society. Rather than rewriting the novel according to contemporary desires, such a reading of Daisy's role merely adds a complementary dimension to our understanding and appreciation of a classic American novel.

A persistent problem for the contemporary critic of *The Great Gatsby* is the reliability of Nick Carraway as narrator, and certainly any effort to revise current opinion of Daisy's role must begin with Nick. Without rehearsing that familiar argument in detail, we can safely suggest that Nick's judgment of Daisy (like his judgment of Gatsby) proceeds from the same desire to have his broken world "in uniform and at a sort of moral attention forever" (p. 2). Returning to a Middle West which has remained as pure as the driven snow he remembers from his college days, Nick flees an Eastern landscape and a cast of characters which have become irrevocably "distorted beyond [his] eyes' power of correction" (p. 178). Life, he concludes, is "more successfully looked at from a single window, after all" (p. 4), and the same tendency to avoid the complexity of experience becomes evident in Nick's relationship to women.[3]

While he is far more circumspect and pragmatic than Gatsby, in his own way Nick maintains a similarly fabulous (and safely distanced) relation to women. In effect, he represents another version of that persistent impulse among Fitzgerald's early protagonists (e.g., Amory Blaine, Anthony Patch, Dexter Green, Merlin Grainger of "O Russet Witch!") to abstract women into objects of selfish wish-fulfillment.[4] Nick, after all, has moved East at least in part to escape a "tangle back home" involving a girl from Minnesota to whom he is supposedly engaged (p. 59). And in New York he has had a "short affair" with a girl in the bond office but has "let it blow quietly away" because her brother threw him "mean looks" (p. 57). In both cases Nick seems desperate to escape the consequences of his actions; he prefers unentangled relationships. Indeed, he seems to prefer a fantasy life with Jordan and even with nameless girls he sees on the streets of New York. "I liked to walk up Fifth Avenue," he admits, "and pick out romantic women from the crowd and imagine that in a few minutes I was going to enter into their lives, and no one would ever know or disapprove. Sometimes, in my mind, I followed them to their apartments on the corners of hidden streets, and they turned and smiled back at me before they faded through a door into warm darkness" (p. 57).[5] Even with Jordan, Nick manifests the sort of attraction to uncomplicated little girls that will seem almost pathological in Dick Diver of *Tender Is the Night*. Jordan, he enjoys thinking, rests childlike "just within the circle of [his arm" (p. 81), and because he has no "girl whose disembodied face floated along the dark cornices and blinding signs" (p. 81), Nick tightens his grip on Jordan, trying to make of her what Gatsby has made of Daisy.

Despite the tendency of critics to view her as a "monster of bitchery,"[6] Daisy has her own complex story, her own desires and needs. "'I'm p-paralyzed with happiness'" (p. 9), she says to Nick when he meets her for the first time, and even though there is a certain insincerity in her manner, Daisy's words do perfectly express the quality of her present life. In choosing Tom Buchanan over the absent Gatsby, Daisy has allowed her life to be shaped forever by the crude force of Tom's money. According to Nick's hypothesis, "all the time [Gatsby was overseas] something within her was crying for a decision. She wanted her life shaped now, immediately—and the decision must be made by some force—of love, of money, of unquestionable practicality—that was close at hand" (p. 151). Yet Daisy discovers as early as her honeymoon that Tom's world is hopelessly corrupt; in fact, Daisy's lyric energy (which so attracts Gatsby) must be frozen before she will marry Buchanan.

In a scene which has attracted remarkably little critical attention, Jordan tells Nick of Daisy's relationship with Gatsby in Louisville and of her marriage to Tom. Despite the $350,000-dollar string of pearls around her neck, when Daisy receives a letter from Gatsby the night before the wedding, she is ready to call the whole thing off. Gatsby's appeal far surpasses Tom's, and the pearls quickly end up in the wastebasket. The important point to recognize is that Gatsby is as much an ideal to Daisy as she is to him. Only Gatsby looks at her—creates her, makes her come to herself—"in a way that every young girl wants to be looked at some time" (p. 76). Thus, it is only after she is forced into an ice-cold bath and the letter which she clutches has crumbled "like snow" that Daisy can marry Tom "without so much as a shiver" (pp. 77, 78). She has been baptized in ice, and with her romantic impulses effectively frozen, Daisy Fay becomes "paralyzed" with conventional happiness as Mrs. Tom Buchanan. Her present ideal, transmitted to her daughter, is to be a "beautiful little fool" because that is the "best thing a girl can be in this world" (p. 17).

Although Fitzgerald certainly depicts Daisy as a traditionally mysterious source of inspiration, even here he dramatizes the limitations of the male imagination at least as much as Daisy's failure to live up to Gatsby's ideal. Gatsby's world is founded on a fairy's wing (p. 100), and as the discrepancy between the real Daisy and Gatsby's dream image becomes apparent, Nick observes, Gatsby's count of "enchanted objects" is diminished by one (p. 94). In effect, Gatsby scarcely apprehended or loved the real Daisy; she was always an "enchanted object": initially as the "first 'nice' girl he had ever known" (p. 148), and then as the Golden Girl, "gleaming like silver, safe and proud above the hot struggles of the poor" (p. 150). The essence of Daisy's promise, of course, is best represented by the magical properties of her voice; yet the process by which Nick and Gatsby research the meaning of that essentially nonverbal sound progressively demystifies the archetype. When Gatsby weds his unutterable vision to Daisy's mortal breath, he immediately restricts the scope of her potential meaning. Much like Hawthorne in *The Scarlet Letter*, Fitzgerald demonstrates the recovery and loss of symbolic vision in *The Great Gatsby*.[7]

Early in the novel, for example, Nick only faintly apprehends the uniqueness of Daisy's voice. Like a fine musical instrument, Daisy's voice produces a sound so impalpable and suggestive that it seems purely formal. "It was the kind of voice," Nick says, "that the ear follows up and down, as if each speech is an arrangement of notes that will never be played again" (p. 9). Full of creative promise, the voice seems to beckon the imagination into a new world of sensation, for "there was an excitement in her voice that men who had cared for her found difficult to forget: a singing compulsion, a whispered 'Listen,' a promise that she had done gay, exciting things just a while since and that there were gay, exciting things hovering in the next hour" (pp. 9–10). Here, in short, Daisy's voice seems full of unrealized possibility.

A vivid expression of an archetype which is fluid in form yet suggests nearly infinite designs, her voice inspires both Nick and Gatsby to wild imaginings. Nick, in fact, hears a quality in Daisy's voice which seems at first to transcend the meaning of words. "I had to follow the sound of it for a moment, up and down, with my ear alone," he says, "before any words came through" (p. 86). Daisy's effect is thus linked explicitly to the kind of auroral effect that a truly symbolic object produces on an artist's mind, "bringing out a meaning in each word that it had never had before and would never have again" (p. 109). She seems able to transform the material world into some ephemeral dreamland in which objects suddenly glow with symbolic meaning. Thus, Gatsby "literally glowed" in Daisy's presence "like an ecstatic patron of recurrent light" (p. 90), and the objects he immediately revalues "according to the measure of response [they] drew from her well-loved eyes" suddenly seem no longer real (p. 92). Existing within a realm of as yet uncreated possibility, Daisy's essential meaning, in short, suggests a psychic impulse too fleeting to be articulated or brought across the threshold of conscious thought. Frantically trying to comprehend the impulse within himself which Daisy's voice evokes, Nick concludes: "I was reminded of something—an elusive rhythm, a fragment of lost words, that I had heard somewhere a long time ago. For a moment a phrase tried to take shape in my mouth and my lips parted like a dumb man's, as though there was more struggling upon them than a wisp of startled air. But they made no sound, and what I had almost remembered was uncommunicable forever" (p. 112).

Like Gatsby with his "unutterable vision," then, Nick admits his failure to realize (and communicate) the essence of Daisy's meaning. Together, both men effectively conspire to reduce that meaning to a "single window" perspective. As successfully as the townspeople of *The Scarlet Letter* in their efforts to confine the punitive meaning of Hester's "A," Nick and Gatsby progressively devitalize Daisy's symbolic meaning until she exists as a vulgar emblem of the money values which dominate their world. Her voice was "full of money," Nick agrees; "that was the inexhaustible charm that rose and fell in it, the jingle of it, the cymbals' song of it. . . . High in a white palace the king's daughter, the golden girl . . ." (p. 120). Paralleling Fitzgerald's sense of America's diminishing possibilities, Gatsby's action has the added effect of forfeiting forever his capacity to reclaim Daisy from Tom's influence. When he tries to become a *nouveau riche* version of Tom, Gatsby ceases to have the power to take Daisy back to her beautiful white girlhood. No longer does he look at her with the creative look the "way every young girl wants to be looked at"; instead, Daisy becomes the victim of what has become Gatsby's irrevocably meretricious look.

Because she, too, seeks a lost moment from the past, Gatsby succeeds momentarily in liberating Daisy from Tom's world. However, just as the shirts in his closet "piled like bricks in stacks a dozen high" (p. 93) signal the disintegration of Gatsby's obsessively constructed kingdom of illusion, Daisy's uncontrollable sobbing with her magical voice "muffled in the thick folds" (p. 94) represents the end of her dream as well. Even as Nick apologizes for its simplicity, Daisy is simply "offended" by the vulgarity of Gatsby's world (p. 108). Thus, although both characters do enjoy the moment "in between time" possessed of "intense life" (p. 97) which they have sought, Gatsby and Daisy inevitably split apart. When Tom reveals the real Gatsby as a "common swindler" (p. 134), Daisy's own count of "enchanted objects" also diminishes by one. She cries out at first that she "won't stand this" (p. 134), but as the truth of Tom's accusation sinks in, she withdraws herself from Gatsby forever. For the second time, Tom's crude, yet palpable force disillusions Daisy about Gatsby, and in spite of the latter's desperate attempts to defend himself, "with every word she was drawing further and further into herself, so he gave that up, and only the dead dream fought on as the afternoon slipped away, trying to touch what was no longer tangible, struggling unhappily, undespairingly, toward that lost voice across the room" (p. 135). Because she cannot exist in the nether world of a "dead dream" which has eclipsed everything about her except the money in her voice, Daisy moves back toward Tom and his world of "unquestionable practicality." Reduced to a golden statute [sic], a collector's item which crowns Gatsby's material success, Daisy destroys even the possibility of illusion when she runs down Myrtle Wilson in Gatsby's car.

Not only does she kill her husband's mistress, thus easing her reentry into his life, but she climaxes the symbolic process by which she herself has been reduced from archetype to stereotype. At the moment of impact—the final crash of the dead dream into the disillusioning body of reality—it is surely no accident in a novel of mutual alienation that Daisy and Gatsby are both gripping the steering wheel. Daisy loses her nerve to hit the other car and commit a double suicide (thus preserving their dream in the changelessness of death); instead she chooses life and the seemingly inevitable workings of history. She forces the story to be played out to its logical conclusion: Gatsby's purgative death and her own estrangement from love. Despite Nick's judgment of her carelessness and "basic insincerity," her conspiratorial relationship with Tom, Daisy is victimized by a male tendency to project a self-satisfying, yet ultimately dehumanizing, image on woman. If Gatsby had "wanted to recover something, some idea of himself perhaps, that had gone into loving Daisy" (p. 111); if Nick had nearly recovered a "fragment of lost words" through the inspiring magic of her voice, then Daisy's potential selfhood is finally betrayed by the world of the novel. Hers remains a "lost voice," and its words and meaning seem "uncommunicable forever."

From *American Literature* 50, no. 2 (May, 1978): 250–257. Copyright © 1978 by Duke University Press. Reprinted by permission of Duke University Press.

Notes

1. Marius Bewley, "Scott Fitzgerald's Criticism of America," in *Twentieth Century Interpretations of The Great Gatsby*, ed. Ernest Lockridge (Englewood Cliffs, N.J., 1968), pp. 44, 45; Robert Ornstein, "Scott Fitzgerald's Fable of East and West," ibid., P. 55; Alfred Kazin, "An American Confession," in *F. Scott Fitzgerald: The Man and His Work*, ed. Kazin (New York, 1950), p. 179; Leslie Fiedler, *Love and Death in the American Novel*, rev. ed. (New York, 1966), pp. 313, 315, 312.

2. *The Great Gatsby* (New York, 1925), p. 2. All quotations from the novel are from this edition and will be cited in the text.

3. Two excellent arguments against Nick's reliability are R. W. Stallman's famous essay, "Gatsby and the Hole in Time," *Modern Fiction Studies*, I (Nov., 1955), 2–16, and Gary J. Scrimgeour, "Against *The Great Gatsby*," in *Twentieth Century Interpretations of The Great Gatsby*, pp. 70–81.

4. In their heavily analytical categorization of "The Evasion of Adult Love in Fitzgerald's Fiction," *Centennial Review*, 17 (Spring, 1973), 152–169, Jan Hunt and John M. Suarez argue that the "Fitzgerald hero accomplishes two basic neurotic goals by ideal-

izing his girlfriend: he evades her even as he consciously believes that he loves her, the process of idealization rendering her realistically unattainable; and, he avoids a mature relationship with other women because he operates under the fantasy that he has already committed himself to the idealized woman" (p. 153).

5. Fitzgerald admitted to a similar tendency in "The Crack Up." He says that he had always had a "secret yen for the Scandinavian blondes who sat on porches in St. Paul" and then notes that he had often gone "blocks to catch a single glimpse of shining hair—the bright shock of a girl I'd never know" (*The Crack Up*, ed. Edmund Wilson, New York, 1945, p. 73).

6. See Hunt and Suarez, pp. 156–162.

7. Charles Feidelson, of course, discusses *The Scarlet Letter* as a study of symbolic perception (*Symbolism and American Literature*, Chicago, 1953, pp. 8–12); and in *The Shape of Hawthorne's Career* (Ithaca, N.Y., 1976), Nina Baym analyzes Hester Prynne's frantic efforts to subvert the oppressive authority of her emblematic letter by embroidering it (pp. 131–133).

RESOURCES

Chronology of F. Scott Fitzgerald's Life _____

1896	Francis Scott Key Fitzgerald is born in St. Paul, Minnesota, on September 24 to Edward Fitzgerald and Mollie McQuillan.
1898 – 1908	After the failure of his furniture business, Edward Fitzgerald takes a job as a salesman at Procter & Gamble, and the family moves to Buffalo, then Syracuse, New York.
1908	Edward Fitzgerald loses his job. The Fitzgeralds move back to St. Paul.
1911	Attends a Catholic boarding school in Hackensack, New Jersey. Writes his first play, *The Girl from Lazy J*, produced in St. Paul.
1913	Enters Princeton. Works on productions for the university's amateur theatrical company, The Triangle Club.
1917	Leaves Princeton without receiving a degree. Joins the U.S. Army as a Second Lieutenant. Begins writing novel, *The Romantic Egotist*.
1918	While stationed at Camp Sheridan, near Montgomery, Alabama, meets Zelda Sayre at a dance. *The Romantic Egotist* is rejected by Scribner's.
1919	After being discharged from the Army, he is hired by an advertising firm in New York. He and Zelda are engaged; later that year Zelda breaks the engagement. Fitzgerald returns to St. Paul to rewrite *The Romantic Egotist*, under a new title, *This Side of Paradise*.
1920	*This Side of Paradise* is published, after being accepted by Maxwell Perkins at Scribner's. Zelda and Scott are married on April 3. Short-story collection *Flappers and Philosophers* published.
1921	Daughter, Frances Fitzgerald ("Scottie"), is born.
1922	*The Beautiful and Damned* published by Scribner's. *Tales of the Jazz Age*, second collection of stories, published.

1925	*The Great Gatsby* is published; receives good reviews, but does not sell well.
1926	A third collection of stories, *All the Sad Young Men*, is published. Fitzgeralds travel to the Riviera.
1927	Zelda begins ballet lessons; Fitzgerald spends two months in Hollywood writing scripts.
1930	They both are drinking heavily; Zelda suffers her first nervous breakdown while they are traveling in Europe.
1931	"Babylon Revisited" published in *The Saturday Evening Post*.
1932	Zelda suffers a second breakdown after the death of her father. She is admitted to a psychiatric clinic in Baltimore and is later discharged. That same year, her novel, *Save Me the Waltz*, is published.
1934	Zelda suffers her third breakdown. Fitzgerald falls into deeper despair, finding himself in dire financial straits; *Tender Is the Night* is published but sales are disappointing.
1935	Publication of *Taps at Reveille*, fourth short-story collection. Declining physical health attributed to heavy drinking. Recuperates in Asheville, North Carolina.
1936	Living in North Carolina, Fitzgerald writes "The Crack-Up," a series of three essays published in *Esquire*. Zelda enters a sanatorium in Asheville, where she remains, intermittently, for the rest of her life.
1937	Moves to Hollywood to work as a scriptwriter for MGM. Begins a relationship with gossip/movie columnist Sheila Graham.
1939	Begins writing *The Last Tycoon*.
1940	"Pat Hobby" stories published in *Esquire*. Suffers a fatal heart attack on December 21.
1941	The unfinished manuscript and notes for *The Last Tycoon* are published.

1945	*The Crack-Up*, edited by Edmund Wilson, published by New Directions; Dorothy Parker compiles *The Portable F. Scott Fitzgerald*.
1948	After dying in a fire at the sanitarium in Ashville, Zelda is buried beside him.

Works by F. Scott Fitzgerald

Long Fiction
This Side of Paradise, 1920
The Beautiful and Damned, 1922
The Great Gatsby, 1925
Tender Is the Night, 1934
The Last Tycoon, 1941

Short Fiction
Flappers and Philosophers, 1920
Tales of the Jazz Age, 1922
All the Sad Young Men, 1926
Taps at Reveille, 1935
The Stories of F. Scott Fitzgerald, 1951
Babylon Revisited, and Other Stories, 1960
The Pat Hobby Stories, 1962
The Apprentice Fiction of F. Scott Fitzgerald, 1907-1917, 1965
The Basil and Josephine Stories, 1973
Bits of Paradise, 1974
The Price Was High: The Last Uncollected Stories of F. Scott Fitzgerald, 1979
Before Gatsby: The First Twenty-Six Stories, 2001 (Matthew J. Bruccoli, editor)

Drama
The Vegetable: Or, From President to Postman, pb. 1923

Nonfiction
The Crack-Up, 1945
The Letters of F. Scott Fitzgerald, 1963
Letters to His Daughter, 1965
Thoughtbook of Francis Scott Fitzgerald, 1965
Dear Scott/Dear Max: The Fitzgerald-Perkins Correspondence, 1971
As Ever, Scott Fitzgerald, 1972
F. Scott Fitzgerald's Ledger, 1972
The Notebooks of F. Scott Fitzgerald, 1978
A Life in Letters, 1994 (Matthew J. Bruccoli, editor)
F. Scott Fitzgerald on Authorship, 1996
Dear Scott, Dearest Zelda: The Love Letters of F. Scott and Zelda Fitzgerald, 2002
    (Jackson R. Bryer and Cathy W. Barks, editors)
Conversations with F. Scott Fitzgerald, 2005 (Matthew J. Bruccoli and Judith S.
    Baughman, editors)

Miscellaneous

Afternoon of an Author: A Selection of Uncollected Stories and Essays, 1958

F. Scott Fitzgerald: The Princeton Years, Selected Writings, 1914-1920, 1996 (Chip Deffaa, editor)

Bibliography

Allen, Joan. *Candles and Carnival Lights*. New York: New York University Press, 1978.

Barrett, Laura. "From Wonderland to Wasteland: *The Wonderful Wizard of Oz, The Great Gatsby*, and the New American Fairy Tale." *Papers on Language and Literature* 42, no. 2 (Spring 2006): 150–180.

Berman, Ronald. *"The Great Gatsby" and Fitzgerald's World of Ideas*. Tuscaloosa: University of Alabama Press, 1997.

_____. *"The Great Gatsby" and Modern Times*. Urbana: University of Illinois Press, 1994.

Breitwieser, Mitchell. "*The Great Gatsby*: Grief, Jazz and the Eye-Witness." *Arizona Quarterly* 47, no. 3 (Autumn 1991): 17–70.

Bruccoli, Matthew. *Some Sort of Epic Grandeur: The Life of F. Scott Fitzgerald*. New York: Carroll & Graf, 1994.

_____, ed. *New Essays on "The Great Gatsby."* New York: Cambridge University Press, 1985.

Bryer, Jackson R., Alan Margolies, and Ruth Prigozy, eds. *F. Scott Fitzgerald: New Perspectives*. Athens: University of Georgia Press, 2000.

Chambers, John B. *The Novels of F. Scott Fitzgerald*. New York: St. Martin's Press, 1989.

Clymer, Jeffery A. "'Mr. Nobody from Nowhere': Rudolph Valentino, Jay Gatsby, and the End of the American Race." *Genre: Forms of Discourse and Culture* 29, no. 1–2 (Spring-Summer 1996): 161–192.

Coleman, Dan. "A World Complete in Itself: *Gatsby*'s Elegiac Narration." *Journal of Narrative Technique* 27, no. 2 (Spring 1997): 207–233.

Dillon, Andrew. "*The Great Gatsby*: The Vitality of Illusion." *Arizona Quarterly* 44, no. 1 (1988): 49–61.

Dixon, Wheeler Winston. *The Cinematic Vision of F. Scott Fitzgerald*. Ann Arbor, MI: UMI Research Press, 1986.

Donaldson, Scott. *Critical Essays on F. Scott Fitzgerald's "The Great Gatsby."* Boston: G. K. Hall & Co., 1984.

_____. "Possessions in *The Great Gatsby*." *Southern Review* 37, no. 2 (Spring 2001): 187–210.

Duffy, Dennis. "To Glow with Bright Colors: Jimmy Gatz's Trip to Oz." *Journal of English Studies* 3 (2001–2002): 65–79.

Eble, Kenneth, ed. *F. Scott Fitzgerald: A Collection of Criticism*. New York: McGraw-Hill, 1973.

Holquist, Michael. "Stereotyping in Autobiography and Historiography: Colonialism in *The Great Gatsby*." *Poetics Today* 9, no. 2 (1988): 453–472.

Kazin, Alfred, ed. *F. Scott Fitzgerald: The Man and His Work.* Cleveland: World, 1951.

Kerr, Frances. "'Feeling Half Feminine': Modernism and the Politics of Emotion in *The Great Gatsby.*" *American Literature* 68, no. 2 (June 1996): 405–431.

Lee, Robert A, ed. *Scott Fitzgerald: The Promises of Life.* London: Vision Press, 1989.

Lehan, Richard D. *F. Scott Fitzgerald and the Craft of Fiction.* Carbondale: Southern Illinois University Press, 1966.

Lockridge, Ernest, ed. *Twentieth Century Interpretations of "The Great Gatsby."* Englewood Cliffs, NJ: Prentice-Hall, 1968.

Long, Robert Emmet. *The Achieving of The Great Gatsby.* Lewisburg, PA: Bucknell University Press, 1979.

Marren, Susan Marie. *Passing for American: Establishing American Identity in the Work of James Weldon Johnson, F. Scott Fitzgerald, Nella Larsen, and Gertrude Stein.* Dissertation: The University of Michigan, 1995.

Meyers, Jeffery. *Scott Fitzgerald: A Biography.* New York: HarperCollins, 1994.

Mizener, Arthur, ed. *F. Scott Fitzgerald: A Collection of Critical Essays.* Englewood Cliffs, NJ: Prentice-Hall, 1963.

Pendelton, Thomas. *I'm Sorry About the Clock: Chronology, Composition, and Narrative Technique in "The Great Gatsby."* London: Associated University Press, 1993.

Phillips, Gene D. *Fiction, Film, and F. S. Fitzgerald.* Chicago: Loyola University Press, 1986.

Piper, Henry Dan, ed. *Fitzgerald's "The Great Gatsby": The Novel, The Critics, The Background.* New York: Scribner's, 1970.

Roulston, Robert, and Helen H. Roulston. *The Winding Road to West Egg: The Artistic Development of F. Scott Fitzgerald.* London: Associated University Presses, 1995.

Samuels, Charles T. "The Greatness of Gatsby." *Massachusetts Review* 7 (Autumn 1966): 783–794.

Seiters, Dan. *Image Patterns in the Novels of F. Scott Fitzgerald.* Ann Arbor, MI: UMI Research Press, 1986.

Trilling, Lionel. "F. Scott Fitzgerald." In *The Liberal Imagination.* New York: Viking, 1950: pp. 243–254.

Way, Brian. *F. Scott Fitzgerald and the Art of Social Fiction.* New York: St. Martin's Press, 1980.

White, Patti. *Gatsby's Party.* West Lafayette, IN: Purdue University Press, 1992.

Whitley, John S. *F. Scott Fitzgerald: "The Great Gatsby."* London: Edward Arnold, 1976.

CRITICAL
INSIGHTS

About the Editor

Morris Dickstein is Distinguished Professor of English at the Graduate Center of the City University of New York and senior fellow of the Center for the Humanities, which he founded in 1993. His books include *Keats and His Poetry* (Chicago, 1971), *Gates of Eden: American Culture in the Sixties* (Basic Books, 1977; Harvard, 1997), and *Double Agent: The Critic and Society* (Oxford, 1992). He also edited *The Revival of Pragmatism* (Duke, 1998). His most recent books are *Leopards in the Temple: The Transformation of American Fiction, 1945-1970* (Harvard, 2002), *A Mirror in the Roadway: Literature and the Real World* (Princeton, 2005), and *Dancing in the Dark,* a cultural history of the Great Depression, to be published by W. W. Norton. His essays and reviews have appeared in the *New York Times Book Review, Partisan Review, The American Scholar, Raritan, The Nation, Literary Imagination, Slate, Dissent,* the *Washington Post,* the *Chronicle of Higher Education, Bookforum,* and the *Times Literary Supplement* (London). He has served as film critic of the *Bennington Review* and *Partisan Review* and was an advisor for a documentary film about four leading New York intellectuals, Joseph Dorman's *Arguing the World.* He was a founder and board member (1983–1989) of the National Book Critics Circle and Vice-Chair of the New York Council for the Humanities from 1997 to 2001. He was a contributing editor of *Partisan Review* from 1972 to 2003 and served as president of the Association of Literary Scholars and Critics in 2006–2007.

About *The Paris Review*

The Paris Review is America's preeminent literary quarterly, dedicated to discovering and publishing the best new voices in fiction, nonfiction, and poetry. The magazine was founded in Paris in 1953 by the young American writers Peter Matthiessen and Doc Humes, and edited there and in New York for its first fifty years by George Plimpton. Over the decades, the *Review* has introduced readers to the earliest writings of Jack Kerouac, Philip Roth, T. C. Boyle, V. S. Naipaul, Ha Jin, Jay McInerney, and Mona Simpson, and published numerous now classic works, including Roth's *Goodbye, Columbus,* Donald Barthelme's *Alice,* Jim Carroll's *Basketball Diaries,* and selections from Samuel Beckett's *Molloy* (his first publication in English). The first chapter of Jeffrey Eugenides's *The Virgin Suicides* appeared in the *Review*'s pages, as well as stories by Edward P. Jones, Rick Moody, David Foster Wallace, Denis Johnson, Jim Shepard, Jim Crace, Lorrie Moore, Jeanette Winterson, and Ann Patchett.

The Paris Review's renowned Writers at Work series of interviews, whose early installments include legendary conversations with E. M. Forster, William Faulkner, and Ernest Hemingway, is one of the landmarks of world literature. The interviews received a George Polk award and were nominated for a Pulitzer Prize. Among the more than three hundred interviewees are Robert Frost, Marianne Moore, W. H. Auden, Elizabeth Bishop, Susan Sontag, and Toni Morrison. Recent issues feature conversations with Salman Rushdie, Joan Didion, Stephen King, Norman Mailer, Kazuo Ishiguro and Umberto Eco. (A complete list of the interviews is available at www.theparisreview.org) In November 2008, Picador will publish the third of a four-volume series of anthologies of *Paris Review* interviews. The first two volumes have received acclaim. *The New York Times* called the Writers at Work series "the most remarkable and extensive interviewing project we possess."

The Paris Review is edited by Philip Gourevitch, who was named to the post in 2005, following the death of George Plimpton two years earlier. Under Gourevitch's leadership, the magazine's international distribution has expanded, paid subscriptions have risen 150 percent, and newsstand distribution has doubled. A new editorial team has published fiction by Andre Aciman, Damon Galgut, Mohsin Hamid, Gish Jen, Richard Price, Said Sayrafiezadeh and Alistair Morgan. Poetry editors Charles Simic, Meghan O'Rourke and Dan Chiasson have selected works by Billy Collins, Jesse Ball, Mary Jo Bang, Sharon Olds, and Mary Karr. Writing published in the magazine has been anthologized in *Best American Short Stories* 2006, 2007 and 2008, *Best American Poetry*, *Best Creative Non-Fiction*, the Pushcart Prize anthology, and *O. Henry Prize Stories*.

The magazine presents two annual awards. The Hadada Award for lifelong contribution to literature has recently been given to William Styron, Joan Didion, Norman Mailer and Peter Matthiessen in 2008. The Plimpton Prize for Fiction given to a new voice in fiction brought to national attention in the pages of *The Paris Review* was presented in 2007 to Benjamin Percy and to Jesse Ball in 2008.

The Paris Review won the 2007 National Magazine Award in photojournalism, and the *Los Angeles Times* recently called *The Paris Review* "an American treasure with true international reach."

Since 1999 *The Paris Review* has been published by The Paris Review Foundation, Inc., a not-for-profit 501(c)(3) organization.

The Paris Review is available in digital form to libraries worldwide in selected academic databases exclusively from EBSCO Publishing. Libraries can contact EBSCO at 1-800-653-2726 for details.

For more information on *The Paris Review* or to subscribe, please visit: www .theparisreview.org.

Contributors

Morris Dickstein is Distinguished Professor of English at the Graduate Center of the City University of New York and senior fellow and the founder of the Center for the Humanities. His publications include *A Mirror in the Roadway: Literature and the Real World* and *Leopards in the Temple: The Transformation of American Fiction, 1945-1970.* He served as president of the Association of Literary Scholars and Critics in 2006-2007.

Michael Adams is humanities librarian at the Graduate Center of the City University of New York. His critical essays have appeared in *Critique, Fitzgerald/Hemingway Annual,* and *Southern Quarterly.* He has contributed numerous essays about literature, film, music, and sports to reference books published by Facts on File, Gale, Greenwood, University of North Carolina Press, Oxford University Press, and Salem Press. He studied Fitzgerald and Hemingway under Matthew J. Bruccoli at the University of South Carolina, where he earned a Ph.D. in English.

Jascha Hoffman is a contributor to *The New York Times* and *Nature.* He lives in Brooklyn.

Jennifer Banach Palladino is a writer and independent scholar from Connecticut. She has served as the Contributing Editor of *Bloom's Guides: Heart of Darkness* and *Bloom's Guides: The Glass Menagerie* for Facts on File, Inc. and is the author of the forthcoming volumes *Bloom's How to Write about Tennessee Williams* from Facts on File, Inc. and *Understanding Norman Mailer* from The University of South Carolina Press. Palladino has also composed teaching guides to international literature for Random House's Academic Resources division and has contributed to numerous literary reference books for academic publishers such as Facts on File, Inc. and Oxford University Press on topics ranging from Romanticism to contemporary literature. Her work has appeared in academic and popular venues alike; her fiction and nonfiction have appeared under the *Esquire* banner. She is a member of The Association of Literary Scholars and Critics.

Amy M. Green is in her final year of studies as a Ph.D. student in literature at the University of Nevada, Las Vegas. Her work has appeared in *Popular Culture Review, Papers on Language and Literature, The Shakespeare Bulletin,* and *The Mark Twain Annual.* Her dissertation focused on the influence of Shakespeare on the works of Henry James and Mark Twain. Although she specializes in both nineteenth-century American literature and Shakespeare, her literary interests are diverse. She remains especially interested in introducing new students to the joys of literary study by means of popular culture. In her literature courses, she often draws her students into reading unfamiliar works of literature by tying them back to their modern popular culture reinventions. She feels passionate about both scholarship and teaching and enjoys discussing literature with her students. She may be reached via her website www.wanderingcow.net.

Dan McCall is Professor Emeritus at Cornell University where he teaches English, American studies, and creative writing. He has published widely on American authors such as Richard Wright, Herman Melville, Nathaniel Hawthorne, and Henry James in journals like *American Literature, College English,* and *The Henry James Review.* His book-length critical works include *Citizens of Somewhere Else* (1999) and *The Silence of Bartleby* (1989). He has also published seven novels, including *Triphammer* (1990) and *Jack the Bear* (1971). He was awarded a Guggenheim Fellowship in 1972, and a PEN Achievement Award in 1985.

Neil Heims is a writer and teacher living in Paris. His books include *Reading the Diary of Anne Frank* (2005), *Allen Ginsberg* (2005), and *J. R. R. Tolkien* (2004). He has also contributed numerous articles for literary publications including essays on William Blake, John Milton, William Shakespeare, and Arthur Miller.

Charles Lewis is Associate Professor of English and Director of the Writing Program at Beloit College. His articles and fiction have appeared in *Arizona Quarterly, Salmagundi,* and *Dreiser Studies.* His most recent book was *A Coincidence of Wants: The Novel and Neoclassical Economics* (2000).

Ruth Prigozy is a Professor of English at Hofstra University and the Executive Director of the F. Scott Fitzgerald Society. Her publications include *F. Scott Fitzgerald: An Illustrated Life* (2004). She has also served as editor for *The Cambridge Companion to F. Scott Fitzgerald* (2001), *F. Scott Fitzgerald: New Perspectives* (2000), and the Oxford University Press edition of *The Great Gatsby* (1998), and as a co-editor for *F. Scott Fitzgerald in the Twenty-First Century* (2003). Her critical essays have appeared in the *Hemingway Review, Twentieth Century Literature,* and *Literature Film Quarterly.*

Robert Roulston and **Helen H. Roulston** are, respectively, Professor Emeritus and Associate Professor of English and Philosophy at Murray State University. They are the authors of *The Winding Road to West Egg: The Artistic Development of F. Scott Fitzgerald* (1995). Helen is also the author of *Love and Nature, Unity and Doubling in the Novels of Maupassant* (1989), and Robert has published numerous articles on American writers in journals like *Modern Fiction Studies, Journal of Popular Culture, Journal of Narrative Technique, South Atlantic Quarterly, American Transcendental Quarterly,* and *Fitzgerald/Hemingway Annual.*

Kenneth E. Eble was Professor of English and University Professor at the University of Utah until his death in 1988. He wrote extensively on American literature in such books as *F. Scott Fitzgerald* (1963), *William Dean Howells* (1982), *Old Clemens and W. D. H.: The Story of a Remarkable Friendship* (1986). He also wrote several highly respected books on higher education and pedagogy, among them *A Perfect Education* (1966), *The Craft of Teaching* (1976), and *The Profane Comedy* (1963).

Dan Coleman is Director of the Master's Program in Liberal Studies at Skidmore College. Formerly, he was Associate Director of the Teacher Education Program at Bennington College. He earned his doctorate in English language and literature from Cornell University.

　　　　　　　　　　　　　　　　　　　　　　　Critical Insights

Matthew J. Bolton is a professor of English at Loyola School in New York City, where he also serves as the Dean of Students. Bolton received his Doctor of Philosophy in English from The Graduate Center of the City University of New York (CUNY) in 2005. His dissertation at the university was entitled: "Transcending the Self in Robert Browning and T. S. Eliot." Prior to attaining his Ph.D. at CUNY, Bolton also earned a Master of Philosophy in English (2004) and a Master of Science in English Education (2001). His undergraduate work was done at the State University of New York at Binghamton where he studied English Literature.

Barbara Will is Associate Professor of English at Dartmouth College. She has written extensively on Gertrude Stein, and her articles have appeared in numerous journals including *Modern Fiction Studies, College Literature, American Literature*, and *Modernism/Modernity*. Her book *Gertrude Stein, Modernism, and the Problem of "Genius"* was published in 2000.

Lawrence Jay Dessner is Professor Emeritus at the University of Toledo. He has published widely on American and British Victorian literature in journals like *Essays in Literature, Studies in the Novel, Critique*, and *Studies in Short Fiction*. He is the author of *How to Write a Poem* (1979) and *Homely Web of Truth: A Study of Charlotte Brontë's Novels* (1975).

Daniel J. Schneider is Professor Emeritus at the University of Tennessee, Knoxville. He is the author of *The Consciousness of D. H. Lawrence: An Intellectual Biography* (1989), *D. H. Lawrence: The Artist as Psychologist* (1984), *The Crystal Cage: Adventures in the Imagination in the Fiction of Henry James* (1979), and *Symbolism: The Manichean Vision; A Study in the Art of James, Conrad, Woolf, and Stevens* (1975).

Leland S. Person, Jr. is Professor of English at McMicken College. He has written extensively on American literature in books like *Aesthetic Headaches: Women and Masculine Poetics in Poe, Melville, and Hawthorne* (1988), *Henry James and the Suspense of Masculinity* (2003), and *The Cambridge Introduction to Nathaniel Hawthorne* (2007). He also served as editor for the Norton Critical Edition of *The Scarlet Letter* (2005), *A Historical Guide to James Fenimore Cooper* (2007), and as co-editor for *Roman Holidays: American Writers and Artists in Nineteenth-Century Italy* (2002). His critical essays have appeared in *Studies in Short Fiction, American Literature, Studies in the Novel, College Literature*, and *Nathaniel Hawthorne Review* (2005).

Acknowledgments_____

"F. Scott Fitzgerald" by Michael Adams. From *Dictionary of World Biography: The 20th Century* (1999): 1161-1165. Copyright © by Salem Press, Inc. All rights reserved.

"The Paris Review Perspective*"* by Jascha Hoffman. Copyright © 2008 by Jascha Hoffman. Special appreciation goes to Christopher Cox and Nathaniel Rich, editors for *The Paris Review.*

"'The Self-Same Song that Found a Path': Keats and *The Great Gatsby*" by Dan McCall. From *American Literature* 42, no. 4 (January, 1971). Copyright © 1971 by Duke University Press. All rights reserved. Reprinted by permission of Duke University Press.

"Babbled Slander Where the Paler Shades Dwell: Reading Race in *The Great Gatsby* and *Passing*" by Charles Lewis. From *LIT: Literature Interpretation Theory* 18, no. 2 (April, 2007). Copyright © 2007 by Taylor & Francis, Ltd. Reprinted by permission of Taylor & Francis, Ltd. http://www.tandf.co.uk/journals.

"Introduction" by Ruth Prigozy. From *The Great Gatsby* (1998) by F. Scott Fitzgerald. Copyright © 1998 by Oxford University Press. Reprinted by permission of Oxford University Press, Inc.

"*The Great Gatsby*: Fitzgerald's Opulent Synthesis" by Robert and Helen H. Roulston. From *The Winding Road to West Egg: The Artistic Development of F. Scott Fitzgerald* (1995) by Robert and Helen H. Roulston. Copyright © 1995 by Bucknell University Press. Reprinted by permission of Bucknell University Press.

"The Craft of Revision: *The Great Gatsby*" by Kenneth E. Eble. From *American Literature* 36, no. 3 (November, 1964). Copyright © 1964 by Duke University Press. All rights reserved. Reprinted by permission of Duke University Press.

"'A World Complete in Itself': *Gatsby*'s Elegiac Narration" by Dan Coleman. From *The Journal of Narrative Technique* 27, no. 2 (Spring, 1997). Copyright © 1997 by Eastern Michigan University Press. Reprinted by permission of Eastern Michigan University Press.

"*The Great Gatsby* and The Obscene Word" by Barbara Will. From *College Literature* 32, no. 4 (Fall, 2005). Copyright © 2005 by West Chester University. All rights reserved. Reprinted by permission of West Chester University.

"Photography and *The Great Gatsby*" by Lawrence Jay Dessner. From *Essays in Literature* 6, no. 1 (Spring, 1979). Copyright © 1979 by Western Illinois University Press. Reprinted by permission of Western Illinois University Press.

"Color-Symbolism in *The Great Gatsby*" by Daniel J. Schneider was first published in *University Review* (now *New Letters*) 31, no. 1 (Autumn, 1964). It is included here with the permission of *New Letters* and the curators of the University of Missouri-Kansas City. Copyright © 1964 by University of Missouri-Kansas City. Reprinted by permission of University of Missouri-Kansas City.

Index

Harlem Renaissance, 87
Harvey, W. J., 168, 187
Hawthorne, Nathaniel, 129, 259
Heart of Darkness (Conrad), 86, 138, 142
Hemingway, Ernest, 3, 14-17, 39, 42,
    100, 103, 126
Herbert Bayard Swope (*The Great
    Gatsby*), 129, 138
Hitchcock, Thomas, 104
Houston, Neal B., 215
Howells, William Dean, 85, 101

Immortality in *The Great Gatsby*, 231,
    233
Immortality Ode (Wordsworth), 6
In Our Time (Hemingway), 103
Iser, Wolfgang, 190, 197

Jakobson, Roman, 161
James, Henry, 4, 14, 17, 99, 101, 119,
    161, 174, 177, 243
James, William, 100
Jamieson, John, 127
Jay Gatsby (*The Great Gatsby*);
    adolescent quest, 221, 253, 255-256;
    character of, 7; consciousness, 199;
    costumes, 52; death, 27, 62, 69, 79,
    81, 134, 155, 183, 185-187, 192, 196,
    219, 222, 243, 250, 262; dream, 37,
    53-56, 110-112, 114-116, 119, 128,
    161, 171, 183, 185, 188, 219, 221,
    232-233, 235-237, 244, 246, 249-
    252, 256, 261; egoism, 63; fate, 205,
    243; father, 138, 155, 232, 234, 240;
    freedom, 230; funeral, 130, 138, 155,
    177, 212; greatness, 205; history of,
    6-7, 35, 59, 63, 69-70, 117-118, 152-
    154, 190, 192-193, 199-201, 215,
    226, 240; mansion, 32, 48, 203, 206-
    207, 211, 233, 247, 253, 256; military
    service, 8, 66, 104, 137, 151, 194;

nature of wealth, 21, 41-42, 51-53,
    64, 69, 106, 112-113, 115, 118-119,
    124, 137, 171, 182, 212, 261;
    obscenity, 207-208, 215, 220, 223;
    parties, 20, 34, 36, 49, 52, 69, 96,
    106, 110-111, 114, 116, 120, 133,
    136-138, 140, 146, 148, 157, 174-
    181, 208, 210-211, 226, 236, 250,
    252; physical presence, 147, 151;
    relationship with Daisy, 8, 20, 26-27,
    29-30, 35, 47, 50, 53-54, 59, 64, 66,
    69-71, 90, 108, 110-111, 114, 118,
    125, 131, 135-136, 140, 146, 153-
    154, 185-186, 189, 192, 198-200,
    205, 210, 214-215, 231, 239, 248,
    252, 255-256, 258-262; rumors, 110;
    theatrical ability, 173, 175; vision, 47,
    50-52, 54, 126, 128-129, 137, 170,
    199, 208, 219-220, 227, 230, 233,
    248, 253, 255, 259-260; youth, 8, 29,
    70, 78, 81, 97, 118, 172, 212
Jazz Age in *The Great Gatsby*, 21, 31,
    42-43
Johnson-Reed Immigration Act, 216
Jordan Baker (*The Great Gatsby*), 29,
    54, 166, 211, 225, 235, 243; color,
    247-248; on Daisy, 135, 256;
    dishonesty and carelessness, 29, 62,
    130, 134, 248-249; relationship with
    Daisy, 153; relationship with Nick,
    33, 82, 194, 196-197, 257; speech,
    147, 172
Joyce, James, 86, 141, 199-200, 213
Jozan, Edouard, 125

Kaye-Smith, Sheila, 85
Kazin, Alfred, 21, 255
Keats, John, 5; influence of, 46, 49-50,
    56, 108, 128, 131, 140, 239;
    language, 47, 49, 52, 54-55; love of
    beauty, 46-48, 56

Shelley, Percy Bysshe, 193
Sister Carrie (Dreiser), 86, 101
Smart Set, The (Fitzgerald), 12
Social realism in *The Great Gatsby*, 241
Sollors, Werner, 74
Spengler, Oswald, 107, 128, 133-134, 140-142
Stallings, Laurence, 40, 98
Stallman, Robert W., 30, 132, 142
Steichen, Edward, 232
Stein, Gertrude, 14, 39, 86, 99
Stern, Milton R., 115, 132
Stieglitz, Alfred, 232
Stoddard, Theodore Lothrop, 72, 78, 89, 133, 142, 214, 216, 218, 226
Stouck, David, 30
Sun Also Rises, The (Hemingway), 100, 103, 127
Swope, Herbert Bayard, 106
Symbolic vision in *The Great Gatsby*, 259

Tanselle, G. Thomas, 41-42
Tender Is the Night (Fitzgerald), 3, 43, 46, 180, 257; autobiographical elements in, 13-14
Tennyson, Alfred Lord, 233
Thackeray, William Makepeace, 99, 127-128, 140, 242
Thalberg, Irving, 15
This Side of Paradise (Fitzgerald), 3, 10, 13, 20, 46, 95, 104, 128, 136, 139-141, 149, 257; publication, 12; success, 13
Three Comrades (screenplay), 15
Three Lives (Stein), 86
Time in *The Great Gatsby*, 97, 106, 116-117
Tom Buchanan (*The Great Gatsby*); affair, 29, 35, 62, 64, 66, 76, 112,
125, 128-129, 131, 136, 150, 170, 181, 196, 231, 249, 253; brutality and jealousy, 19-20, 34, 63, 67, 129, 132, 150, 173, 185, 237, 251, 255; character and wealth, 8, 19-20, 34-35, 63-65, 107, 113, 125, 171, 192, 201-202, 214; corruption, 112, 196, 256, 258; influence, 258, 260-261; racist, 72, 74-75, 78, 81-82, 84; relationship with Gatsby, 6
Triangle Club, 11
Trilling, Lionel, 36, 46, 56, 205
Twain, Mark, 101, 131

Ulysses (Joyce), 86, 213

Valley of ashes symbolism (*The Great Gatsby*), 32, 35, 53, 55, 107, 114, 129, 150, 168-170, 188, 247, 249, 251, 253
Vanity Fair (Thackeray), 99
Vechten, Carl Van, 87
Vegetable, The (Fitzgerald), 14, 97, 140

Wald, Gayle, 75, 89
Waste Land, The (Eliot), 9, 107, 129, 133
Wells, H. G., 100
Wescott, Glenway, 100
West, Dorothy, 87
Weston, Edward, 232
Wharton, Edith, 128
Wilde, Oscar, 128, 141
Wilson, Edmund, 3, 11, 16, 19, 133, 217, 226
Wilson, Woodrow, 103-104
"Winter Dreams" (Fitzgerald), 257
World War I, 11, 31, 61, 100-101, 194, 232
World War II, 19